Energy and Environmental Hedge Funds

The New Investment Paradigm

Energy and Environmental Hedge Funds

The New Investment Paradigm

Peter C. Fusaro
Gary M. Vasey

John Wiley & Sons (Asia) Pte Ltd

Published in 2006 by John Wiley & Sons (Asia) Pte Ltd
2 Clementi Loop, #02-01, Singapore 129809

This publication is designed to provide accurate and authoritative information in regard to the subject matter covered. It is sold with the understanding that the publisher is not engaged in rendering professional services. If professional advice or other expert assistance is required, the services of a competent professional person should be sought.

Other Wiley Editorial Offices

John Wiley & Sons, 111 River Street, Hoboken, NJ 07030, USA
John Wiley & Sons, The Atrium Southern Gate, Chichester PO19 8SQ, England
John Wiley & Sons (Canada) Ltd, 5353 Dundas Street West, Suite 400, Toronto, Ontario M9B 6HB. Canada
John Wiley & Sons Australia Ltd, 42 McDougall Street, Milton, Queensland 4064, Australia
Wiley-VCH, Boschstrasse 12, D-69469 Weinheim, Germany

Library of Congress Cataloging-in-Publication Data

ISBN-13   978-0-470-82198-5
ISBN-10   0-470-82198-1

Typeset in 10.5/13pt Minion by Laserwords Private Limited, Chennai, India.
Printed in Singapore by Saik Wah Press Pte Ltd.

10 9 8 7 6 5 4 3 2 1

Contents

Introduction

T he rising power of hedge funds has continued to reshape both Wall Street and the City of London during the past several years. While hedge fund returns generally disappointed investors in 2004 and 2005, their movement into the energy complex has not. It now seems likely that their advance into energy is primed to follow throughout the world as the globalization of financial markets accelerates. Rapid economic growth in China and India, coupled with rising energy demand, is leading a sustained thrust into the energy hedge fund universe. This financial model is now changing to include more equity investment, as well as commodity trading, and begins to blur the line with investment banking, venture capital, and hedge funds. The second thrust of this powerful financial change will be the emerging environmental financial markets as drivers of both change and investment opportunities. The environment now overlays the energy value chain, as the recent emergence of "green" hedge funds attest to this investment opportunity.

Hedge funds seek new areas of investment where returns may be stronger, and that opportunity is in the global energy business and emerging environmental financial markets. This book is envisioned as a road map to identify investment opportunities in these new and volatile markets. It is a primer for investors and other hedge fund managers to take a hard look at this complex sector, which is now rife with both investment opportunities and risk. The relative immaturity of both energy and environmental financial markets point to much opportunity in this sector than is currently realized, but it does not fit tidily into the macro models and more sophisticated trading of foreign exchange and corporate debt trading, which is the traditional realm of hedge funds.

Today, there are more than 8,700 hedge funds with over $1 trillion at work, which could be levered to at least $2 trillion. This is double the number of hedge funds that existed in 1999.[1] The flat or sideways trading of global equity markets for the past several years since the dot com crash has not shown the rates of return that investors have become accustomed to. Meanwhile, the energy complex is volatile, capital intensive, and just plain interesting. You can't put down the newspaper or watch television today without every angle of the energy complex being under intense scrutiny and investor interest.

Our research has revealed that there are over 450 energy hedge funds and perhaps that number could be as high as 600, with many new funds emerging on a daily basis. These funds run the gamut of strategies from energy equities, commodities, distressed assets, debt, and alternative energy (environmental) such as renewable energy and emissions trading, and increasingly, funds of hedge funds. Investors are looking for better returns every year as they abandon one financial sector for another, and they have now turned to the energy patch for those financial rewards – but energy is a risky and physical business that cannot readily be compared with other investment opportunities.

In this book we make the case for energy and later the environment, as it relates to energy, as the place to invest. It is an area where hedge funds in particular offer investors exposure to a wide variety of innovative and profitable opportunities. Our thesis is that a lack of investment in the entire energy complex over the last 20 years since the price collapse in 1986 has now teed up a sustained period of supply–demand tightness in all energy commodities. We argue that there will be no mean reversion in energy prices, and offer the view that energy markets are behaving differently this time around. Something has fundamentally changed in energy.

For the last couple of decades, energy commodity prices moved sideways within a narrow range, but then suddenly began an inexorable rise about two years ago. We feel that many in the industry were lulled into a false sense of security around market fundamentals, while many skills simply left the industry altogether during the past two decades. Many in the industry today, including Wall Street and other analysts, have no experience of anything but low and relatively stable energy prices. Indeed, after the collapse of Enron in late 2001 and the energy merchants in 2002, many predicted the demise of energy commodity trading and markets altogether. But, it was this event that accentuated opportunities in energy and even provided many of the trading skills that allowed the new energy speculators to enter these complex and risky markets. And so we have seen the new triangle of trading emerge these past two years, which includes investment banks, hedge funds, and multinational oil companies. We have not seen the predicted globalization of electric utilities, but instead foreign utilities retreated from American power markets. We have also witnessed the Wall Street power companies rise as they bought distressed assets and began to trade those assets through various asset optimization strategies. We have seen the resurfacing of the financial institution/utility joint ventures such as Calpine and Bear Stearns, as well as Merrill Lynch's purchase of Entergy/Koch, and more recently we have seen the entrance of financial hedge funds focusing on the energy industry for a variety of reasons, including acquiring and trading distressed generation assets.

It has been the rise in energy commodity prices and volatilities, the lack of investment in infrastructure, and the credit and debt issues of the collapsed merchants that have uniquely combined to create today's opportunities. Somewhat simplistically, the lack of investment in infrastructure across the complex this last 20 years, combined with the surge in global demand for energy, has resulted in a rapid rise in energy commodity prices and volatilities. In turn, this has created a situation where energy companies across the complex have seen profits rise. This is now resulting in increased spending on long overdue projects and activities. Meanwhile, the abundance of relatively cheap assets for sale, and the need for various energy companies to restructure debt, has created a variety of other opportunities. Finally, higher energy prices and the tightness in supply–demand dynamics across all energy markets is driving increased interest in alternative forms of energy and energy efficiency investment.

Although a small number of hedge funds have specialized in energy equities for several years, and many more general equity funds had a component of energy in their portfolios, it was the entrance of hedge funds into energy commodity trading that really spurred the interest on the part of investors in hedge funds. These early energy commodity funds, staffed with expert energy traders from the old merchant segment, produced extraordinary returns in 2003 and 2004. As a result, investor interest increased and many ex-traders and investment bankers created new hedge funds across the space. Existing funds, especially larger macro funds, also exposed more of their assets under management to the energy complex. Of course, it wasn't just hedge funds that got into energy – it was all of the investment banks as well.

While many hedge funds concentrate mostly on price risk, there are almost unlimited risks in the physically oriented energy business. There is operational risk, geopolitical risk, event risk, regulatory risk, weather risk, tax risk, and others that add multiple additional dimensions to the more linear and traditional thinking of hedge fund operations. These externalities are also about to be overwhelmed by "environmental risk," which is the wave beyond the current energy hedge fund euphoria. Therefore, trying to put the traditional hedge fund financial overlay into the energy complex is really putting the proverbial square peg into the round hole. Why? Because energy is the world's largest business with over \$4 trillion in annual trade, but it is also a very immature financial market.

The notional value of the financial energy market is $2.2 trillion according to our estimates. Since commodities traditionally trade six to 20 times the physical market, we still have a long way to grow toward market maturation. Moreover, the Enron and energy merchant debacle set back natural gas and power trading a good three years. Today, the natural gas market is over $400 billion – where it was when Enron went down in December 2001. Oil trading still predominates energy trading and is the most liquid financial business. It also predominates in the energy commodity hedge fund business as it is still the only global energy market today.

Energy is a business that hedge funds really have just entered in large numbers during the past two years. Of course, it can be argued that commodity pool operators (CPOs) and commodity trading advisors (CTAs) have been around for decades, but the movement into energy trading by hedge funds has really accelerated in the more recent time period. In our Energy Hedge Fund Center (www.energyhedgefunds.com), we have counted more than 120 energy commodity trading hedge funds with over $50 billion or more in assets under management in our universe of over 450 energy hedge funds. Just 18 months ago there were less than 20 commodity trading hedge funds.

Energy trading activities such as electric power trading look attractive and bold, but they are fraught with unexpected risks – especially for those used to more mature financial markets. And that's the problem with energy for people and organizations more used to such markets. It's a very complex physical market. Superficially, it seems straightforward enough, but the more you probe into the business transactions required to make the industry work, the more complex and risky it becomes. Even crude oil markets are not as simple as just supply and demand. One has to consider transportation issues, crude quality issues, storage levels, refining capabilities, weather risks, and so on.

Certainly, there is a rapidly developing investor appetite for energy, but energy doesn't neatly fit the hedge fund business model and we observe some issues around that fact, particularly with respect to funds in energy and the institutional investor. However, we see an ongoing bull market for energy for some time to come and the results speak for themselves. Where there is a will, there is a way.

WHAT'S ON THE HORIZON?

Today, the energy hedge fund arena is ramping up, due to the need for higher returns for hedge fund investors. Our book attempts to frame this financial opportunity for them, but energy hedge funds are still only about 5% of the hedge fund universe – and growing. New York and London continue to be the twin capitals of both energy trading and energy hedge funds. Houston, Calgary, Chicago, Singapore, and Switzerland play second fiddle. More hedge funds and fund of hedge funds are in formation as the energy bull market continues with rocky price spikes and collapses.

After this investment window begins to close, watch out for the surge of environmental hedge funds coming into play that is just now surfacing. While carbon trading is the current focus of attention, there are also markets for sulfur dioxide (SO_2), which causes acid rain, nitrous oxides (NOx), which cause urban ozone, and renewable energy credit trading (as it is called in the United States). There are also opportunities in alternative energy market caps, ethanol trading, and alternative energy project equity plays. The emissions market formation is global as we recently learned of emissions credit trading for sulfur dioxide in China, which burns a lot of coal. Thus, the energy wave is superceded by a "green wave" of environmental hedge fund trading. Its genesis is still the United States, but now it is spreading globally. Watch this space expand, contract, and mature.

The energy hedge funds have the trading talent, better credit, and risk-taking acumen to really roil markets. They already have in day trading in both West Texas Intermediate (WTI) and Henry Hub Natural gas on the NYMEX, and Brent on the International Petroleum Exchange (IPE), making more traditional energy traders squeamish about all that intra-day price volatility. More is coming. The energy hedge funds are a double-edge sword for energy trading, since while they bring more liquidity to markets they also bring more price volatility. They also bring in more speed in day trading that traditional energy traders are not used to. Our belief is that more traditional players will have to live with the new market dynamics of what we dub the "trading triangle" of multinational oils, investment banks, and the funds. What is really occurring is a rising financialization process in the energy complex. This transition is not without risks and market changes are seldom greeted with open arms.

In this book, we will also disclose our thinking on what is driving energy markets and the attendant investment opportunities, picking apart myth from reality as we see it. The media and politicians try to simplify energy to a sound bite, but it is far more complex than that. There are a multitude of views as to where energy is headed from the apocalyptic theory of "peak oil" to the idea that this is just another dot com bubble. To us, it is about the fundamentals. Fundamentals have driven energy commodity prices these last two years, and the evidence suggests nothing much has changed as we reached the end of 2005. We hope to demonstrate that in this book.

For many years, the floor traders on the NYMEX have complained about hedge funds entering energy markets. For the most part they were wrong. Today, the funds have really arrived. They are looking for greater returns on equity for their investors than the flat trading of stock market equities. The missing ingredient is the understanding of energy markets and its complexity. Funds like to "move money in and move money out," as one experienced energy trader commented to us recently. However, what they are missing is that there are now fewer opportunities for that type of trading. Second, there are greater risks in the market because they have arrived to trade. A seasoned energy trader we know commented that "there is a billion fund with three traders, the oldest is 29 years old." The funds often lack knowledge and experience in energy markets, but they are gaining it. Energy trading is the most volatile and complex of any commodity. Energy prices are driven by supply–demand fundamentals, technical trading, weather, events, geopolitical issues, and regulatory issues. Credit risk is still an important risk to manage in the energy industry, particularly since this industry has less creditworthiness. The funds have better credit but less knowledge. They also sometimes have a "know-it-all" attitude. These factors bode for more impending energy trading disasters, and some have already occurred during 2005. Expect more to come.

Energy and the environment provide both opportunity and risks for hedge funds, fund of hedge funds, and investors to show much better than average returns. This book is an attempt to decode this new market. This is the beginning of a ramping up of energy and environmental hedge funds. It is sustained due to market uncertainty, supply constraints, and just plain old risk factors. We think it's a good thing as hedge funds are starting to provide the risk capital for investment in new technology that the venture funds are used to. This book should provide some insights into how these markets operate, where the hedge funds are entering, and where this all might ultimately lead us.

Peter C. Fusaro and Dr. Gary M. Vasey
April 2006

NOTE

1 Vann Hedge Fund Advisors, LLC website.

Acknowledgements

It is said that behind every good man is an even better woman. In this instance that would be Carmen and Maureen – who constantly ask us to strive for greater things but complain at the hours we put in!
    Love and thanks for their tolerance and patience.

Peter C. Fusaro and Dr. Gary M. Vasey

Abbreviated Terms used in this Book

ANWR   Arctic national wildlife refuge
CAT   Cumulative average temperature
CBOT   Chicago Board of Trade
CCX   Chicago Climate Exchange
CDDs   Cooling degree days
CFTC   US Commodity Futures Trading Commission
CME   Chicago Mercantile Exchange
COT   Commitment of traders
CPO   Commodity pool operator
CTA   Commodity trading advisor
E&P   Exploration and Production
EHFC   Energy Hedge Fund Center (www.energyhedgefunds.com)
EIA   US Energy Information Administration
EPRI   Electric Power Research Institute
ETF   Exchange traded fund
EU ETS   European Union Emissions Trading Scheme
FERC   Federal Energy Regulatory Commission
FoF   Fund of hedge funds
GDDs   Growing degree days
GHG   Greenhouse gas
HDDs   Heating degree days
HNW   High net worth
IEA   International Energy Agency
IGCC   Integrated gas combined cycle
IPE   International Petroleum Exchange
IPO   Initial public offering
IPP   Independent power producer
LCH   London Clearinghouse
LME   London Metals Exchange
LNG   Liquefied natural gas

M&A	Merger and acquisition
MLP	Master limited partnership
NAV	Net asset value
NWS	National Weather Service
NYMEX	New York Mercantile Exchange
OTC	Over the counter
PAI	Palo Alto Investors
REC	Renewable energy credit
ROI	Return on investment
RPS	Renewable portfolio standard
SEC	Securities and Exchange Commission
SUV	Sports utility vehicle
WTI	West Texas intermediate
WRMA	Weather Risk Management Association

CHAPTER 1

The New Investors in Energy

F or the average investor the energy industry has always offered opportunities to profit through the publicly traded securities available on
the world's stock markets. Indeed, many multinational oil companies have
long been considered "blue chip" stocks with both reasonable dividend and
appreciation characteristics. Mutual funds have also provided investors
opportunities to indirectly invest in the energy equities, although until
recently usually as part of a more diversified approach. More sophisticated
investors have had other options, including the use of options on securities
and access to commodity trading through CTAs, hedge funds, and other
alternative investment vehicles.

However, over the last two years, the energy industry has literally
been transformed into the "hot" investment sector. Today, with high and
volatile energy commodity prices impacting everyone, energy is in the
news headlines 24/7. On a daily basis, new investment opportunities in
the energy industry are offered in the form of energy or natural resource-
specific mutual funds, exchange traded funds (ETFs), income and royalty
trusts, master limited partnerships (MLPs), and other vehicles. The average
investor now has a broader set of opportunities to participate in the
booming energy sector. Yet these new vehicles only scratch the surface of
the opportunities provided through the alternative investment universe via
energy and environmental hedge funds.

NEW ENERGY INVESTORS

The new investors in energy are what we refer to as "the triangle of trading."
These comprise investment banks, hedge funds, and multinational oil
companies. Today, utilities are being increasingly marginalized in energy
markets as they drop back into trading around their assets and pursue a
strategy of optimizing those assets for shareholders if they trade at all. With

the energy merchants long gone after the fall of Enron and the others, a vacuum was left that these new investors have stepped in to fill.

The investment banks have been in and out of energy over the years to varying degrees, but over the last 18 months, the banks have increased their interest in and exposure to energy across the board. Almost every sizable investment bank now has a position in energy, while only Goldman Sachs and Morgan Stanley have had some form of presence for over 20 years. Other banks, including UBS, Barclays Capital, Lehman Brothers, Citigroup, Deutsche Bank, and ABN AMRO, among others, have all increased the size of their energy trading desks; and others, such as Merrill Lynch and Bear Sterns, have created joint ventures with, or even acquired, existing energy trading firms.

Investment banks continue to play a role on the distressed asset side of the energy business, too, while some have actually acquired significant energy assets and now operate those assets. For example, Goldman Sachs added to its energy portfolio with the purchase of East Coast Power and the acquisition of Cogentrix Energy in the United States. Both Goldman Sachs and Morgan Stanley can handle physical trading and take actual physical delivery of product. Goldman also holds a large renewable energy generation portfolio, too. Some investment banks have even bought oil and gas reserves in the ground.

The multinational oils have also moved in to fill the space left by the energy merchants in recent years. British Petroleum (BP) is now the largest trader of natural gas in North America, and it and other multinational oil companies have reported huge profits from their energy trading activities over the last 12 months.

However, the key area of interest and the topic of this book is the ever-growing and "secretive" hedge fund community. Despite increased interest from regulators such as the US Securities and Exchange Commission (SEC) and others, hedge funds are being funded at a record pace. Once the exclusive domain of private wealthy individuals, institutional money is now flooding into hedge funds seeking promised better returns (Figures 1.1 and 1.2). The $38.2 billion that flowed into the funds in Q1 2004 was a record and that pace has continued as public and corporate pension funds now allocate an average of 5–7% of their assets for investment in hedge funds. Van Hedge Fund Advisors[1] recently issued a report in which it expects assets under management at hedge funds to double to $2 billion by 2009.

But as hedge funds gain access to increasing amounts of capital, so too has the average hedge fund return declined to something less than spectacular. Hedge funds returned less than 9.64% in 2004, compared to 15.44% in 2003, and under-performed more conventional asset classes according to the CSFB Tremont hedge fund index.[2] Hedge fund managers attributed their lower performance in 2004 to low volatility and low interest rates. As a result, hedge funds have been looking for other asset classes to invest in. Seeking new opportunities where the sparkle can be put back on their reputation for producing a significant return on investment, they have identified the energy industry as having that potential. Early indications have only served to raise energy's profile since some of the better performing funds last year were focused on energy.

As a result, those ex-energy traders from the merchant era are now back in demand. Energy traders are being snapped up by hedge funds, multinational oil companies, and investment banks, and, in some instances, they have formed their own hedge funds based on their energy trading expertise. Indeed, the number of specialist energy commodity trading funds with between $1 million and $25 million in assets under management is growing rapidly. Not all the energy funds are so small. Several of the better known energy-focused funds are quite large, between $400 million and over $1 billion in assets under management. But we are also seeing a trend for much larger (greater than $1 billion under management) macro funds to switch more of their assets into energy, too. Today, our research has identified over 450 hedge funds that are active in the energy industry and that number continues to grow. Their assets under management range from $1 million to $2 billion.

WHY NOW?

Perhaps those of us in the energy industry have been too comfortable and too close to the business to notice the lack of sustained investment in our industry over the last 15 or so years. Whether it is oil and gas exploration, development of new reserves, or investment in the power industry, we are now seeing supply–demand tightness in all energy commodity markets and a historical under-valuation of energy companies and their assets. At the same time, demand has continued to grow robustly, and we are now at a stage where unforeseen events such as acts of terrorism, industrial disputes or accidents, weather-related events, and transmission constriction can be enough to create considerable concern about supply. This has resulted in increased price volatility, particularly in oil markets, and the funds love that price volatility.

There is now a growing awareness and even acceptance that in global oil markets supply tightness is such that OPEC no longer holds the swing vote on oil price formation. Today, oil prices are set by the trader's views on the NYMEX as much as anything else. News events such as those that occur in Iraq, Nigeria, Russia, and Venezuela over the potential for or actual supply disruptions, combined with reserve estimate reductions by major oil companies and the lack of transparency into the true nature of OPEC's own reserves, are now sufficient to cause $2+ daily swings in the oil price. Over the last two decades, oil companies have been more interested in buying back their stock to increase share price and please shareholders than in investing in new exploration or production activities. Wall Street just hasn't rewarded explorers and risk-takers, and the majors have not significantly increased their exploration and production budgets partly because other commodity markets, like steel, have also risen accordingly, adding to the expense side.

For each energy commodity the picture is similar. While oil is a global market and impacted by global events, regional natural gas, coal, and electric power markets are now often subject to similar supply tightness. The rush to natural gas-fired generation has helped to increase the perception of supply tightness in gas markets and the 2003 black outs did likewise for electric power.

Hedge funds like volatility. They like to identify trends and bet on those trends. Today they see that the trend in commodity prices has been largely up, and as they place their bets they are accentuating those trends. They are also followers and will follow each other, chasing the money and the returns. Some of the energy commodity trading funds had returns of over 40% during the past year and that has not gone unnoticed.

Similarly, as oil companies made money on increased commodity prices, their equities looked undervalued. Energy stocks, including oilfield services, looked the same. Also, the collapse of the merchant sector in the industry has created a significant distressed asset and debt play for the funds. As ex-merchants seek to raise cash by selling perfectly good assets, so the hedge funds have seen their opportunity, and today hedge funds are among the leading holders of ex-merchant debt backed by valuable collateral. Even as the industry seeks answers to its own problems, the hedge funds see opportunities in renewables and green trading, for example.

WHAT IS A HEDGE FUND?

A hedge fund is a type of "alternative" investment. The term "hedge fund" is a general, non-legal term that was originally used to describe a type of private and unregistered investment pool that uses sophisticated hedging and arbitrage techniques to trade in the corporate equity markets. While hedge funds have traditionally been limited to sophisticated, wealthy investors, over time, their activities have broadened into other financial instruments and activities. Today, the term "hedge fund" no longer really refers to their hedging techniques, which they may or may not use, but it simply refers to their status as private and unregistered investment pools. They are usually unregulated.

Hedge funds are somewhat similar to mutual funds in that they are both pooled investment vehicles that accept investors' money and generally invest it on a collective basis. However, hedge funds differ significantly from mutual funds because they are not required to register under all of the federal securities laws. They have this status because they generally accept only financially sophisticated investors and do not publicly offer their securities.

Hedge funds are also not subject to many of the numerous regulations that apply to mutual funds for the protection of investors, such as those requiring a certain degree of liquidity, that mutual fund shares be redeemable at any time, protecting against conflicts of interest, assuring fairness in the pricing of fund shares, disclosure regulations, limiting the use of leverage, and more. This freedom from regulation allows hedge funds to engage in leverage and other sophisticated investment techniques to a much greater extent than mutual funds. Hedge funds are subject to the antifraud provisions of the federal securities laws.

Part of the difficulty in defining what constitutes a hedge fund is that other investors engage in many of the same practices. For example, investment bank proprietary trading desks take positions, buy and sell derivatives, and alter their portfolios in the same manner as hedge funds. Individuals and institutions buy stocks on margin, and even commercial banks will use leverage. For these reasons the line between hedge funds and many other types of institutional investors is blurred.

However, there has been a change in the status of hedge funds recently. On December 2, 2004, the US SEC adopted Rule 203(b)(3)-2 and related amendments under the Investment Advisors Act of 1940. The new rules will require most hedge fund managers to register as investment advisors with the SEC. The effective date for many of the provisions of the new rule was February 10, 2005, and all hedge fund managers had to be in compliance by February 1, 2006.

The United States is not the only country looking more closely at a variety of hedge fund regulation issues. The French Regulator has also adopted new hedge fund regulations, providing for the creation of single manager funds and revising the rules regarding the criteria applicable to investment by French funds in hedge funds. Other nations are following suit or have already acted.

Hedge funds are often labeled in the press as secretive and by inference as sinister. They have been blamed by the media, politicians, and others as being behind the run-up in energy commodity prices, but, as we will show, this is grossly unfair on both counts. In the United States, hedge funds are not allowed to market themselves. They have to show that potential investors are properly qualified before they can send fund materials. This means that hedge fund websites are stark password-protected pages offering no explanation of what or who they are. It means that it is exceedingly difficult to obtain any information about the fund, its manager, and its strategy for making money. However, this is simply a legal requirement of being a hedge fund.

These funds have been justifiably criticized because of the lack of transparency in investment methods. For hedge fund investing to become more widespread, the issue of transparency has to be approached. A fine balance has to be achieved between risk exposure information for investors without position-level transparency, which may be detrimental to a fund's performance. A fund may also use proprietary strategies and trading tactics that are vital for the manager's success.

Outside of the United States, marketing and solicitation rules are different and more information can be readily obtained on funds in the United Kingdom, for example. In fact, several hedge funds, such as London-based RAB Capital, are actually publicly traded in the United Kingdom and therefore offer a significant level of transparency to potential investors and shareholders. The supposed secretive and therefore sinister nature of the funds is in fact something largely dictated to them under law and regulation. We suspect that they would like nothing better than to build their own brands, profiles, and investor base if they were permitted to, just like any other business.

Alternative investments, and hedge funds, in particular are now widely acknowledged as a source of enhanced return compared to traditional portfolios. A number of strategies are available to the hedge fund manager to take advantage of declining as well as rising markets. Alternative asset managers aim to generate high rates of return for a given level of risk, regardless of market trends. Contrary to the sometimes prevailing public opinion, intelligent and effective risk management is a core component of each hedge fund strategy.

Hedge funds offer investors a number of advantages over other types of investment including, for example:

- instant portfolio diversification
- products can be created and structured quickly to meet the demands of a client

- they have traditionally offered superior risk-adjusted returns over the long run, with better downside protection over other investments
- absolute performance orientation, which can deliver positive return in all market conditions
- the potential for low correlation to traditional asset classes, particularly fixed income.

Another type of fund that has gained in popularity among certain types of investor is the fund of fund (FoF) or multi-manager fund. A fund of fund is a managed portfolio of other hedge funds designed to provide greater risk diversification among a set of strategies, and investors in funds of funds are willing to pay two sets of fees, one to the fund-of-funds manager and another (usually higher) to the managers of the underlying funds. The fund of fund may be actively managed, meaning that the actual investments in other funds can change through time. The fund of hedge funds will be dealt with in more detail in Chapter 9, but according to Vann Hedge Fund Advisors[3] there are now over 3,000 fund of hedge funds compared to less than 50 in 1990, holding about 40% of the industry's assets. There are also investments known as fund of fund of funds, where investors of fund of funds invest in other fund of funds.

US HEDGE FUND REGULATION – A BRIEF UPDATE

As stated above, on December 2, 2004, the US SEC adopted Rule 203(b)(3)-2 and related amendments under the Investment Advisors Act of 1940. The new rules will require most hedge fund managers to register as investment advisors with the SEC. The effective date for many of the provisions of the new rule is February 10, 2005, and all hedge fund managers must be in compliance by February 1, 2006.

The new rules essentially require that advisors of "private funds" with more than 14 clients (more than 14 investors on a look-through basis) during the previous 12 months are required to register as an investment advisor if they have at least $30 million in assets under management. Also, they would be permitted to register if they have at least $25 million in assets under management. The SEC defined a "private fund" as an entity that:

1. Would qualify as an investment company under the US Investment Company Act of 1940 as amended if not for the exemption in either section (c)(1) or 3(c)(7) of the Investment Company Act;

2. Permits investors to redeem their interests within 2-years of purchase (lock up period); and
3. Offers its interests based on the investment advisory skills, ability or expertise of the investment advisor.

The new rules also require offshore advisors to look through all funds that they manage, whether or not those funds are located offshore and count as clients any investors that are US residents. Any offshore fund that had more than 14 US resident investors over the past 12 months would generally have to register also. The US resident designation is made at the time of investment in the private fund. An exception to the definition of "private fund" is included for a company that has its principal office and place of business outside of the United States, is regulated as a public investment company under the laws of a country other than the United States, and makes a public offering of its securities outside the United States in the same jurisdiction in which it is regulated as a private investment company.

Additionally, a registered investment advisor is generally prohibited from charging a client fees based upon capital gain or appreciation (meaning performance fees), unless the client is a "qualified client" (meaning a person or entity that has at least $750,000 under management with the advisor, has a net worth of more than $1.5 million at the time of the investment, or is a "qualified purchaser" as defined in the Investment Company Act). There is a "grandfathering" provision to allow investment advisors to maintain current fee arrangements with existing clients.

The new rules include a number of other provisions, such as modified record-keeping requirements, custody rules, and that readers should review the complete SEC rules for themselves.

Registration with the SEC as an investment advisor includes full compliance with the Advisors Act such as:

1. the preparation and filing of form ADV
2. the prohibition against charging performance fees to new investors who do not qualify as "qualified clients"
3. the adoption of written compliance procedures and the appointment of a chief compliance officer
4. the adoption of a written code of ethics
5. certain disclosure requirements upon payment of a cash referral fee to third-party placements agents
6. enhanced record-keeping requirements

7. additional reporting and audit requirements if the advisor has custody of its clients' assets
8. periodic inspections by the SEC.

One potential impact of the SEC registration requirement is a move to lengthen lock-up periods. Historically, lock-up periods had been 12 months, but recently managers have begun offering reductions in performance fees for longer lock-up periods. By lengthening such periods beyond 24 months, funds might avoid being defined as a "private fund," and hence work around the new rules. The two-year lock-up rule was apparently intended to distinguish between hedge funds and private equity funds, but may now be potentially used to avoid registration.

WHO INVESTS IN HEDGE FUNDS?

It is generally estimated that 80% of all hedge fund assets belong to high net-worth individuals. This group of investors was the first to massively allocate assets to hedge funds. Currently, US "accredited investors" (minimum $1 million net worth) are reported to have 8–10% of their portfolio allocated to hedge funds. But institutions have been increasing their allocations to hedge funds at a rapid pace, too.

According to Van Hedge Fund Advisors,[4] about 60% of US foundations and endowments, and around 20% of pension funds, have invested in hedge funds. European financial organizations are also known to allocate on average 1.3% of their total assets under management to hedge funds, and researchers believe that this percentage will rise above 5% in the future.

Some institutions are going still further. Some actually buy an entire fund; for example, Unicredito's purchase of Momentum Asset Management and JP Morgan Chase's purchase of Highbridge. Yet others set up an in-house fund of hedge funds (for example, the traditional manager Jupiter) or chose to establish an independent alternative investment firm. Institutions investing in hedge funds encompass many different sectors: portfolio managers (including private banks), insurance companies, corporate treasuries, pension plans, college endowments, and foundations. In all cases, the growing acceptance of hedge funds as a vehicle for institutional investment means that the available capital will continue to grow significantly.

Another survey by Prince & Associates[5] also shows that about 45% of family offices are invested in fund of hedge funds, and this is set to grow significantly. Family offices are the world's private investors who invest the monies of high net worth (HNW) individuals. Since the 1980s most hedge fund investing came from HNW individuals and private banks. This is also now changing with the bulk of the new exponential growth coming from insurance companies, pension funds, and endowments.

The 8,700 hedge funds with around $1,000 billion in assets under management is double the number of hedge funds in 1999. It demonstrates the rapid growth of the hedge fund as a popular investment vehicle among particular groups of wealthy investors. The asset management industry is changing rapidly. The poor performance of traditional and index tracking funds in past years and the success of many individual hedge funds with different strategies, have shown that alternative investments are a plausible means to invest. Alternative asset management differs from traditional asset management in its dynamic investment strategies, and hedge funds form the most dynamic sector of asset management today.

Stimulated by strong interest from sophisticated investors, this sector continuously attracts highly creative talented managers and enjoys sustained growth. The low correlation of hedge funds to equity and bond markets has become an increasingly important consideration for investors. Additionally, the effects of globalization have reduced the investor's ability to achieve meaningful diversification through geographical spreads across traditional markets.

Over the past decade, hedge fund assets expanded dramatically; from US$20 billion to almost $1 trillion today, and estimates are that they will reach over $2 trillion in five years.[6] There may be another 7,000 funds by then. In this decade the number of hedge funds has increased from 200 to more than 8,000 equally divided between the United States and offshore funds. However, some experts argue that hedge funds are experiencing a phase of consolidation, after which only 1,000 funds with an average size of $200 million (instead of $50 million today) may remain. That is highly debatable.

Hedge funds can take both long and short positions, and use leverage through financial derivatives in concentrated investments in order to maximize their profits. Their fund managers typically have a portion of their wealth tied up in the fund so that their relationship is in alignment with their investors.

Hedge funds have become a standard allocation class for corporations such as General Motors, educational institutions such as Harvard and Duke Universities, and state and local government pension funds. In Europe and Asia the boom is also underway. Germany has loosened its requirements so that there is no minimum investment requirement. In effect, they sell them to the retail market. But in reality there are only two hedge funds there at

FIGURE 1.1   Growth of global hedge funds

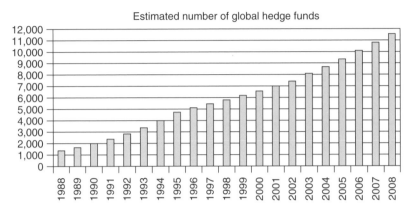

Note: Estimates for 2005–2008 are projections based on current data and may be revised in the future. © 2005 Van Hedge Fund Advisors International, LLC and or its affiliates, Nashville, TN.

Source: www.hedgefund.com

FIGURE 1.2   Growth of hedge fund assets under management

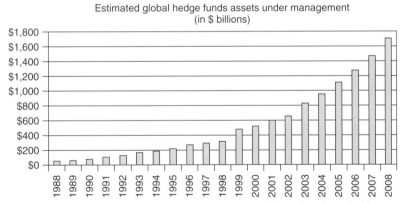

Note: Estimates for 2005–2008 are projections based on current data and may be revised in the future. © 2005 Van Hedge Fund Advisors International, LLC and or its affiliates, Nashville, TN.

Source: www.hedgefund.com

present. Singapore is allowing a tax holiday in order to attract hedge funds to establish there.

It should be pointed out that over 70% of hedge funds have less than $100 million to invest and are thus not necessarily good candidates for institutional investors, although that criterion may change for energy hedge fund investing. In the past, investors waited for funds to develop a 3- and

5-year track record, and could wait for funds to grow to acceptable size before investing. However, that is now changing and huge capital inflows coupled with the relatively few number of "institutional quality" funds will cause funds to grow very quickly. Therefore, investment decisions will need to be made quicker with less reliance on long-term track records. This is creating new investment criteria for the hedge fund industry.

According to Strategic Financial Solutions,[7] of the 8,000 or so distinct hedge funds and funds of hedge funds in 2004, approximately 5,500 were single manager hedge funds and accounted for over $1.5 trillion under management. They also found that nearly 175 of these funds have already surpassed the $1 billion assets under management mark, but that the majority manages less than $25 million. About 2,600 funds of hedge funds exist and manage approximately $415 billion in assets, but the majority of funds of hedge funds manage less than $50 million. The survey also found an additional 650 commodity trading advisors managing approximately $81 billion, with over 40% managing less than $25 million.

Worldwide financial assets are estimated at $126 trillion and the funds are now estimated to engage 0.8% of that amount. It is still really quite small.

THE BASICS OF HEDGE FUND INVESTING

As potential investors in a hedge fund, individuals first have to meet certain standards as HNW individuals, including, for example, having a net worth of $1 million or at least $500,000 under management with the advisor. Under Section 205(a) and Rule 205-3 of the Investment Advisors Act, investment advisors are prohibited from receiving hedge fund-like compensation based on a share of the gains, unless certain conditions are met. One of those conditions is that the advisor's clients are "eligible investors."

Should you be eligible to invest in a hedge fund you will then be subject to certain fees and conditions. The fees will include a management fee of between 0.5 and 2% (although some high-performing energy funds are charging more) on your entire holding in the fund, and a performance fee of around 20% assessed on gains over a 12-month period. Performance fees may include a hurdle rate that is usually tied to a benchmark rate, and/or a high watermark. For the manager to take a performance fee the return on the fund must be more than the hurdle rate and the fee will be paid on the portion of the return that is above the hurdle rate. A high watermark may also come into play. This provision means that investors only pay a performance fee on the actual gain in the 12-month period. So, for example, if the fund's net asset value (NAV) fell 10% during the year and then recovered to return a 15% return for the year, the investor pays performance fees only on the 15%, as opposed to the 25% gain that the fund experienced from its lowest NAV during the year.

For funds of hedge funds, the fees are generally lower to the fund of hedge funds manager; typically around a 1% management fee and a less than 10% performance fee. However, the investor is in effect paying two sets of fees: one for the fund of fund manager and another for the underlying hedge fund investment. Over the last year or so, fund of hedge fund fees have been facing some downward pressure from investors.

Additionally, the investor may be subject to a lock-up period during which monies may not be withdrawn from the fund. Typically, this has been three to six months, but lock-up periods are widely variable and may extend as much as two or more years, depending on the fund's strategy. The lock-up period is designed to insure that new investors give managers sufficient time to put their money to work. Recently, some funds have considered more than two-year lock-up periods to avoid SEC registration via a loophole in the regulation. After the lock-up period, investors are also subject to a redemption notice period of a month to three months or so, with a penalty payment for early redemption.

Terms and conditions vary from fund to fund and may include other restrictions and provisions beyond those general ones discussed here. We recommend that you fully understand all of the terms and conditions prior to making any investment in a hedge fund.

TYPES OF FUNDS

Of course, there are many different types and styles of hedge funds to choose from. But, according to Eichengreen and Mathieson[8] there are really three major classes of funds:

- macro funds, which take large unidirectional positions based on a top-down analysis of macroeconomic and financial conditions
- global funds, which take positions worldwide but employ bottom-up analysis
- relative value funds, which take bets on the relative prices of closely related securities.

Despite these, hedge funds usually follow a strategy. Most hedge fund strategies are market neutral as they make their money on the arbitrage between markets or individual securities, rather than betting one way or the other. That may not be true of energy hedge funds as the energy trader's mentality is often to take a "view on the market."

The following list defines a number of strategies employed by hedge funds.

Relative Value Strategies

- Equity market neutral – This seeks to profit by exploiting price inefficiencies between related securities, neutralizing exposure to market risk by combining long and short positions.
- Convertible arbitrage – This involves purchasing a portfolio of convertible securities and hedging a portion of the equity risks by selling short the underlying common stocks.
- Fixed-income arbitrage – A market neutral hedging strategy that seeks to profit by exploiting pricing inefficiencies between related fixed-income securities, while neutralizing exposure to market rate risk.
- Fixed-income – This invests in non-investment grade debt. Objectives may range from high current income to acquisition of undervalued instruments. Emphasis is placed on assessing credit risks of the issuer. Some of the available high-yield instruments include extendible/reset securities, increasing rate notes, pay-in-kind securities, step-up coupon securities, split coupon securities, and usable bonds.
- Fixed-income, mortgage-backed – Invests in mortgage-backed securities. Many funds focus on AAA-rated bonds.

Event-driven Strategies

- Distressed securities strategies invest in, and may sell short, the securities of companies where the security's price has been impacted by a distressed situation such as reorganization, bankruptcy, distressed sales, and other corporate restructuring.
- Merger arbitrage/Risk arbitrage – Merger arbitrage is also sometimes called risk arbitrage and involves investment in event-driven situations such as leveraged buy-outs, mergers, and hostile takeovers.

Other Strategies

- Equity hedge – Comprises long stock positions with short sales of stock or stock index options/futures. Has a long market bias.
- Sector composite – Invests in specific sectors. Primarily long energy, financial, healthcare/biotechnology, real-estate, and technology sectors.

- Emerging markets – Invests in the securities of companies or the debt of developing or emerging countries. Investments are primarily long.
- Global macro – Involves leveraging investments on anticipated price movements of stock markets, interest rates, foreign exchange, and physical commodities.
- Short selling – Involves the sale of a security not owned by the seller. It is a technique used to take advantage of an anticipated price decline.

Additional characteristics of hedge funds that should be borne in mind are as follows:

- many, but not all, hedge fund strategies tend to hedge against downturns in the markets being traded
- they are flexible in their investment options (can use short-selling, leverage, derivatives such as puts, calls, options, futures, and so on)
- they benefit by heavily weighting hedge fund managers' remuneration toward performance incentives, thus attracting the best brains in the investment business.

Additionally, as mentioned above, there are funds of funds too.

AN INTRODUCTION TO ENERGY AND ENVIRONMENTAL HEDGE FUNDS

The energy industry has come into sharper focus for hedge fund investing over the last 18 months because of the lack of opportunity in other markets and more recently the bull run in energy. Lower hedge fund returns are sparking much of the interest, but many of the larger macro funds view energy as an asset diversification play where they have been traditionally underweighted in investment. For example, the CAN$550 million Sprott Canadian Equity Fund significantly shifted its portfolio over 2004 to become more deeply involved in the energy segment by increasing its exposure to these markets to 40% of its assets.

Generally, the traditional classifications of hedge funds don't fit energy hedge funds very well. For that reason we have developed our own classification of energy hedge fund strategies that is discussed in more detail in Chapter 2. In fact, despite the interest in energy and the existence of more than 450 hedge funds with some energy interest, the energy industry as an investment opportunity poses some problems for traditional hedge fund managers and investors. Sophisticated investors, fund managers, and the financial press still do not appear to understand what is happening in the energy patch and in energy hedge funds. In private meetings with fund managers interested in energy, we still have had the uphill task of explaining that no track record in the hedge fund industry is not necessarily such a bad thing. Capable traders at banks and energy companies can show returns and have track records outside of hedge fund "land" to review.

Energy doesn't fit the traditional hedge fund mold. And yet there are over 450 funds out there, and growing in the energy and environmental fields. In our meetings with existing hedge fund managers, we have found that the opportunities in the energy complex are still relatively misunderstood and that to leverage these opportunities might well require a slightly non-traditional approach on the part of many investors. The most insurmountable barrier to entry into energy hedge fund land is the lack of knowledge of the world's largest and most complex business, which is rife with opportunity. Energy is the new kid on the block and it is still unfamiliar territory to many in the financial community. Yet the interest is there.

Another thing that we have learned is that investors, particularly institutional investors, like to look for younger managers early in their careers. This means a manager in his or her early thirties who has just started a fund. The theory is that the manager is hungry and the strategy will pay its largest returns earlier in its history. Interestingly, however, in discussions with other hedge fund managers we have heard conflicting opinions, such that the lack of at least a 24-month track record was considered a significant impediment. Perhaps this is simply related to the potential investor appetites on the parts of the funds and investors we have met with, but in energy, particularly energy commodities, our preferred managers would have some gray hair! Energy is a complex business and it has been moving sideways for 15 years or so. What we would want to see is someone who has been around long enough to have experienced both bull and bear energy markets and who understands these markets very well. On the other hand, as fund managers they need not have a long track record in managing a fund so long as they have a good track record as energy traders! In fact, given that most energy commodity funds have less than a two-year track record this is the only way to consider investing in the fund.

Notwithstanding the interest in the energy complex and its emerging environmental overlay, energy hedge funds are in something of a class of their own. Energy is an attractive asset class, but it is one that is just different enough to traditional investment opportunities to require a slightly different classification of strategies, a slightly different approach to manager selection, and due diligence. Energy is a risky business and neither those risks nor the underlying physical complexities are adequately understood by many in the financial community. However, as the number of energy funds grows and as the quality of the returns are observed, the interest and the willingness to change the model slightly will be there.

NOTES

1 "Hedge Fund Demand and Capacity 2005–2015," the Van Companies, August 2005.
2 CSFB Tremont hedge fund index, www.hedgeindex.com.
3 See (1) above.
4 See (1) above.
5 See (1) above.
6 See (1) above.
7 Strategic Financial Solutions, LLC – Database Study 2004.
8 Eichengreen and Mathieson, "Hedge Funds: What Do We Really Know?", International Monetary Fund report, September 1999.

CHAPTER 2

What are Energy and Environmental Hedge Funds?

H edge funds are not necessarily a new phenomenon in energy markets, nor indeed are commodity traders, who have been around since the late 1970s in the form of commodity pool operators (Cpos) or commodity trading advisors (CTAs). Equity-oriented hedge funds owning energy merchant stocks made money after the collapse of Enron by shorting the merchant segment of the industry during 2002. At that time, a number of very large commodity trading hedge funds also saw their opportunity to recruit talented and experienced energy traders from the collapsed merchant segment. However, there were just 20 or so hedge funds actively trading energy commodities two years ago. Today, there are more than 120 energy commodity hedge funds[1] and they have significantly impacted oil and gas futures trading on the NYMEX, and oil trading on ICE Futures (formerly the IPE). In our universe of energy hedge funds, we have counted more than 450 such funds in the energy and environmental space,[2] and we have been reliably informed from other hedge funds and investment banks that we have undercounted. There may be another 100 or more funds. So what happened to create this influx of new hedge funds in the energy sector?

Energy is the new game in town and it is already experiencing hedge fund market maturation dynamics. That is, some funds have already blown up this year in trading oil, gas, electric power, and weather. Undoubtedly more will follow. The reason is simply price volatility. Many hedge fund managers want alpha and low price volatility, and they will need to throw their rigid rule book out the window for the energy sector. Energy traditionally has exhibited high price volatility, and today it is exhibiting more than historical levels of price volatility across the complex. The point is that trying to construct an energy portfolio of 7 or 8% price volatility will leave you mostly with energy equities, but they too are starting to behave more like commodities due to the continued strength of the natural resource bull market; that is, they too are now exhibiting greater price volatility. Higher highs have bamboozled many financial analysts as they haven't figured out that everything has now changed in energy markets and that the mean reverting price models of the past are dead. The past no longer predicts the future in energy markets. Backward-looking models can't capture the new market dynamics.

Investors are looking for better returns, and they have turned to energy for those financial rewards since 2004. However, energy is a risky business. While many hedge funds concentrate mostly on price risk, there is almost an unlimited risk in the physically oriented energy business. There is operational risk, geopolitical risk, event risk, regulatory risk, weather risk, tax risk, volume risk, and other risks that add multiple dimensions to the more linear and traditional thinking of hedge fund manager. These externalities are also about to be overwhelmed by the emerging "environmental risk" that, as we will show, is the wave beyond the current energy hedge fund euphoria.

As the energy space becomes more attractive to investors, we have also observed the entrance of energy and natural resources funds of hedge funds during 2005. By investing in a portfolio of energy managers, funds of hedge funds can expose investors to a wider range of energy opportunities. We now see more than 25 natural resource and energy funds of hedge funds,[3] with more in formation, targeting energy for their returns. A problem with funds of hedge funds, however, is once again the accurate appreciation of the risks involved in energy and the volatility of the sector in general. Manager selection has to be performed carefully with additional due diligence steps that require detailed knowledge of energy markets.

From the outside looking in, activities such as electric power trading are attractive and bold, but power trading is particularly fraught with unexpected risks. The North American power markets are regional, immature, and largely physical, with day ahead financial markets being the most liquid. Power is real-time, non-storable, and as a consequence, a highly volatile commodity. Power plants are complex beasts with a wide array of fuels, types, and operating parameters to consider. Demand is equally difficult to predict as anyone in the load profile and forecasting business can tell you. Electric power trading is best performed with generation assets in the portfolio today, and a detailed understanding of the market and its risks and complexity.

And that's the problem with energy for people and organizations more used to traditional financial markets. It's simply a complex physical market. Superficially, it seems straightforward enough, but the more you probe into the business transactions required to make the industry work, the more complex and risky it becomes. Even crude oil markets, which are global and fairly mature, are not as simple as supply and demand. One has to consider transportation issues, crude quality issues, storage levels, refining capabilities, and so on.

A key feature of energy markets, due to their underlying physicality, is known as "volume" risk. Put simply, this is related to the need to actually deliver the physical commodity at some point. It is about the risks implicit with being unable to deliver or produce the commodity. In actuality, volume risk is intimately related with many other risk factors and it has been this type of risk that has been on the mind of oil traders as tropical storms have recently moved across the Gulf of Mexico, for example. The questions include: How would supply be impacted? What damage might be done to the infrastructure? How long might repairs take? Volume risk serves to remind us that this is fundamentally a physical and complex industry.

In discussing the uniqueness of energy risks, we ought to mention environmental issues, too. Already, environmental issues are having a bigger impact on energy than might initially be considered. They impact on project costs requiring compliance with environmental regulations, such as having to consider the removal of oil production facilities in the North Sea for example. They impact on transportation, such as the requirement to scrap single-hulled tankers and replace them with multi-hulled versions. They impact on refining capacity as refiners have to change set-ups for seasonal gasoline varieties to meet more severe and complex standards. The environment will continue to have an ever-larger impact on the energy industry.

WHY NOW?

In considering this question, there are a number of issues that bear consideration. First, the hedge fund universe has seen returns diminish considerably over the last two to three years as existing strategies in established markets became overcrowded. An average 8% or so return during 2004 for hedge fund investors is simply not considered an adequate reward for the risks that investors take by placing their money with a fund. Meanwhile, those early energy-focused funds returned between 40% and 100% to investors during the same period in 2004. While these types of returns are not sustainable for the longer term and have certainly come back to earth in 2005, energy-focused strategies provide an opportunity to make better returns in the 15 to 20% range, which is better than the average fund.

A second reason behind the energy upsurge is that there were many experienced and talented energy traders let go by the merchants and utilities during the past several years since the Enron bankruptcy and the demise of energy merchant trading. As the investment banks and hedge funds moved in, many of these skilled resources were snapped up by existing hedge funds, while others saw the opportunity to set up their own hedge funds to trade energy commodities. However, the energy trading talent pool isn't and never was very deep. Already there is a shortage of good trading talent.

But the overwhelming reason for the rush to energy has been the supply–demand dynamics across energy commodities that have driven commodity prices higher than ever before. Similarly, volatilities have increased and hedge funds like trading volatile and not flat markets. The bull run in commodities has resulted in higher profits for energy companies that produce energy, and spilled over into other segments of the industry such as oilfield services, refining, and tanker markets, as activity levels have increased, creating an opportunity in equities, too. Additionally, restructuring across the industry as cash-strapped merchants sold off assets has created secondary debt, distressed generation assets, and other investment plays across the industry in which hedge funds are now playing a role.

Rising oil and other energy commodity prices have had the additional effect of focusing minds on energy efficiency. While current oil prices do not seem to have had much impact on economic growth rates and buyers' behavior today, there is a realization that increased energy efficiency programs will be needed and also a renewed interest in other technologies that might provide alternative energy sources and investment in the alternative energy equities, which now number over 350 stocks in the United States and Europe. This change has also to be set against the growing consumer interest in all things environmental that has resulted in new regulations around emissions in particular, but it has added burden, cost, and complexity across the energy industry as well. The confluence of energy and environment is really just now beginning, but it too provides a wealth of opportunities for investors and hedge funds.

TYPES OF ENERGY AND ENVIRONMENTAL HEDGE FUNDS

Many of the existing macro funds pursue long/short commodity strategies, taking bets in a variety of commodity markets such as grain, metals, soft commodities (such as coffee, sugar, and cocoa), and energy. These funds tend to be larger and well established with significant assets under management (often greater than $1 billion). Some of the macro funds engage in playing the spread between commodity markets and equities, going long energy commodities and short energy equities for example. While the amount of money coming into these funds is growing, they have also shifted their investment mix toward a heavier energy component.

Another indirect indicator of hedge fund activity is the formation of energy-specific hedge funds. Ex-energy traders from the merchant sector have set up hedge funds specifically to trade energy and energy-related commodities such as weather and uranium. Although most are still relatively small in comparison to the macro, largely commodity-based, funds, the new energy hedge funds are often actively trading physical energy as well as derivatives, using their prior experience in energy markets to attract investors. Many new energy-specific funds are in formation and range in size from $1 million to $2 billion. In fact, traders with prior energy experience are now in great demand from the funds and investment banks, attracting hefty salaries and bonuses.

Trying to put the traditional hedge fund financial overlay into the energy complex is difficult. No matter how hard the quantitative analysts try, it just doesn't happen that way. Why not? Because energy is the world's largest business with over $4 trillion in annual trade, but energy is also a very immature financial market. In fact, it is probably behind agriculture, the world's second-largest business, in terms of financial maturation.

We developed our classification of hedge funds in energy (see Table 2.1) simply because traditional classification models say little or nothing about energy hedge funds. We classify energy funds in terms of their style (equities long/short), commodities, diversified (equities and commodities, debt, distressed assets, and alternative energy for example), and industry sector or commodity focus. While the tendency may be to look to recently high-performing and sexy commodity-focused hedge funds, the danger is that these are often the most risky strategies. Meanwhile, the relative boring energy equity long/short strategies have also performed well over the last 2+ years, and may even be outperforming commodities this year.

ENERGY COMMODITY FUNDS

Energy commodity funds trade all of the energy commodities, as well as energy-related commodities such as uranium, sugar, and steel. Some commodity funds trade a variety of different commodities, including metals, agricultural commodities, softs, grains, and so on, but also have a significant exposure to energy commodities in their portfolio. Some have

Table 2.1 Energy hedge fund styles and strategy terms

Style/Strategy	Description
Energy specialist fund	A hedge fund that invests only in the energy industry or in energy-related investment opportunities.
Energy-oriented fund	A hedge fund that does not focus exclusively on energy but has a proportion (more than 20%) of its assets under management (AUM) exposed to various energy investments.
Equity	A fund that invests in energy company (public or private) equities and other securities, or options on equities for example. May seek general energy exposure or be energy sector specific
	Often the equity fund will utilize energy ETFs or other instruments for hedging purposes, too.
Equity long/short	An energy equity fund that takes both long and short positions. Most equity long/short energy funds have a long bias.
Equity long only	An energy equity fund that takes long positions only.
Commodity	An energy fund that trades energy commodities. The commodities traded may be exchange traded future and options, via over the counter transactions or through passive indexes. It can trade financial and/or physical energy. The fund can trade any set of energy and energy-related (for example, weather, sugar, and uranium) commodities.
Alternative energy (or "green")	An energy fund that specializes in environmental investment strategies. It may focus on equities, commodities or both. The fund's environmental component, however, is around the energy industry (for example, emissions, renewable energy, energy efficiency, and so on.)
Water fund	A hedge fund that is targeting the water industry either through equities or through other investments such as water rights.
Diversified	A predominantly equity fund that uses up to 20% of its assets under management to invest in energy commodities either through exchange-traded futures and options, or in some instances oil and gas reserves in the ground. The exposure to commodities can provide an arbitrage opportunity against the equities.

Table 2.1 *(continued)*

Style/Strategy	Description
Distressed debt and assets	A fund that specializes in distressed assets in the energy and other industries, and engages in corporate restructuring and debt restructuring.
Fund of fund	A fund that invests in other hedge funds seeking a lower risk/return than through an investment in a single hedge fund. See Chapter 9.

been set up by ex-merchant traders or ex-investment banker energy traders, and have a more focused energy commodity approach. We find that many are considering or are already trading emissions, particularly in Europe. Many of the energy commodity trading funds follow more fundamentally based strategies, as opposed to the trend-following strategies commonly used by CTAs. They are also involved in energy spreads trading, which is a less risky manner to trade the energy commodity markets.

During the past two years, we have seen some issues arise with commodity trading strategies. Already, a small number of newer funds have exited the business as they discovered that their strategies were not paying off for crude oil options trading, natural gas trading, and financial power trading. In particular, problems have arisen in funds trading highly volatile electric power markets in the United States, or those that simply pursued a traditional merchant-type strategy without the help of the merchant company behind them; that is, owning physical assets such as generation assets. Energy is a risky business and a commodity trading strategy is the most risky strategy for hedge funds. Nevertheless, hedge funds have significantly impacted both North American oil and gas commodity markets. They now account for over 50% of the open interest in energy contracts, as evidenced by the trade of non-commercials as defined by the US Commodity Futures Trading Commission (CFTC). (This will be analyzed in greater detail in Chapter 6.)

Energy commodity markets are behaving differently today, and there is no historical precedent for some of this behavior. We argue that there is a structural change underway in energy markets. As a result, history is no longer a predictor of the future. The speed of hedge fund trading is one example of the power of hedge funds to influence energy markets.

Today, we are seeing the rapid financialization of energy trading. Electric and gas utilities, particularly in the United States, and some in Europe, are mostly continuing to exit energy trading. Their place is taken by both investment banks and hedge funds. Natural gas trading, which broke down after the demise of Enron and the energy merchants, has taken three years to be reestablished in energy trading markets. Today, BP is the largest natural gas trader in North America. Similarly, the new financial risk entails ownership or access to physical assets in many cases. Financial trading, thus, has become reestablished on both the established energy exchanges (NYMEX and ICE Futures), and the deeper over-the-counter (OTC) markets through new participants.

This new triangle of trading includes multinational oil and gas companies, investment banks, and hedge funds with electric and gas utilities increasingly marginalized in the North American markets. Energy markets in Europe are a little different to those in North America and tend to be dominated by large national oil, gas, and power companies. As a result, commodity hedge fund participation in the energy space has mostly been confined to the United Kingdom, Switzerland, and Scandinavia, as opposed to continental Europe where there are insufficient counterparties. Scandinavian hedge funds are almost all related to trading electric power derivatives in the fairly mature regional NordPool, and one has started trading CO_2 emissions credits there as well. In Asia, there are a few energy-specific hedge funds, and some entrance by more established macro funds. We think Asia will become a hotbed of rising hedge fund activity in the energy and environmental market, probably led by Chinese and Indian participation in these markets.

EQUITY FUNDS

There are now over 125 energy equity funds in our Energy Hedge Fund Center data base. Generally, the funds have a long bias, and track the entire energy complex by taking long and short positions in energy equities. The funds often diversify by seeking exposure to different segments in the industry, such as exploration and production (E&P), MLPs, or utilities for example. Others may diversify by seeking out early opportunities with private companies pre-initial public offering (IPO) and helping those companies float on markets like the AIM in the United Kingdom, as has been seen for both energy, carbon trading, and clean technology companies.

Recently, there has been a trend among newer energy equity funds to diversify their portfolios even more by seeking some exposure to energy commodities via exchange-traded futures and options. Generally, these funds limit their commodity exposure to just 10–20% of their portfolio, and they are seeking "arbitrage" between equities and commodities. Other funds, particularly those focused more on the E&P side of the business, may also seek to become owners of oil and gas reserves in the ground via acquisition of producing properties, or by farming in to exploration activities. In fact, the hedge fund model is changing as their equity participation makes them lenders of project finance capital for both oil and gas exploration and production, as well as clean technology and carbon finance.

During 2005, the equity-focused funds have had better performance on average than the commodity funds. In part, this is due to the behavior of energy commodity markets this year, as this behavior has become dislocated from historical trends. Largely, this is due to the impact of greater profits and greater activity levels in the industry impacting on the perceived value of energy and energy-related equities. Not only have energy equities thrown off some good dividends, but they have also appreciated considerably this year, except for a sell-off in early October 2005. Energy equities may still be undervalued in certain industry segments, given the need for majors to replace reserves (via the acquisition of independents) and the anticipated upsurge in M&A activity in the North American utilities segment after the repeal of PUHCA (the Public Utility Holding Company Act, which has thwarted large utility consolidation in the United States), due to the passage of the US Energy Policy Act of 2005.

DEBT, DISTRESSED ASSETS AND OTHER INFRASTRUCTURE STRATEGIES

The counterparty credit crisis that impacted on the industry after the collapse of the merchant sector of the industry has meant that assets have been sold off to provide cash to pay debts. These assets run the entire gamut of the complex from producing properties through gathering systems, gas plants, pipelines, electricity generation, and more. The hedge funds have seen opportunities in this arena too and are now one of the largest providers of debt financing to the old merchants.

The most obvious activity in this area of the energy business on the part of the funds has been in the MLP area to date. The MLP is a tax efficient structure created two decades ago by the US government, primarily for the E&P sector; however, it has become one of the vehicles of choice for investment banks and hedge funds to purchase industry assets in the midstream as well as the upstream side of the business. The MLP structure allows funds to participate in debt financing in order for it to purchase more assets and to convert that debt to equity in the form of units as it is floated. By owning declining assets that throw off cash, the unit-holders benefit from price appreciation and healthy earnings. We are also hearing talk of "Green MLPs" for biomass plays in the green financial markets.

Hedge funds have been primary lenders and buyers in the distressed generation asset arena, and actually own several utilities like MidAmerican Energy, which is owned by billionaire Warren Buffet. We expect more utility asset ownership by hedge funds in the short term, but they will eventually sell the utility assets back to other utilities. We have already seen this in the NRG transaction where NRG and Texas Genco LLC entered into a definitive agreement on October 2, 2005, for NRG to acquire all the outstanding equity of Texas Genco LLC for approximately $5.8 billion, comprised of approximately $4 billion in cash and $1.8 billion in common and preferred stock. In addition, NRG will assume approximately $2.5 billion of Texas Genco debt. KKR, Blackstone Group, Helman and Friedman, and Texas Pacific Group were the hedge funds that were instrumental in acquiring these assets only 15 months before and then selling them to NRG.

Recently, a number of funds have been evolving into a hybrid investment model of private equity capital and a hedge fund structure. Investors face an elongated lock-up period for their money in these investment structures. In part, the supply–demand dynamic in the industry today has been brought on by a lack of investment in the industry. Now that the obvious investors on the part of the merchants have gone, these funds see opportunities to finance capital projects related to infrastructure such as generation facilities, for example.

A fall out of this activity by hedge funds has also been the influence of the funds at the board level. For example, hedge funds now own a substantial piece of Aquila and have sought board-level appointments with that company; while in the United Kingdom, hedge funds sought to block the restructuring of British Energy. Such funds have also been involved with the Drax power station in the United Kingdom and in numerous other situations where they have forced management into restructuring or other activities.

The energy industry is rich with possibilities along the value chain for hedge funds that can pressure companies to restructure by taking a significant equity interest. The hedge funds seek undervalued or under-performing companies where restructuring will result in increased share prices, or debt restructuring where the hedge funds will profit in the longer term.

ALTERNATIVE ENERGY OR GREEN HEDGE FUNDS

The number of environmental or green hedge funds is also growing substantially, and we now see more than 20 funds in this area with more in formation. These funds are seeking, through a variety of strategies, to invest in and profit from emissions trading, carbon credits, investment in environmental company equities and debt, investment in renewable energy schemes, and in trading the more established SO_2 (acid rain) and NOx (urban ozone) markets in the United States. There are a few that invest in clean technology or alternative energy equities only, and some in both equities and commodities.

These so-called green hedge funds are taking a somewhat different tack than usual in emerging markets, so that the hedge fund business model is changing to more of a hybrid venture capital/hedge fund strategy to lock down investment from two to four years and trade the monetized credits for projects. Some big macro hedge funds in New York like the illiquidity of the emerging environmental financial markets, as they see wide arbitrage opportunities for emissions and renewable energy trading specifically. There are also a number of nascent exchanges for trading of emissions in both Europe and the United States. And most importantly, there is obvious cross-commodity arbitrage for energy hedge funds trading oil, gas, power or coal. We continue to expect the green space to really heat up further as the European Union Emissions Trading Scheme (EU ETS) and Kyoto generate more interest in green trading during the next two years. (This area will be covered more extensively in Chapter 7 of this book.)

FUND OF HEDGE FUNDS

The most recent marker of the ongoing investor interest in energy has been the emergence of funds of hedge funds focused on energy and natural resources. We have tracked more than 25 funds of hedge funds with more information. By investing with different hedge fund managers and running a portfolio of energy hedge funds, the fund of hedge funds attempts to reduce risk and volatility, but delivers slightly less return after fees. This approach is popular with privately wealthy individuals, family offices, and institutional investors such as pension funds.

Additional benefits for investors are a lower minimum investment amount (perhaps $25,000, as opposed to $100,000+ for single hedge funds, although we have seen as low as $5,000 for one European hedge fund) and the fund of funds' ability to gain access to hedge funds that are closed to individual investors. In the latter case, many of the better known earlier energy hedge funds are now closed to investors.

WHERE THIS IS ALL GOING

While energy hedge funds have often been the scapegoat for the run on energy commodity prices, there is little evidence to support that. We estimate that the commodity funds control only about $50–$60 billion in assets, and with many of them focused on more fundamentally driven strategies, they have little impact on price formation even with leverage. However, they do impact intra-day volatility in the way that they trade. What is often missed by the media is that energy hedge funds are endemic to the industry and pursue a wide variety of strategies that have little impact on commodity price formation.

We expect to see hedge funds and other investment vehicles entering the energy industry. After all, energy is in the news on a daily basis and the opportunities to make money in the complex are increasingly obvious as a result. The issue for investors, however, is can these funds make money in a down market, too?

Traditionally, hedge funds have played in the energy equity markets and they made a mint shorting equities of energy merchant power companies and electric utilities in 2002. In 2003 they looked for opportunities in the equity markets, especially after the August blackout, but found little to invest in on the equity side. In 2004 they entered commodity trading in energy in a big way. Starting in the well-established and liquid oil markets they migrated into natural gas and electric power trading, as well as other energy commodities. There are several plays that they are interested in. One is the pure commodity trading play. The second is the energy equity/energy commodity arbitrage. And third is the distressed asset play on merchant generation, which they are now beginning to acquire. They have the credit and risk appetite to pull off this trifecta.

What many hedge funds often don't have is the deep energy knowledge base to be successful. Some will be, but many will blow up. While traders love volatility, the energy trading complex is the most volatile on earth, and electric power wins first prize due to its lack of storage capability, multi-fuel capability, and endemic weather risks. It can bring spectacular profits for a month or quarter, followed by even more spectacular losses.

Speculative energy trading is back. The guys with the "black boxes" and the deep pockets are going to shake up the markets. Expect more price volatility in the future. The added liquidity that they bring to markets is a double-edged sword in that they also bring much more unpredictability and volatility to the short end of the markets. The new energy markets promise to become more volatile and increasingly dominated by financial players. Many will not be able to manage the risks of the energy complex, but their attitude is that they are masters of the universe.

The energy hedge fund arena is ramping up due to the need for higher returns for hedge fund investors. Energy hedge funds are still only about 5% of the hedge fund universe, but continue to grow in North America and Europe predominantly. It can be said that New York and London continue to be the twin capitals of both energy trading and energy hedge funds. Houston, Calgary, Singapore, and Switzerland play second fiddle.

Also, watch as the investment interest in energy migrates to interest in environmental plays. A trip to London during 2005 revealed that every single European hedge fund that we spoke to (and there were more than a dozen), was either engaged or interested in carbon emissions trading. While carbon trading is the current focus of attention, there are also markets in the United States for sulfur dioxide (SO_2), nitrous oxides (NOx), and renewable energy credit trading. Watch the environment as investment opportunities expand, contract, and mature. Risk is how the funds make money. Welcome to the energy and environmental hedge fund club where risk is endemic.

There is a school of thought that the funds will enter energy trading and leave. We don't believe it as there is a real sustained business here. The scale and momentum that is now underway is unprecedented and signals a structural change in energy trading itself. The new triangle of trading is energy hedge funds, investment banks, and multinational oil companies who have the balance sheet, risk appetite, and trading acumen to bring energy trading to the next level.

MANAGED FUTURES AND COMMODITY POOLS

Some old-time brokers and traders think that the entrance of hedge funds into energy is no big deal. They point to the fact that investment management professionals have been using managed futures for more than 30 years. More recently, institutional investors such as corporate and public pension funds, endowments and trusts and banks have made managed futures part of a well-diversified portfolio. In 2001 it was estimated that more than $35 billion was under-management by trading advisors according to the Chicago Board of Trade (CBOT). The growing use of managed futures by these investors may be due to the increased institutional use of the futures markets. Portfolio managers have become more familiar with futures contracts. Additionally, investors want greater diversification in their portfolios. They seek to increase portfolio exposure to international investments and non-financial sectors, an objective that is easily accomplished through the use of global futures markets.

The term "managed futures" describes an industry made up of professional money managers known as CTAs. These trading advisors manage client assets on a discretionary basis, using global futures markets as an investment medium. Trading advisors take positions based on expected profit potential. There are over 450 CTAs actively trading the energy complex, managing almost $70 billion in assets according to Tremont's TASS Research,[4] up from $20 billion in 136 funds four years ago.

Commodity pools are enterprises in which several individuals contribute funds in order to trade futures or futures options collectively. They are analogous to mutual funds in that many investors pool their assets to gain the power to make trades that they could not make individually. Additional benefits include bypassing margin requirements and limiting risk to the amount invested in the pool. The trade publication, *Energy Risk*,[5] estimates that 68 of the top 100 hedge funds are registered as CPOs.

DIVERSIFICATION OF RISK AND HEDGE FUND COMPOSITION

Diversification of risk-based portfolios now includes energy as an asset diversification strategy. While global stock markets remain relatively flat, the smart money has decided to chase commodities such as energy and metals. Commodities are now the asset class that is proving enticing for global portfolio investors.

Since hedge funds can engage in complex trading strategies, are secretive and largely unregulated, they're often a convenient whipping post for events in the market. In 1998, for example, they were accused of playing a pivotal role in the Asian financial crisis. And during the bear market of 2001 and 2002, hedge funds were criticized for fueling the declines by shorting stocks and corporate bonds. Today, they are blamed for the run up in oil prices to a large degree. In reality it's hard to know how much hedge funds have contributed to previous market declines or how much they're fueling the rise in oil today.

In fact, their impact is almost impossible to quantify since it is hard to factor out what hedge funds did and did not do to the oil complex. The reality is that they have had some impact and the bigger reality is that with the ramping of trading operations all over the world, their impact will grow in coming years. However, they are definitely a contributing factor to energy market psychology on a daily basis.

It is however disingenuous to say they are having no impact and that floor traders on the NYMEX are having a greater impact. In fact, the days are passing when the floor ruled oil price formation. Today, the funds are here and they are here to stay. It can be argued that the funds are not doing anything that large investment banks such as Goldman Sachs and Morgan Stanley have been doing in racking up record-breaking commodity trading profits. Like the funds, the banks don't talk about their proprietary trading desks, but their volume is increasing.

Some analysts claim that these oil speculators aren't hedge funds *per se*, but commodities trading advisers, or CTAs, which are regulated by the US Commodity Futures Trading Commission (CFTC). Still, the distinction between CTAs and hedge funds is somewhat nebulous. Frankly, it is splitting hairs as CTAs are hedge funds, too. Basically, highly levered pools of capital through either managed funds accounts by CTAs or hedge funds are getting significant cash injections to trade in the energy complex. The obvious fact is that hedge funds are highly levered. Financial leverage is an important component of the trading strategies.

A QUICK GLOBAL ASSESSMENT OF ENERGY FUNDS

Germany really only has two funds now, although it is looking at entry strategies for more fund participation. One senior analyst who recently went to Germany called it the "monopoly of Deutsche Bank." But right next door is Switzerland, and there is lot of activity to enter the energy sector with funds such as Harcourt AG. Recently, we have observed a number of new funds with an energy or commodities focus in France.

In Japan, we still see no energy hedge funds yet, but the maturation process is actually farther progressed than Germany. Japan has seen a rise of almost 40% in hedge fund money in the past year. There are also high price correlations between the Nikkei and oil prices. The recent rise in oil prices has lead to a downward trend on the Nikkei. Portfolio diversification demands that they expand into energy.

Singapore is currently the oil trading center in Asia. The Singaporean government has recently given a tax holiday, but we have found one energy trading hedge fund surface so far.

Hong Kong regulators may allow hedge funds for retail investors. Hedge fund managers and investment advisers may have an easier time meeting various licensing and qualification requirements in Hong Kong if the city's securities regulators agree to relax guidelines governing the sale of investment products to retail investors.

The Chinese have been on fire in oil futures trading since the end of April. They have their single energy futures contract on the Shanghai Futures Exchange. However, they are very much like what Chicago is to New York: a much more speculative town with smaller capital markets, but growing.

As far as we are able to learn, there has been some entrance of energy hedge funds in Australia as pension fund monies are known to be looking for homes. Given Australia's heavy commodity exposure in energy and mining, and well-developed capital markets, we expect more funds next year.

TECHNICAL ANALYSIS AND ITS ROLE IN ENERGY TRADING

Timing is the key to any successful trading or hedging program. But getting the timing right will always be more of an art than an exact science. However, there are some tools that can help to build up a clearer picture of when the market price trend may change, which in turn should provide an idea of market direction and timing. There are two main types of analysis that can be carried out: fundamental analysis and technical analysis.

Fundamental analysis deals with the supply and demand factors of the physical energy world, whereas technical analysis is concerned with the price history of the market. In reality, most people use a combination of the two. In other words, when a general technical picture of market direction and timing has been established, any new fundamental information can be incorporated into the picture as it is announced. Hedge funds generally often seem to be more technical traders and do not heavily rely on fundamentals. They follow trends.

There are a number of ways of defining technical analysis, but, in a nutshell, it is the study of market prices, with price charts being the primary tool. It is based on the idea that historical price movements of a commodity can be used to predict the sentiment and the expectations of market participants with regard to the future price trends. It fits the black box trading of certain hedge funds like a glove.

One thing is certain, technical analysis can help when making timing and market direction predictions. However, it is not enough to rely on a single technical tool, and therefore a combination of five or six technical tools and approaches is needed to help build up a good picture of market trend price targets and timing. It should also be remembered that there are certain types of market price movement that can render some technical analysis tools useless and too unreliable to follow.

Technical analysis works on some key principles. These are:

- that all known market fundamentals (news in the market) are accounted for and reflected in market prices. The market has absorbed all the news, and the price represents a consensus on which it should be based on all known data. This is certainly true in efficient markets that have good trading volume (liquidity)
- that prices move in trends and that the trends persist
- that market action is repetitive or cyclical.

The key is that technical analysis reveals price trends. Generally, the trend is simply the direction of the market. More precisely, market moves are usually a series of zigzags, resembling a series of waves with fairly obvious peaks and troughs. It is the overall direction of these peaks and troughs that constitute market trend. Most of the time, traders watch for a change in trend, and subsequent confirmations that the trend is changing or has changed, before acting on that information. Trend lines play an important part in illustrating that a change has been made. Also, they give traders an indication of the price levels that might trigger a price change or a new buying or selling interest. Trend lines should be drawn off two price points: a high or low, and the earliest price points that can be found.

Energy futures markets (that is, NYMEX or IPE, the International Petroleum Exchange) tend to reverse or consolidate once they reach one of these ratio levels (measured from the distance of the previous trends reversal). This means that they can be very useful at position entry and exit levels.

There are many types of mathematical indicators in the technical analysis field, but here we focus on some key ones that work on a consistent basis for the energy futures markets. These indicators can give a trader a simple, yet very effective tool for building up a view on price direction and timing, when used in parallel with bar charts, support/resistance levels, gaps, trend lines, volume, and open interest information.

There are a large number of tools that can be used for technical analysis of the market and it is important that they be used in combination with each other. But even if the five or six most appropriate analytical tools have been chosen to study the prevailing conditions, the results may still not always prove reliable. The truth is that in the real world there are some days when technical factors drive the market and others when it is driven by fundamentals.

Some hedge funds have moved from technology to energy, thinking that all the world works according to models. This is a very mechanistic approach to energy trading. As they rise up the learning curve, hedge fund managers will get more cautious, based on both fundamental values and in terms of money management algorithms. These factors will lead to fund managers taking smaller positions as prices become more volatile.

One fundamental factor that is never going to go away, and thus makes energy attractive to speculators, is that there is a lack of transparency on reliable supply and demand due to OPEC's secrecy and the inability of the International Energy Agency to produce reliable and accurate data. The erratic nature of supply–demand data and OPEC's lying about their actual production will keep markets volatile. The speculator is attracted to this price volatility that the lack of market transparency breeds. It will continue to be a self-perpetuating cycle in oil markets and will increase trading liquidity.

While CTAs and CTA-like hedge funds in energy commodities tend to follow a more technical trading pattern, we have observed that many of the energy hedge funds formed by ex-energy traders are following a more market fundamentals-based approach. In reality, as discussed above, all are essentially a mixture of the two approaches, but the emphasis on approach tells you a lot about the fund, its strategy, and its manager. In either case there are problems and these problems have come home to roost in recent months. Technical traders using models often use past history as a predictor of future trends. On the other hand, a more fundamental approach relies on information about macro and micro trends and will, by necessity, take into consideration historical precedent as well. Therein lies the issue. The energy markets this last summer and fall have shown a tendency not to repeat historical patterns and a structural change is underway. As a result, neither of the trading approaches has performed well recently.

NOTES

1 "Directory of Energy Hedge Funds," November 2005 issue, The Energy Hedge Fund Center.
2 See (1) above.
3 See (1) above.
4 TASS Asset Flows Report, Tremont TASS Research, www.hedgeworld.com.
5 Stella Harrington, "A Good Bet for 2005," *Energy Risk*, February, 2005, vol. 2, issue 4, pp. 14–17.

CHAPTER **3**

Why are Hedge Funds Attracted to Energy and the Environment?

This chapter will set the stage for the changes underway in energy markets and where investors can play in these markets. Today, the most amazing thing about the energy industry is the lack of accurate and experienced analytical support offered to investors from its Wall Street and City of London energy analysts. By and large, the analysts have followed a crowd mentality and therefore have been out of touch in painting an accurate picture of what is really happening in the global energy sector this year and last. Frankly, they have been plain wrong in expecting prices to revert to historical means. In fact, with oil prices where they are, there is a continued lack of recognition that the energy sector may go still higher. Something has changed this time and many of these analysts missed the investment opportunity.

Today, the energy sector is in focus because of many changes and factors. It is not something that can be distilled into a sound bite for the TV news. Its complexity has scared off investors who should look at energy as an asset class for investment diversification and one where they should be more heavily weighted in. And guess what? It's still not too late. The energy bull market in oil, gas, power, and coal will continue for at least the next two years. After that, all bets are off; but the sector may get an unexpected uplift from the nascent and surging global environmental financial markets, which are just starting to take root in both the alternative energy sphere and emissions trading. Already, the Emissions Trading Scheme (ETS) in the European Union has caused a stampede of investment in to carbon hedge funds and emissions trading in Europe in 2005. The environmental play is actually much wider than that. But once again, the linear thinking of the media is to get it down to one sound bite. This is not the dot com bubble and bust of several years ago that many claim energy now is. This is real and it is driven by market fundamentals!

Energy is now being driven by the fundamentals of the tremendous global under-investment in the oil and gas industry, electric power industry, and transportation sectors, coupled with rising global demand for fossil fuels. This is a global phenomenon of industrialization and globalization trends that have now accelerated throughout the world. New commodity price moves continue to accelerate with no "conservation effect" to speak of, with oil reaching all-time highs of $70 per barrel in 2005, and it may reach higher prices in 2006. The reality is that the energy sector now is a tremendous investment opportunity for investors, and the question becomes how do investors play this sector.

There are many factors driving higher energy prices. Energy in current dollars is cheap compared to the 1970s. This has made oil consumption a one-way street; that is, continuously higher consumption with little economic braking due to price. Price has so far been almost irrelevant, having little impact on the US economy and for that matter the global economy. While China and now India are continually blamed for their higher consumption, the reality is that the US economy consumes over 20 million barrels of oil per day, or over 20% of global oil demand. Also, the US economy has effectively eaten up all the energy efficiency gains of the past three decades. The 1990s saw a period of relatively stable and not very volatile energy prices. This led to the purchasing by Americans of both larger and less energy-efficient cars and homes. Cost concerns are beginning to develop, but energy, even at these higher price levels, is still relatively cheap in real dollars. This demand-driven market just won't quit, for as the world more rapidly industrializes and globalizes it uses more fossil fuels year after year.

These factors have led to the current high oil price world where reserve capacity is increasingly constrained, global refining capacity is tight, and transportation markets are also tight – as exhibited by higher than normal tanker rates. Overlaying all these important energy concerns are the rising environmental and other cost factors that are also now increasing in importance. The energy industry, which is mature and has a high cost base, has also brought with it higher price volatility due to globalization of markets, the weaker US dollar, and endemic geopolitical risk in many oil-producing countries. In addition, more speculators in the form of both hedge funds and investment banks have increased their trading activity and caused more price volatility. This additional price volatility has laid the groundwork for trading liquidity, as the adage "liquidity begets liquidity" is very true. The bottom line is that we are in the middle of a demand-driven bull market in energy commodities like we have never seen before and probably won't see again. Annual oil company profits for 2005 were at record levels and may be even higher in 2006. They were already the highest on record for 2004 and 2005.

What has been the hardest obstacle for many energy analysts and investors to comprehend is that it is different this time. Most energy companies and governments have continued to look backward and wait for the expected mean price reversion to lower energy prices. It has not occurred and will not this time. There is no surplus supply cushion in these demand-driven markets. As the fourth quarter of 2005 ended, the profit picture was substantially higher for all energy companies, and the perception may change into one that this is the greatest energy bull market of all time. Each market sell-off is actually a buying opportunity or, as one European fund manager told us, "the lows get higher." It's still true. And there are a variety of financial tools to play this market. While it may be buyer beware, savvy investors know a good thing when they see one. Energy is that new asset class.

The next play for investors will be greener investments in the energy space as the environmental financial market matures over the next few years. Once again, investment opportunities will be alternative energy equities, environmental companies, green hedge funds, green financial investible indexes, and green MLPs.

FACTORS IMPACTING ON OIL AND NATURAL GAS PRICES

There are many factors influencing high oil and other energy commodity prices and volatility. These include unusually high geopolitical risk among OPEC producers, continued economic growth in China and Asia tied to oil, the continued rise in US gasoline demand, and the lack of substantial investment in oil and gas exploration and production by the oil majors (that is beginning to change – see Chapter 11). Each of these factors is interconnected and is leading to the current high energy price environment.

Oil demand has surprised many analysts to the upside on the extent of its growth in both 2004 and 2005, and that should continue through 2006 and 2007. The International Energy Agency is now projecting that oil demand growth will rise to 119 million barrels per day by 2025[1] from the estimated 82.63 million barrels per day consumed in the first quarter of 2005. It seems that the world economy has finally recovered from the shocks of 9/11 and associated reduction in world travel.

China and Asia

China is undergoing tremendous economic growth tied to energy consumption and increased industrialization, and it is now the second-largest oil consumer in the world. Inadequate energy supply is seen by the Chinese as a constraint on their economic growth, and energy security is seen as a key to maintaining this growth. They feel that a failure to ensure adequate supply could discourage foreign investment. China's economy continues to grow at a rapid pace (9.4% in 2004), and even though that growth rate is predicted to slow to around 8%,[2] it is increasingly in need of an overseas oil supply. While coal is still the predominant fuel at 68% of its energy market, oil demand appears to be headed significantly higher, rising by around 1 million barrels a day through 2004 toward a projected 6.56 million barrels per day in 2005, and growing at 6% or more annually after that according to International Energy Agency estimates (Figure 3.1).[3] Moreover, the shifting of manufacturing from the West and Japan to low-cost China adds to Chinese oil demand.

While the United States continues to be an energy glutton, the emerging and rapidly growing economies of Asia continue to demand energy, too. Indeed, China has emerged as a natural global competitor to the United States for sources of energy, pursuing an aggressive and unique strategy. In entering global oil markets to secure supply, China is faced with some serious issues. Historically, it has not played much of a role in oil exploration and production outside of the mainland, and it has to seek opportunities

FIGURE 3.1   China's oil demand 1980–2004

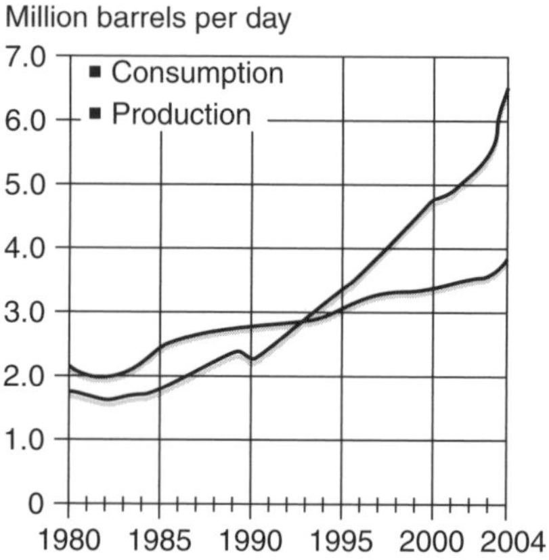

Million barrels per day

Source: US EIA

as it can. As a consequence, the nation finds itself increasingly at odds with Western politics and policies, as it is forced to seek opportunities in countries and regimes shunned by the West. Its approach to entering these markets and opportunities has been different, too – building railways in Nigeria, paying for a port project in Gabon, helping to provide electric power to Angolan slums, investing in a major Sudanese oil company, investing in Iran's largest onshore oil field, funding road projects in Rwanda, and more. Similarly, China has shown that it is quite prepared to aggressively engage in exploration for, and the exploitation of, politically sensitive areas, including the Strait of Malacca, and by calling for joint exploration in disputed territory near the Philippines.

In its search for oil supplies, China has also played off disagreements with US policy in nations on the United States' border. It has taken a $150 million share via CNOOC in the Alberta oil sands and PetroChina has signed a memorandum of understanding with Enbridge Inc. for half of the supply from a proposed $2 billion pipeline project to take oil from Alberta to Prince Rupert in British Columbia. With negative sentiments to Chinese investment in the United States, Canadian oil companies are now attractive to Chinese oil companies. PetroChina made a recent successful bid for Calgary-based PetroKazahstan in a deal worth $4.18 billion. But Chinese interest is also known to be in western Canadian projects. It has even been active in trying to secure supplies in US administration-critical Venezuela, where it has signed 16 petroleum agreements with the government of Hugo Chavez.

Like the United States, China's energy issues are further complicated by environmental issues. About two-thirds of its current electric power generation is from coal and, like the United States, the country has tremendous coal reserves. However, crude oil is cleaner than coal burning. Besides, oil is needed for other reasons, such as to provide gasoline to its growing automobile market and to provide the fertilizers, plastics and other materials that its industry needs. The country uses middle distillates such as gasoil and diesel fuel for heating, power generation, and transportation.

Chinese demand for oil will continue to play a role in oil price formation and, one suspects, world politics. While Chinese demand growth is certainly not the only factor at work behind today's oil price, it will remain a key factor in global oil markets. Consider this quote from a recent issue (August 5, 2005) of the *Economist*.[4]

> China has accounted for one-third of the increase in global oil demand since 2000 and so must bear some of the blame for higher oil prices. Likewise, if China's economy stumbles, then so will oil prices. However, with China's

oil consumption per person still only one-fifteenth of that in America, it is inevitable that China's energy demands will grow over the years in step with its income. There is currently only one car for every 70 people in China, against one car for every two Americans. That implies a huge increase in oil demand, which could keep prices high for the foreseeable future, because of scarce global spare capacity. China's consumption per person of raw materials, such as copper and aluminum, is also still low, so rising demand will continue to support commodity prices.

China is also known to be stockpiling oil and has begun filling a strategic petroleum reserve similar in concept to the US Strategic Reserve (which now holds almost 700 million barrels of oil). This stockpiling has apparently magnified China's presence in international oil markets during the past two years and will continue to do so in the future. Ironically, India too is also stockpiling oil, and other non-OECD countries may follow suit. That may keep a floor under the demand side of the balance if Chinese stockpiling ends.

Another factor that is often overlooked in energy markets is that the Chinese are known to be very aggressive oil traders. Since April 2004, Beijing has allowed oil futures trading to be done in China. Specifically, the Chinese are trading NYMEX and IPE oil futures contracts. China Oil, for example, was known to be setting up trading in New York with 20 oil traders, quite a large number for a start-up. The speculative risk appetite of Chinese oil traders cannot be underestimated and has not been followed by any energy analyst. They are having some impact on oil price volatility.

The key conclusions are that growing energy demand and oil in particular threaten to constrain economic growth; therefore, security of energy supply is increasingly viewed by the Chinese government as a strategic imperative. Because of past severe power shortages, diesel demand is more important to fuel generators while gasoline demand is more elastic as personal cars are still a luxury in China. The sheer volume of Chinese demand for foreign oil, as well as the erratic nature of this demand, has had and will continue to have significant impacts on world oil markets. More importantly, China is now a growing presence in the Atlantic Basin, particularly in West Africa, which is not its traditional market as Beijing is interested in diversifying its oil supply mix. This trend will continue.

While the focus is usually on China's economic growth and financial clout, India is now rising faster than imagined. India's economy has grown 5.7% since 1980, with 6.9% growth in 2004–2005.[5] By 2050, it will be the world's third-largest economy after China and the United States. India has less political risk than before as in theory democracy and rule of law diminishes political risk. It has a young, well-educated population that speaks English and a middle class as large as the US population.

Economic reforms in India have continued since 1991 with 100 multinational companies now doing business in India. Previously, its socialist government was highly protective and backward looking. Its banking sector is more established than China's and attracts a disproportionate share of the $40 billion in foreign investment (like 77% in portfolio investments). It has a dynamic securities market with 5,000 companies listed and one of the largest electronic exchanges in the world with the Bombay Stock Exchange. It also has another exchange: the NSE. Its markets are one of the fastest growing in equity derivatives in the world. It has foreign exchange reserves of $140 billion and was largely untouched by the Asian financial flu of 1997, due to the limited access of its market to foreign markets.

But the country is still hard to do business in. India is still protectionist. It needs $150 billion in infrastructure investment – infrastructure needs to be seriously upgraded. However, the financial system is now open for business as more institutional investors are attracted to the returns and its continued market liberalization. The investment story sounds great. The question is can this be sustained. We hope so.

North America

US demand for energy in all forms remains robust. The penetration of sport utility vehicles (SUVs), which sell more than other automobiles and are very fuel inefficient, is leading to higher than expected gasoline demand. Moreover, Americans are taking more domestic vacations, which includes mostly car and air travel. The increased air travel has fueled more jet fuel demand.

The lack of US energy policy over the past decade has led to very little in the way of conservation efforts. Today, the United States consumes more than 20 million barrels of oil per day, including over 9.5 million barrels per day of gasoline.[6] It has not increased gasoline taxes significantly in decades to try to limit consumption. US auto-makers do not build energy-efficient vehicles. They build highly inefficient, expensive, and profitable SUVs. The likelihood of increased efficiency in the US fleet of more than 200 million cars and trucks is nonexistent. The bottom line is that the United States is a prodigious energy consumer that continues to build for an unsustainable future of more cars, trucks, and energy consumption across the board. Its economic power in energy markets cannot be understated.

The outlook for natural gas demand, moreover, seems to be headed the way of oil, as there is more demand, less supply, and higher costs. Liquid natural gas (LNG) may be a long-term panacea, but today there are supply constraints. There are also geopolitical risks in many of the producing countries that need to be added to this equation. Fuel-switching opportunities from gas to oil are limited, due to environmental rules (low sulfur fuel oil can only be burned in many facilities in the United States). In effect, oil prices may drive natural gas prices higher as usually gas is capped to oil prices. In recent months, US natural gas prices have largely hinged on oil prices. Gas prices during the fall of 2005 went to all-time highs on the NYMEX and have matched the continued oil price rises.

OPEC

OPEC's under-investment in its oil infrastructure over the past two decades cannot be understated. OPEC nations are also very suspicious of Western oil companies and only allow limited participation in their upstream oil and gas exploration and production activities. Consequently, OPEC's capacity has actually declined from 34 million barrels per day to around 30 million barrels per day, and it is currently producing around 29.6[7] million barrels per day. OPEC has 76% of the world's oil reserves. Production cuts by OPEC producers over the past several years have provided a further disincentive to produce more oil. Moreover, it should be remembered that all OPEC countries are in budget deficit with oil being their most important export.

Production declines due to wars and political instability in Iraq, Iran, Libya, Nigeria, and Venezuela have added to production actually falling in these countries. This leads us to the current situation, where really only Saudi Arabia has spare sustainable oil capacity that is estimated at one million barrels per day on top of its current production of around 9.5 million barrels per day.[8] Other estimates are that the Saudis could boost production to 12 million barrels per day if they invested in some of their other oil fields. That capacity is not readily available at the moment.

The current demand-led market is also underpinned by the fact that observed inventory build-ups have not kept pace with implied surplus demand. This may mean that many analysts have been overestimating OPEC production reaching the market. There may be upward revisions to commercial oil inventories to narrow the gap for these unaccounted barrels in coming months.

The Oil Majors

Besides the lack of investment by OPEC producers, the oil majors have not stepped up their oil and gas exploration and production since 1999, but will do so in 2006. It should be recalled that in late 1998, oil prices were reaching $10 per barrel, and there was a fear that OPEC would flood the market with more supply. The majors cut exploration and production budgets at that time. They wisely decided in the late 1990s that it was more important to merge than grow organically.

Today, we see the results of that mega-merger strategy. They have bought and continue to buy paper assets; that is, the stocks of energy companies. They are extremely risk averse and have cut their exploration and production budgets over the past several years. They would rather buy other companies than drill for oil as they are rewarded for earnings per share and not for increased production or taking more financial risks by Wall Street.

The scandals by Shell and El Paso Energy over counted oil reserves in recent years are just reflective of the problem of pleasing Wall Street stock analysts by inflating their reserve base. The fact is that the major oil companies have not so far significantly increased drilling in this high price environment. They have, however, stepped up their hedging activities, as they want to lock in higher production prices.

One anticipated impact of higher sustainable prices should be an increase in exploration activities. However, until recently the E&P sector, which operates on a long cycle time, has not responded to higher oil prices with increased drilling activities. The industry has been "burned" in the past by responding to periods of higher prices with increased drilling activities, only to see prices fall to levels that would make any future developments uneconomic. If energy prices continue to rise, exploration companies will continue to make paper profits on increasing stock valuations. Ironically, there have also been price increases in other commodities, such as steel, that impact on exploration and production budgets, as well as increase the cost of tankers.

Exploration, development, and production are extremely expensive and time-consuming. The International Energy Agency (IEA) estimated earlier this year that some $2,188 billion would be needed for investment in exploration and development between now and 2030 if expected oil demands were to be supplied.[9] This averages out at some $81 billion per year of additional investment. While in the past, sustained high prices encouraged investments in exploration and production, those increased investments also tended to result in increased supply and reduced energy prices just as new developments were brought on stream. As a result, oil companies are now more reluctant to open the investment floodgates.

According to Dr Paul Stevens of Dundee University:[10]

> ... the explanation for the potential lack of investment lies in the dominance of value-based management theories as the driving force of financial strategy in the major oil companies. This view of corporate finance began to gain credence in the 1990s. Its basis is simple, although the logic is based upon quite complex concepts such as the capital asset pricing model and later variations. If the company cannot provide a rate of return at least equal to the general stock market and to its appropriate sector, it should return funds to the shareholders rather than investing them itself. This is achieved either through higher dividends or share buy-backs pushing up the share price.

As companies in a maturing industry, such as the oil industry, are challenged to maintain shareholder value, this is exactly what they are doing. For example, BP announced a program to return around $18 billion to its shareholders over a three-year period. In 2003, BP invested $9.7 billion in exploration and production activities. ExxonMobil is also expected to return some $6.4 billion to shareholders.[11] This strategy is a self-fulfilling prophecy as it becomes a source of competition between companies to keep their shareholders happy. The danger is that the very short-term benefits to share price will be at the expense of future investments in maintaining and developing crude capacity. On the other hand, national oil companies are unaffected by this phenomena. For example, PetroChina recently announced a 13% spending increase on the back of increased profits.

While simple economics might suggest that high prices produce a supply response, thereby creating a self-correcting mechanism, this simplistic assumption neglects the long lead times involved in developing upstream oil. As a result of short-term thinking and strategies on the part of the oil companies designed to sustain share prices, the upturn in investment in exploration and development activities required to bring more supply may well be delayed and in turn this will have a forward impact on prices.

For the independent oil companies, higher sustained oil prices may also spell a period of danger. The easiest way for larger oil companies to increase reserves is to buy them. In so doing, smaller producers become their prey.

Ironically, the higher energy prices and the larger oil companies' response to them provide another opportunity for hedge funds. Many of the larger macro funds specialize in equity investment plays and potentially see all of this activity as another speculative profit opportunity by investing in the oil companies. Hedge funds are investing across the E&P sector. For example, Palo Alto Investors (PAI), a private, value-oriented hedge fund in northern California, is the largest institutional investor in Canadian Superior Energy at 6.5% of the outstanding shares. The fund sees optionality in its investment, meaning that the stock is like a call option. In fact, PAI has also invested in a number of other exploration ventures and seeks low-cost finders of oil, a successful strategy evidenced by the funds compounding 25% returns over the last 14 years.

An additional activity in E&P is for investment banks to buy the rights to oil in the ground from oil companies, essentially providing the bank with its own reserves and bringing forward revenue for the oil company. Examples include an announcement by Morgan Stanley to buy 24 million barrels of oil to be produced over four years from Anadarko for $775 million, and an earlier deal in which Morgan Stanley acquired oil and gas reserves in the Gulf of Mexico for around $300 million from Apache. Morgan Stanley and Deutsche Bank also recently bought equity production in the North Sea for the period 2007 to 2010. They obviously anticipate sustained higher prices as these deals are way out on forward price curves.

Supply Situation

The oil market today can be described as very fragile with little spare supply capacity. Today's oil inventories can be drawn down quite quickly, leading to a scramble for supplies of gasoline and heating oil (gasoil). The fragility of the world system was exposed during the fall hurricane season in the United States.

What is happening today is a paradigm shift in supply–demand patterns for energy commodities. A lack of investment in energy infrastructure over the last two decades or more has combined with surging demand to support growth in not just Asian economies such as China and India, but also closer to home in the United States. India, China, and other oil consuming countries are now competing with the United States for supply around the world, including in Canada and other traditional US suppliers.

Added to that are a number of other largely overlooked issues. These include the huge potential impact of growing and often complex environmental regulations on the prospect for reinvestment in energy; a genuine shortage of skills and talent in the industry for everything from geologists to oil traders; and supply changes that require reinvestment in refining, processing, and other facilities.

Contrary to popular media opinion, there are plenty of fossil fuels to be exploited throughout the world using new technologies and the higher cost base of today's markets. Let's look, for example, at sub-Saharan Africa. Angola is now a major oil producer with Sonagol producing 1.2 to 1.3 million barrels per day. New developments will increase that to two million barrels per day in the 2007–2008 timeframe.[12] It is the second-largest producer in sub-Saharan Africa after Nigeria and ranks behind Saudi Arabia and Iran in recent oil discoveries. All this oil is offshore in 34 blocks. Most of the current production is in shallow water but deep-water drilling is where the next phase of development will commence. The country also has 1.6 ten cubic feet (TCF) of gas, which will be exported as LNG. Two other former Portuguese colonies with oil and gas resources are San Tome and Equatorial Guinea. San Tome is an island off the coast of Nigeria. Conservatively, it has four billion barrels of oil in nine blocks called the Joint Development Zone. This oil will be exploited in joint ventures with Nigeria, but Western companies such as ExxonMobil, ChevronTexaco, and Total will produce the oil. There are also plans for LNG development. Guinea has 1.5 billion barrels of proven reserves.

Today, Angola supplies 7% of US oil supply, but by 2009 the three former Portuguese colonies could produce 15% of US oil imports. Oil reserves globally continue to be exploited as US production declines. Looking at ANWR (Arctic national wildlife refuge) is not where the ball is. It's almost every other international oil play out there. The United States will never be energy independent, which is just a political slogan tested by the White House to play well in the media (they actually did focus groups on this). The United States is actually energy interdependent. The energy industry is resilient and will bring more supply to the United States from all over the world in competition with China and other countries whose energy demand is also growing.

Also, consider the independents such as Calgary's junior oil companies as they bring incremental supplies to market. Canadian juniors are oil and gas companies such as Duvernay Oil Corp and Real Resources, which produce over 10,000 barrels per day. Another junior company is Highpine Oil & Gas, which hopes to reach 14,000 barrels per day at the end of 2005. It has plans to eventually reach 40,000 barrels per day. Another is Cyries Energy, which had 2,800 barrels per day in the second quarter and hopes to reach 8,000 barrels per day by the end of the year 2005. Many of these production gains have been fueled by shareholder money to finance exploration. Expectations are that the Canadian junior oil and gas companies will continue to surge in equity prices until we reach a market peak. Also, expect takeover plays by larger companies.

Russian Oil Production

Russia was the largest oil producer in 1990 at 12 million barrels per day, including all of the independent states. Then, we saw the collapse of oil production as the production methods of the 1980s, such as water flooding, damaged oil fields. We now see a resurgence of the Russian economy, led by oil and gas production and imports. Russian oil production has reached 9.3 million barrels per day.[13] It will go higher. In a recent 2005 meeting in New York, the Russian Finance Minister stated that they are capable of going to 14 million per day. Russia's Far East has unknown oil and gas reserves. The issue is not that Russia does not have the supply base, but how soon can new Russian and, for that matter, Caspian production, be brought on line. We now see Russia offering Sakhalin oil and gas (as LNG) production to the United States, as well as northeast Asia.

While it would seem that Japan, South Korea, and China would be the natural markets for Russia's Far East oil and gas production, the United States will remain the high-cost gas center. It seems very likely that Russian oil and gas will find its way to this market. ExxonMobil will be pumping 250,000 barrels per day of Sakhalin oil production. Some of that oil may come to the US West Coast. Russian oil production will increase in coming years. LNG exports will also come to the United States, most likely through Baja, Mexico, and the Sempra Energy LNG receiving facility there.

Examining the Peak Oil Argument

Given the current supply–demand situation it is not surprising that the concept of peak oil has resurfaced in some quarters. Peak oil theorists follow the argument that at some point, a peak output of oil and gas is reached that cannot be exceeded, even with improved technology or additional drilling. After the peak, oil production slowly but increasingly tapers off. After the peak, but before an oil field is empty, another significant point is reached when it takes more energy to recover, transport, and process one barrel of oil than the amount of energy contained in that barrel. At that point, the oil is not worth extracting and the field may be abandoned. Hubbert's peak theory proponents claim that this is true regardless of the price of oil. The theory predicts that future world oil production will soon reach a peak and then rapidly decline. The actual peak year will only be known after it has passed, but, based on available production data, proponents have predicted the peak years to be 1989, 1995, 1995–2000, or, according to one influential group, 2007 for oil and somewhat later for natural gas.

However, a review of the definition of "peak oil" will find that it refers to "conventional" crude oil; that is, oil found and recovered by the drill bit.

Peak oilers largely dismiss non-conventional sources as doing little other than to delay the actual onset of the problem. Of course, the media likes to get hold of material like this because the potential impact of peak oil on humanity, and the United States in particular, will be catastrophic. It's a good scare story, and the media eats it up because it's a simple explanation of a complex problem.

Have we reached the peak or is the peak close? No one really knows. The theory really cannot be proved or disproved, based on available data, because there isn't sufficient accuracy in it. Reserves are often difficult to estimate and for a whole variety of reasons they may be under- or overestimated. For example, since individual OPEC country quotas are determined, based on reserves, there have been some dramatic swings in reserve numbers put forward by individual OPEC countries. Even major oil companies have problems with reserve estimates, including Shell, who recently downgraded its own reserve estimates. Whatever you hear about peak oil, it is likely to be an opinion and not a fact as to when it may occur.

It is true that new major conventional oil fields have not been found for quite some time and that it is getting harder and more costly to find new oil reserves. Much of the new reserves, such as the North Sea, added after the last major oil price shock, are now in decline and the world is increasingly beginning to look to OPEC again as its major supplier. And therein lies the crux of the matter, in that there have been views put forward and taken up by the media that Saudi Arabian reserves may not be as reported. They may either be close to peak oil or, as Saudi Arabia increases production rates to cater for increased demand, it may be damaging its reservoirs by bringing its peak production closer. A further review of this discussion will quickly demonstrate that it is a minority view perpetuated by the press.

What the peak oil theory doesn't allow for is human ingenuity. As oil prices rise, increased efficiencies and conservation ought to follow. It certainly did after the last oil price shock. Second, as oil prices rise so does the interest in finding more of the stuff. It is true that the majors have been late in increasing E&P budgets, but increased E&P activity is generally led by the independents. And the evidence we see in the market shows that once again, it is the independents and the "junior" oil companies that are now driving rig utilization rates back up.

Despite all the talk of technology and geology/geophysics, many of the world's giant oil fields were found by accident! Ask the geologists and they will tell you that this is so. Consider also that prior to exploration in the North Sea the then head of a major oil company is reputed to have said that he would personally drink every barrel of oil extracted from the North Sea because he didn't believe there was any prospect of oil there. Our point is that oil discovery is often not a just question of good science but also of good fortune. Peak oil theorists will say that the technology and the science have not produced much incremental oil and that there are few areas left to explore. Nonsense. The Falklands area is thought to have huge potential and there are other basins still to be properly explored by nature of their depth or accessibility. The lure of oil revenues is simply too large and the world's oil companies have shown no loss of appetite for exploring and producing in the most remote and/or dangerous places on earth.

Unconventional sources are also usually glossed over as simply adding a small amount of cushion prior to peak oil. But today the Canadians estimate tar sand reserves at 1.6 trillion barrels and 178 billion barrels recoverable, and with rising oil prices and improved technology, the recoverable reserves could be more than 300 billion barrels.[14]

Are we saying there is no such thing as peak oil? No, our ability to produce enough supply to meet growing demand will one day falter and oil production will peak. But to use this period of supply–demand tightness as evidence of the onset of peak oil now is false logic. There are many reasons for today's surge in oil prices and we think that reflects infrastructure problems throughout the value chain from exploration through production to transportation and refining. The real crisis is an energy crisis brought on by a 20-year period of under-investment.

Finally, we have seen this all before. We saw these same stories in the 1970s; the news was full of such accounts. The problem is that no one remembers anymore. The industry has lost much of its institutional memory due to two decades of consolidation. Government knows even less.

The Environment as a Risk Factor

The world's growing concern over protecting the environment is a key difference between the situation today versus that of the last oil price spike that resulted in conservation and reinvestment. Today, a plethora of environmental considerations govern the plant siting and planning of new facilities, their construction and operation costs, the technologies utilized, and even the cost of final removal of the facility. Cost of compliance with environmental regulations is an ongoing burden for the energy industry and they impact on costs.

The new emphasis on the environment adds cost, complexity, and time to any planned energy project in the short term, and it will reduce the industry's ability and flexibility to solve the supply-side issues rapidly. In the short term, it has impacts that are not often covered in the media, too. For example, tanker fleets are being scrapped faster than they can be built as a result of new regulations governing tanker design, and most new oil discoveries and projects are for heavy sour crude that require additional investment in refining facilities in order to process them. On the one hand, such issues are helping to reinforce the idea that oil prices will continue to rise and on the other they are creating an active trading market in freight rates.

Commodity Interdependence

The supply–demand tightness in almost all markets is having a knock-on effect in other commodities, too. Consider heating oil as an example. Heating oil prices set record levels during June 2005, when traditionally they were at their lowest. According to the US Energy Information Administration (EIA), the average retail price of a gallon of home heating oil nationally has been 12.8 cents lower in June than December during the past 10 years. In part, the run up in prices may be as a result of a shortage of refining capacity, something that OPEC and even the Bush administration have recently pointed to as a cause of high oil prices.

What has changed is the fact that there are a number of changed fundamentals behind this pricing behavior. Europeans use more diesel for automobiles than in the United States, but additionally the Germans were 40% under-filled on heating oil (gasoil) at the beginning of June 2005, which is their heating oil filling season. Moreover, the Chinese use half of their distillates for power generation, and power demand in China is also up dramatically. Additionally, the United States driving season uses both gasoline and diesel fuel. Demand is driving that price behavior.

Also, coal prices have been impacted with eastern coal spot prices 25% higher since the start of 2004, according to the Electric Power Research Institute (EPRI). EPRI points to increased demand for coal for power generation, but also to consolidation in the coal mining industry and other issues. Again, environmental issues potentially aggravate the situation in coal too, as available supplies of high-quality clean coal are diminished. Similarly, the interdependence between commodities is having its impact as natural gas prices rise, compelling a switch to coal for power generation. This drives rising demand. Higher levels of coal burning increased the value of emissions allowances for both sulfur dioxide and nitrous oxide.

The supply-side issues impacting on global and regional commodity markets include not just a sustained lack of investment in facilities and prospects, but transportation, environmental, and global policy issues, too. We are seeing the "perfect storm" in many of these global or regional commodity markets, as increased demand has outstripped industry investment to create supply–demand tightness.

A Lack of History and Experience

Another reason behind today's commodity markets price rise and the industry's apparent slowness to catch on to the paradigm shifts that have, and are taking place, may well be to do with a skills issue. After a sustained period (two and a half decades excepting short price spikes) of almost sideways movements in energy commodities prices, the fact is that many people have simply left the industry. Oil companies have been public in their concern over the "generation gap" in the industry where today's participants have no experience of markets and market fundamentals like those we are experiencing today. Discussions at the 2005 Offshore Technology Conference focused in on "the lost generation" and it is a growing concern that many in the industry are looking to the history that they know in order to try to predict where these markets are going. If history is no longer the predictor of the future, then we need to return to a more fundamentalist approach in our analysis.

Hedge Funds and Speculation

During the past two years we have seen the entrance of many hedge funds into oil and gas trading in the United States, as well as oil trading in Europe. These well-capitalized funds are trading both the New York Mercantile Exchange oil futures contracts, as well as the International Petroleum Exchange's oil contracts. We have seen a 55% increase on NYMEX for open crude oil, heating oil, and gasoline, primarily due to hedge fund trading activity. (Open interest is a better indicator of futures contract liquidity than daily trading volumes.) Simply put: open interest is the futures contracts that have not been closed in their positions. Because of this increased futures trading activity for oil, there is more price volatility in markets. Hedge funds have also at times made costly bets that oil prices would decline and have had to cover their positions.

There has been much discussion about the energy price volatility and the presence of speculators a.k.a. hedge funds. Some of this discussion has naturally resulted in a rush to judgment and, in some instances, calls for investigation. Much of the furor has been caused by both the general background of rising commodity prices, but specifically by natural gas prices. In Congress, members have periodically asked the US Federal Energy Regulatory Commission (FERC), Commodity Futures Trading Commission (CFTC), and NYMEX for investigations of trading by hedge funds after receiving complaints from energy companies and consumers.

While there are many who potentially benefit by placing the blame on speculation for price volatility or perhaps more truthfully on increasing energy commodity prices, we believe that there is little or no evidence that speculation by hedge funds is the primary factor at work in energy price formation. Energy industry officials, faced with consumer distaste for higher prices, and government leaders who might wish to veil the lack of investment in energy infrastructure and lack of a real energy policy, are among the most likely to attempt to place blame on speculation. OPEC too has consistently sought to point to speculation as the primary reason for oil price volatility. Ironically, hedge funds, which are usually very private, have said nothing in their defense.

Our research shows that this view is false. At the time that the US Energy Information Administration (EIA) released an inaccurate gas storage report in the fall of 2004, hedge funds were net short according to the CFTC Commitments of Traders report, indicating that the funds were betting on a decrease in natural gas prices. Indeed, movement in spot markets at the time was more likely to be the result of the end-users in spot markets, since most of the speculator's money is bet in the futures market where volatilities typically are of a lower magnitude. In North America, natural gas supply dynamics have also tightened considerably over recent years as generators switched to natural gas-fired generation. This has lead to higher than normal prices, which have been sustained.

Hedge fund speculation has played a role in price volatility, but this is a small price to pay for the considerable benefits that the speculators and their money bring to energy commodity markets. Apparently, others agree with our analysis. Tom Mathews of Kinder Morgan recently published an article citing various academic research that showed an inverse relationship between outstanding futures contracts on the NYMEX and spot market volatility.[15] We believe that the benefits of hedge fund activity far outweigh any negatives, including providing the market with more market information, providing greater liquidity for hedging and risk shifting, and potentially over time for reduced volatility. They are most definitely increased price volatility, particularly intra-day price volatility, for oil and gas futures.

The US Dollar

The US dollar has been substantially weaker during the past three years, due to $500 billion annual budget deficits, low interest rates, and the highest monthly US trade deficits on record. Consequently, since all OPEC producers are in budget deficit, they must buy their goods and services in international markets in weaker US dollars. They need more dollars to do so. It is fair to say that US dollar purchasing power has decreased by at least one-third in the past three years. This is another factor to consider in the current situation of higher oil prices, although the dollar has rallied in 2005.

Dollar-denominated oil means that $30 oil or $40 oil may be the new average price when markets settle down. But it seems apparent that the days of $20 oil are over for the foreseeable future. Oil producers continue to complain that their spending power in non-dollar markets suffer more in a weak dollar environment.

Socioeconomic Impacts

The world still runs on oil. There is a high correlation between economic growth and oil. However, countries such as China or India are much more impacted on than the United States. It should be remembered that today in the United States, energy costs are only 2% of GDP, not the 6% of 1980. Although the United States is twice as energy efficient as the 1970s, the danger is that sustained higher prices will cut economic growth. In effect, higher oil prices are a tax on consumer spending for lower and middle-class people as they now have less disposable income – a larger portion of their household budget must be spent on energy. This will lead to a softening of retail sales.

Higher energy costs are slowing earnings growth by corporations. Oil prices peaked at more than $70 per barrel during 2005 and, while that has not brought us to a world recession, it is impacting on the purchasing power of consumers. Oil price increases today tend to disrupt economic growth rather than add to inflation. Sustained higher oil prices could do much economic damage. A $5 increase in oil prices can shave as much as 0.5% off global economic growth in the next year or two. A 1% cut in output for the world economy is now forecast for 2006. A $10 oil price increase can curb US growth by 0.3%.

However, in reality the oil–economic relationship is much more complex. The oil price affects economies in different ways. For example, expectations are that we could see robust growth in oil producer countries in a high price environment and conversely lower growth in oil consumers. Energy-intensive industries are particularly impacted on and suffer more from higher prices.

Talk of demand destruction in energy markets has now entered our daily headlines as profit taking in energy equities also pushed down the energy sector during the fall of 2005. Basic economics tells us that markets are cyclic. Increasing prices, at some point, start to impact on demand growth. While there are disagreements over timing and the data, the fact that demand destruction is now in the news suggests that psychologically we are near the top of the market. While OPEC reduced its forecasts for oil demand, growth for 2005 by about 17% compared against its previous report,[16] it remains skeptical about lasting demand weakness. Hurricane-driven gasoline prices have had an impact on US gasoline demand, which according to sources declined by 2 to 3% in the weeks following the hurricanes, as compared to 1 to 2% growth for the same period in 2004. Every industry analyst offers conflicting views. From their comments read uncertainty. Why? Because no one is quite sure how to read the data this time around and history, as we have said, has no parallel this time.

So what is the difference this time around? It's the global competition for supplies of energy. Whether this is competition for oil, natural gas, or coal; or whether it be global or regional, it is this competition for supply that will overlay any argument regarding demand destruction. Yes, there will be demand destruction in some markets, but it will be compensated for by others. Take for example the United Kingdom, which some believe may face a three-day week sometime during the winter of 2005 due to a natural gas supply issue. Despite taking in imported LNG, the United Kingdom will still face shortages and in its search for LNG cargoes, it will be in competition with others.

The historical lack of investment in industry infrastructure means that supplying regional markets can be a problem. Bottlenecks mean that at any time the industry is vulnerable to outside events causing shortages in various regional markets for different energy products. Post-storm US gasoline prices reflect this issue. And let's see what happens over the winter (2005–2006) with heating oil. Talk of the end of high-energy prices is just that – talk. Energy prices will remain high (compared to recent history) and very volatile for some time to come. What we are hearing today may well be wishful thinking, but we think it is based on an ignorance of the details.

Energy and related environmental plays are now the hottest ticket in town for investors. This includes not just hedge funds, but private individual investors, too. Funds are flooding into energy stocks and other investment vehicles. For many in our industry, this is a new boom time that will spur increased activities, increased employment, and increased profits. It will drive new investment in exploration and production, new facilities, new technologies, and it may change some long-held biases against other sources of energy including nuclear power. But for consumers, this is likely to herald a sustained period of increased energy costs, and at some point it will act as a drag on economic growth (though there is little evidence that this has happened yet).

It will also encourage buyers of energy to look for increased hedging opportunities to protect against future price rises. Those that get their hedging strategies right will benefit, such as Southwest Airlines, for example. The irony is that it will likely be the media scapegoat for rising energy prices in the form of the hedge funds that provides an increased ability to hedge!

THE ATTRACTION OF POWER TRADING

Any profit potential in electricity trading has until recently been beyond the strategic reach of US banking firms. Institutional interest in the power markets has been limited by various regulatory restrictions placed on controlling the underlying physical commodity. Under Regulation Y, the US Federal Reserve Bank only authorized bank holding companies to take principal (that is, ownership) positions in commodity contracts, which were exchange-traded. (In energy trading that means trading on the NYMEX.) Furthermore, Regulation Y stipulated that banks could only engage in contracts, which were cash settled. Both regulations practically limited commercial banking institutions from engaging in physical energy trading. Non-commercial banks were further restricted by FERC statutes, which imposed a 1% utility stock ownership limitation on a bank's ability to trade energy with a utility counterparty.

These combined statutory restrictions discouraged financial institutions from seriously exploring the power sector as an avenue for expansion in commodity trading. Since the electricity wholesale markets are primarily physically settled, Regulation Y was a major impediment to any institution with a commercial banking function. The FERC rules were impediments to the investment banks that actively trade in utility stock. Moreover, conglomerate institutions (such as JP Morgan/Chase and Citigroup) have been impacted on by both Federal Reserve and FERC guidelines, since their businesses are a mix of commercial and investment banking functions.

Within the past year, these restrictions have been materially loosened, attributable to active financial community lobbying and the depressed state of the US power markets. The Federal Reserve has relaxed Regulation Y to permit institutional trading in the physical commodity. In a related event, FERC has increased the utility equity ownership threshold from 1 to 5%. These recent rulings remove significant regulatory roadblocks and enable US financials to pursue power trading within the contact of their wider business interests. As a result, power trading initiatives have emerged at almost all major institutions in the United States.

The US electric power markets have gone through tremendous upheaval since the Enron bankruptcy in December 2001 (see Figure 3.2). While the

FIGURE 3.2   Recent dislocation events in the US energy industry

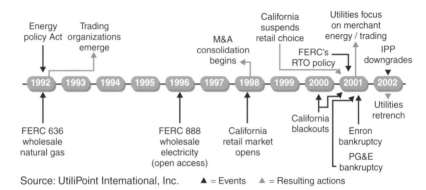

Source: UtiliPoint International, Inc.   ▲ = Events   ▲ = Resulting actions

Enron model of "asset light" seems to have been discredited, the asset-heavy strategy today is much more of an opportunistic occurrence than the execution of a well-defined investment strategy by financial institutions. Today, the financial energy markets have changed and are being rebuilt with financial players such as investment banks and, to a lesser degree, hedge funds. Some of these financial institutions own generation assets but most do not.

Serious problems that arose in the energy sector in the wake of the Enron scandal focused attention on all energy-trading operations. Credit ratings agencies such as Fitch, Moody's, and Standard & Poor's have downgraded the ratings of companies that have indulged in such deceptive practices as round-trip or wash trading in order to give the illusion of a higher volume of trading activity. Merchant plant operators also gave poor financial incentives to energy traders in paying quarterly bonuses based on volumes.

As a result of the credit downgrades of energy companies such as Williams, Aquila, Mirant, El Paso, Reliant, and Dynegy, and the subsequent decline in the number of counterparties willing to trade wholesale energy products, many industry observers asked who would step in to fill the vacuum. These energy merchants inevitably had to sell assets to meet the looming debt maturities that they agreed to under their refinancing packages. In effect, the only companies that are selling assets are ones that are looking to exit the merchant business. Moreover, many power marketers exited the business due to credit downgrades and the fact that those ongoing credit concerns substantially shrank overall market liquidity.

Many companies such as Duke and AEP exited all proprietary trading for gas and power, and instead limited themselves to the simple exercise of marketing power directly from their regulated and unregulated merchant assets. In the new financial environment, the credit community is suspicious of proprietary trading ventures and, as a rule of thumb, insist that proprietary traders have single A ratings or better. The only exceptions to this rule are Sempra Energy Trading (BBB+) and PSEG Power (BBB+); both also have additional credit support from their regulated utility parents. (Sempra bought the former AIG trading operation many years ago.)

Banks have either become reluctant owners of generation assets or have purchased assets opportunistically. Both motivations stem from the credit crunch that brought the power sector into crisis after the collapse of Enron. The credit woes of the sector either forced ownership on to financial institutions or created opportunities where financial institutions could take opportunistic advantage of the vast gap between the borrowing capability of the power sector and the borrowing capability of banks.

Regardless of how they got there, banks are the newest owners of energy assets and the next major players in the energy trading space. Banks, which pioneered the use of important new-risk management tools in the financial services sector, are a natural for shoring up the public's confidence in energy trading as well. Their tougher metrics are needed to guard against credit and liquidity risks. Banks have the credit to take on these financial risks and are taking advantage of the distressed credit of independent power producers (IPPs) or merchant generators.

Given the increasing importance of liquidity for margin purposes, another issue is the proper relationship between credit exposure and profit margins. To be profitable, power plant assets are heavy consumers of capital (and credit capacity). Generation assets are expensive assets to construct. It is sometimes forgotten that they are also large consumers of capital in order to simply operate the asset.

In order to illustrate this point, we will examine the relatively simple example of a contracted (that is, not traded) asset. Given the high capital cost and long capital recovery period (measured in decades), this asset needs to contract its output in significant volumes over a relatively long period. The buyer of this contract will naturally want financial assurance that the asset will perform as contracted. To provide the assurance, the asset must be in a position to offer financial guarantees (thereby eating into its credit capacity). Because of the maturity and size of a typical power contract, this guarantee will be in the tens or hundreds of millions of dollars. Multiply this credit support for a single asset by the multiple assets in the portfolio, and the magnitude of required borrowing capacity becomes evident (merely to support output off take). The credit consumption of non-contracted (that is, traded) assets becomes even larger, since the traded asset will have multiple counterparties over multiple maturities. Interestingly, the process of reducing credit consumption by "netting" transactions with counterparties has only very recently caught on in the power sector.

Financial and physical valuations are not the same because physical assets are not valued on a mark-to-market basis as are financial positions by equity analysts and the ratings agencies. The difficulty with mark-to-market valuation of physical assets is generally attributable to the plant operational risk factor, and model risk, or manipulation of the spark spread valuation. Industry observers tend to agree that power prices and energy asset values have been depressed and will take time to burn off all the excess generation built in the past five years. The days of big profits by the energy merchant companies are over, and organizations will have to add such value-added services as risk mitigation to survive. Although asset prices are currently depressed far below their fair value, it is widely thought that distressed sellers will have to significantly lower their asking prices before any sales are made. This has been occurring substantially this year and will continue. Asset sales or no asset sales, many banks believe they will soon be forced to foreclose on substantial energy assets, including power generating plants and natural gas pipelines. The unanswered question is what will be the new role of the banks in the energy industry. Because of this phenomenon, the hedge funds have also focused on this distressed asset sector. It is opportunistic investing.

Power Trading and Asset Ownership

There are two groups of financial institutions that have taken ownership interests in assets: those who purchased the assets and those who had the assets transferred to them (because of financial distress). These are as follows:

- Asset purchasers – The purchasers consist largely of private equity investors (who do not have active energy trading capabilities) and selected investment banks with energy trading capabilities.
- Owners-by-default – This class of investor consists of the banks and institutional investors who were lenders to the power sector and assumed equity ownership through financial distress. These institutions never contemplated ownership. Adverse industry credit developments, industry capital structures, and the process of financial distress left them with little choice.

The two classes of investors are linked through the power sector's financial distress. The credit crisis that forced the owners-by-default into equity ownership created the opportunity for the asset purchasers. The power sector's liquidity crisis forced the industry to divest assets (something that the players would not have done willingly). The generally forced nature of the divestitures enabled purchasers to buy assets at favorable prices. In short, the power sector ran out of credit. The financial institutions had a great deal of credit and were able to close transactions based on their credit strength.

Several financial institutions have stepped into physical energy asset acquisition. Banks have traditionally shown interest in both securitization and asset-backed trading. Hedge funds are there primarily for risk management opportunities. Partnerships are generally aimed at leveraging financial strength and the physical operations expertise. Finally, we are seeing consortiums of foreign banks, energy companies, and niche players in the market buying distressed assets for future arbitrage and trading around those assets. However, as indicated above, the opportunity has been presented because of the collapse of the merchant energy sector not by any grand strategic design. Asset purchasers also got a boost from changes in the regulatory arena such as the amendment to Regulation Y by the Federal Reserve, and the FERC raising the utility stockholding limit to 5%. These moves have been made recently.

The FERC regulates the sale of natural gas and electricity involved in interstate transactions and continues to intervene in gas and power markets. They feel that competitive markets will continue to benefit consumers by providing information, incentives for efficient production, allocating scarce resources, creating incentives for efficient investment, and providing customer's choice. The FERC now has an Office of Market Oversight. Its function is to monitor markets, as FERC is still worried about the financial performance of energy companies.

There is a third route to asset control that is worth mentioning – the energy trading joint venture. Here a financial institution will team up with a power sector company for the purpose of energy trading. The conventional rationale for such a venture is that the financial institution brings trading capability and risk management expertise. The power sector company provides the physical assets (which the venture will use as a trading platform). This is the route that Merrill Lynch took with its purchase of the Entergy/Koch joint venture.

While Morgan Stanley and Goldman Sachs have remained active in commodity trading for more than two decades, many financial institutions have entered and exited these markets from time to time. Other financial houses such as Merrill Lynch and Credit Suisse First Boston (CSFB) have either quit commodities or let their divisions wither. Today, these banks and Lehman Brothers, Citigroup, Barclays, UBS, and others have built up their commodities businesses. It has been two good years for trading commodities. The oil price surge has attracted the banks' attention once again.

Many investment banks today are solely concentrating on the financial trading of electricity and gas. It is assumed that those with access to physical product may have an edge. The potential for serious trading profits is also drawing in hedge funds. Such funds are also busy hiring former big name energy traders from energy producers. D.E. Shaw, Ritchie Capital Management, and Citadel have raided the former energy trading operations of producer Aquila Inc., and another fund, Alpha Energy Partners LP, is run by former energy traders at American Electric Power.

This drive for profits in energy trading is also altering the nature of taking risks. Banks are feeling more confident that they can place longer term bets on which way oil and gas prices will go, and are starting to do the same for electric power. For example, in the past, power traders have felt comfortable going out only about 18 months in the future. Yet with a longer contract there is a greater chance to earn revenues on a well-chosen trade. Armed with sophisticated risk management and modeling systems that have been honed in the derivatives markets, banks are hoping to push out the futures market for power further into the future.

To put this in some recent perspective, some banks, such as Goldman Sachs and Morgan Stanley, had been trading energy throughout the Enron years, but the majority of banks had steered clear or even bailed out of energy trading in recent years. Morgan Stanley and Goldman Sachs had the luxury of building their commodity franchises over decades. Rivals to the investment banks wonder if those returning to commodities, especially energy, are willing to stick with the business this time. Now, there is a sense that the field is wide open. Hedge funds may have the capital but will need time to develop the in-house expertise to trade the electric power sector effectively.

The cost to play in energy trading is rising however, with power company officials estimating that it takes roughly a $1 billion balance sheet to be an effective counterparty in today's market, up from a $400 million average during the Enron years. Players are too susceptible to market shocks and credit events. The new Wall Street energy traders come in all varieties, ranging from those sampling the market to those willing to make a massive commitment in terms of balance sheet and hiring. Banks typically fall into two broad categories – those with some sort of physical ownership in energy production as well as a trading desk, such as Goldman Sachs, and those that are only trading energy, serving as middlemen between producers and buyers, such as Barclays' trading operation.

However, the road will be tough and expensive for those looking to get into the business, given the cost of acquiring people and assets. Whether the current interest in commodities will prove lasting remains to be seen, but banks are making big commitments.

Having access to physical power distribution might prove to be a key competitive strength. According to bankers and analysts, those traders with actual ties to production will have an advantage in terms of predicting future price estimates. Access to physical assets is said to be necessary for longer term transactions, since there is exposure in the physical market. Without physical assets, there is greater financial exposure. However, many financial institutions will assume that risk.

Marking to model is essentially sophisticated guesswork. Banks have elaborate models that can take current market pricing, product volatility, and future demand, and then calculate what prices are going forward, and compare that to the contracts they now have in place.

It's clear that everyone is gunning to make money by taking on trading risk. Long-timers Goldman Sachs and Morgan Stanley have continued to put up attractive numbers through 2005. Tight supply and rising demand in energy markets drove prices and volatilities higher for oil and gas primarily. While neither bank breaks out their energy trading component, market sources and analysts believe it has been a substantial chunk of the totals over the past year. We will refine these trading models as some hedge funds are trying to replicate them.

Analysts have noted that these two institutions' impressive results come from long-term relationships and established standards in energy trading. Whether a start-up could get similar results is still unknown. Banks have formidable risk-taking abilities and a well-disciplined expertise in managing risk and volatility across many commodities and financial products. In effect, energy trading becomes one of many components to their overall book. No matter how sophisticated the financial model, it is still a matter of taking a calculated risk. Banks just have a greater ability to hedge, due to their stronger balance sheets, and understand risk better than some of the energy merchants. It should also be remembered that no one knows where commodity prices will ultimately go.

Many energy players expect hedge funds also to try to push contracts outward as the funds are now changing how we go from a high to a low price, not only changing price volatility. While the funds have actually increased daily price volatility in oil and gas trading, their influence on power trading is still negligible.

As more banks and hedge funds enter energy trading, it is unsurprising that many long-term players view the newcomers with suspicion, arguing that their presence is causing increased volatility. Because hedge funds and banks have made leveraged bets that prices will stay at high levels, the argument is that something of an energy bubble has been created. When things start to go wrong in the financial markets, or when someone is hurting, hedge funds often get the blame. It is still too early to evaluate the true impact of the hedge funds. The point is that they have entered the energy commodity markets in a big way for the first time. Previously, they had confined most of their trading activities to energy equity trading.

MIDSTREAM ASSETS

The midstream segment of the industry (pipelines, gathering systems, and associated processing assets) has also recently been the center of mergers and acquisitions (M&A), and construction activities. As the energy merchants look to sell off hard assets for cash to restore damaged balance sheets, many such assets have changed hands and local supply–demand dynamics have created opportunities for new construction.

In many instances where energy firms are offloading assets, hedge funds are replacing banks as leading lenders, providing billions of dollars in credits in return for rich returns. More than $10 billion in refinancing have been arranged in 2004 for companies including Centerpoint Energy, Reliant Resources, Allegheny Energy, Dynegy, and Aquila, and hedge funds are buying pieces of short-term loans to these entities. For example, Berkshire Hathaway was part of a group of investors that provided $900 million to Williams and received 34% returns in interest and fees. Additional evidence for these types of activities comes from the sale of Texas Genco Holdings, Inc., a unit of Centerpoint Energy that caused media speculation when it was discovered that a group of unnamed hedge funds had made it to the final round of bidding in the deal.

While many of the acquisitions are being made by investment banks and private equity, the hedge funds are also playing a role as they partner in some of these deals. In fact, new distressed-asset strategy and energy-specific hedge funds are emerging. This includes 2003 Houston Energy Partners, which was launched to invest in all levels of the energy business, including securities, stock, debt, and MLPs. There continues to be an influx of non-energy firms acquiring natural gas assets across North America, often led by investment banks, private equity groups, and hedge funds. How long this activity will continue will be dictated by both the appetite of companies to acquire assets and the completion of business strategy adjustments by energy companies.

While there has already been substantial M&A activity in the midstream segment of the industry, the tendency for hedge funds and investment banks to get involved encompasses the entire energy value chain. Recently, for example, plans by British Energy to approve a rescue deal involving a $650 million government bail-out that would ultimately give 97.5% of the company to its bondholders have been challenged by a group of investors led by British hedge fund, Polygon. Additionally, hedge fund Stark Investments also owns 8% of British Energy, along with a substantial interest in the bonds of Drax, the coal-fired station in Yorkshire that generates 7% of the United Kingdom's electricity. Stark Investments, founded in 1986, manages funds totaling over $4 billion and has averaged returns of more than 20% since then, mostly from distressed asset plays in the energy industry.

On the buy side of this M&A activity is a resurgence of publicly traded MLPs. These have two major advantages over other corporations that make them attractive in today's environment. First, the MLPs' earnings are taxed only once at the unit-holder level. Most other publicly traded corporations are actually taxed twice: once at the corporate level and once at the shareholder level. MLPs can therefore pay out significantly more of their cash flow to unit-holders than an ordinary corporation can. Second, the non-tax expenses of an MLP, such as depreciation, directly benefit the unit-holder since such expenses diminish the taxable income passed through to them.

ENERGY TRADING GROWING

According to Energy Hedge Fund Center research estimates, the notional value of the energy and environmental trading markets today is only $2.2 trillion. We predict that this will grow to $10 trillion by 2010, which is still small in size compared to the over $200 trillion foreign exchange and interest rate swaps and futures markets. This is not the daily volume of trading on the energy futures exchanges, but the outstanding number of contracts on both the futures exchange (called open interest) and all bilateral OTC contracts. Our breakdown is provided in Table 3.1 on page 66.

Today, the twin capitals of energy trading and hedge funds continue to be New York and London, where most of the hedge funds and investment banks reside. This trend will continue to grow and include more energy trading developments in Houston, Calgary, Rotterdam, Dubai, Singapore, Tokyo, and Shanghai. As the financial markets for energy and environmental financial products mature, we will see more financial futures, but

Table 3.1 Total energy trading
notional value

Commodity	2005
Crude oil	$1.5 trillion
Natural gas	$400 billion
Heating oil/Gasoil	$100 billion
Gasoline	$50 billion
Jet fuel	$50 billion
Electricity	$20 billion
Weather	$ 7 billion
Coal	$15 billion
SO_2	$10 billion
CO_2	$10 billion
Renewables	$1 billion
Petrochemicals	$1 billion
Tanker rates	$1 billion
Total	**$2.2 trillion**

Source: Energy Hedge Fund Center
(www.energyhedgefunds.com)

more importantly for energy and environmental hedge funds, we will see more indices to trade off. Related to this, the recent carbon-centric IPOs on the London Stock Exchange's AIM show that there is an appetite for more mainstream derivatives for institutional investors by issuing more alternative energy and carbon-oriented equities. In Chapter 10 we will enter into further discussion on commodity trading indices, ETFs, and other passive and active means for hedge funds to trade these emerging markets. Many of these new commodities will also be traded bilaterally as OTC swaps and options contracts that will clear on NYMEX Clearport and ICE's London Clearinghouse relationship. This will in effect make them quasi-futures contracts, as they are cleared on regulated exchanges. This growth should be exponential.

A good rule of thumb for commodity markets is that they should trade six to 20 times the underlying physical market. Since energy is over a $4 trillion physical global market, we think that energy derivatives have a long-term growth trajectory ahead of them. Add to that market size the projected growth of the global emissions market to $3 trillion, as well as its market immaturity, and we have a tremendous business opportunity for hedge funds to enter the energy and environmental trading space. Today's market inefficiencies, as well as high price volatility, are continuing to attract risk and investment capital into this financially immature market sector. The new triangle of trading includes major energy companies, investment, and hedge funds. This structural change in energy trading now encompasses more participation by both hedge funds and fund of hedge funds to participate in energy commodity markets.

NEW FUND PLAYS IN THE ENERGY PATCH

While we continue to see most of the funds focus on oil and gas as a commodity, there is no doubt that their interest in energy commodities is increasing. In Europe this has already meant diversification into carbon dioxide trading. Coal also fits their commodity diversification profile after many years of being ignored by investors as coal prices have also become more volatile due to global energy supply tightness as well as its lower (but rising) costs. Coal has become a global commodity and it has attracted investment banks such as Morgan Stanley and Goldman Sachs' J Aron, but also hedge funds such as Ospraie. One senior coal analyst told us that 25% of coal trading is institutional and fund driven in North America.

Another area of activity has been in the weather derivatives area, which in 2005 blossomed on the Chicago Mercantile Exchange. (In Chapter 8 we will discuss weather derivatives in greater detail.) There has been tremendous interest in weather derivatives, particularly following the big Chicago-based hedge fund, Ritchie Capital. Also, several new weather hedge funds have launched at capitalizations of $10 to $20 million. One weather risk management fund is Ramsay's Parthelion Fund based in Kansas City.

There has also been noticeable interest in launching alternative energy or green hedge funds in 2005. (In Chapter 7 we will go into detail about these investment opportunities.) These funds invest in long/short equities of alternative energy companies such as fuel cells, flywheel, biomass, wind, and solar energy companies that are listed on US and European exchanges. One fund that was launched on December 1, 2004, was also interested in trading REC credits (renewable energy certificates). Other funds are trading ethanol derivatives. And some funds will be involved in renewable energy projects. The EU ETS allowed many funds in the European Union to start trading carbon dioxide emissions during 2005. While green hedge funds are still a small part of the energy hedge fund universe, there is interest for both "fund of fund" macro investors and those who want to broaden their energy market exposure. One interesting anecdote for a "green hedge fund" was that an investor asked the fund manager if he was an environmentalist and the manager replied that he was a trader. The trader said "good," and the investor put $20 million in the fund.

We are beginning to see other hedge fund interest in other less-developed and emerging markets, such as freight derivatives (that is, UK shipbroker Clarkson has launched a hedge fund), uranium, sugar (for ethanol trading), and water.

SUMMARY

Energy has arrived at the perfect time for this switch in strategies to an emerging market that is now entering the perfect storm in energy tightness and price volatility, due to decades of under-investment in its upstream, midstream, downstream, and transportation markets. The world has now entered a time of sustainably higher energy prices and investors need to capitalize on this trend. Accelerated global demand coupled with severe supply constraints and more geopolitical risk have brought the underlying volatility that hedge funds have exacerbated in daily trading in both oil and gas futures and OTC markets. They are forcing a structural change in energy trading that is now primed for more hedge fund participation throughout the world.

Traditionally many investors look to bonds, real estate, and commodities during inflationary times to protect the purchasing power of their capital. Adding diverse asset classes to their portfolios, investors seek to have multiple degrees of downside price protection to capture upside potential. Commodities traditionally have had a negative correlation to traditional asset classes such as stocks and bonds, and therefore are a good part of any long-term portfolio. They are a good bet for portfolio diversification.

Hedge funds are looking for market anomalies such as undervalued assets, credit spreads, and commodity plays. Energy is the place for the funds to be, as drivers of hedge fund performance are always returning on investment. High economic growth and low interest rates equal their length in energy markets.

This drive for profits in energy trading is also altering the nature of taking risks. Banks are feeling more confident that they can place longer term bets on which way oil and gas prices will go. For example, in the past, power traders have felt comfortable going out only about 18 months in the future. Yet the longer the contract, the greater the chance to earn revenues on a well-chosen trade. Armed with sophisticated risk management and modeling systems that have been honed in the derivatives markets, banks are hoping to push out the futures market further into the future.

There are many positives in bringing the larger financial players as new participants bring more market liquidity to the table. Banks and funds not only have increased liquidity; in the banks' case, they also have greatly improved the risk profile of the entire sector. Instead of trades being conducted by companies teetering on junk-level ratings, many deal counterparties are now highly rated financial institutions with large balance sheets.

Of course, the big question is whether banks and funds are truly here to stay in trading, or whether they are just pursuing the latest bubble that, when it bursts, could leave some players on the wrong end of a trade, with costly repercussions. But this time it is different as the banks combine energy commodity hedges with capital through other value-added products. Other banks are content to incorporate energy trading as part of a growing overall commodities desk.

As more banks and hedge funds enter energy trading, and try to push the envelope, it is unsurprising that many long-term players view the newcomers with suspicion, arguing that their presence is causing increased volatility. Because funds and banks have made leveraged bets that prices will stay at high levels, the argument is that something of an energy bubble has been created. The banks also benefit, acting as a prime broker for the hedge funds, and in fact, many banks active in the more established and mature foreign exchange markets are now stepping up efforts in their prime brokerage function in the energy trading area. The banks also provide leverage capital to hedge funds, and this function should not be overlooked either, as leverage as high as a factor of 20 has been heard in energy markets. This is exceedingly dangerous. Many more traditional hedge funds are leveraged three to four times. About 30% of hedge funds do not use leverage, which is considered sub-optimal. The pullback in energy markets in the fall of 2005 has reduced leverage and added to a more mature approach to trading the energy markets due to its attendant risks.

Some investors have changed their perspective on investing in energy commodities and energy futures. While they traditionally invested in the energy equity markets, they have shied away from the energy commodity complex. One driver of more funds into energy has been the twin drives of deregulation of the hedge fund industry in Europe and the rapid growth of the hedge fund industry in Asia. While energy is not generally well understood by these investors either, it has become an attractive place to be for those capacity-limited hedge funds looking for new opportunities. Since hedge fund managers are generally very quantitative at both the technical and fundamental level, they spend significant resources on sources of statistical arbitrage, looking for correlations, cross-market arbitrage such as credit versus event exposure. They are also aware of event risk exposures in energy markets such as plant outages or pipeline damage.

Historically, energy futures contracts have had a very low correlation with energy-related and non-energy-related stock/bond markets. Energy as a commodity has usually been used as an inflation hedge, just like real estate. Thus, futures or options based on energy contracts can be used as an alternative asset class that represents fundamental returns for a diversified investment portfolio.

NOTES

1 "International Energy Outlook 2005," US Department of Energy, Energy Information Administration, July 2005.
2 "Wen Lowers 2005 Economic Growth Target," *China Daily*, December 6, 2005, www.chinadaily.com.cn/english/doc/2005-03/06/content$_{422130}$.htm.
3 See (1) above.
4 "How China Runs The World Economy," the *Economist*, July 20–August 5, 2005, pp. 61–3.
5 "Indian Budget 2005–2006," the full text is available on the website www.banknetindia.com.
6 See (1) above.
7 "Oil Market Report," November 2005, International Energy Agency, November 10, 2005.
8 See (7) above.
9 See (1) above.
10 Dr Paul Stevens, "The Future Price of Crude Oil," www.mees.com.
11 See (10) above.
12 See (1) above.
13 Jason Bush, "What's Holding Back A Flood Of Russian Oil," *Business Week*, July 25, 2005, www.businessweek.com/magazine/content/05_30/b3944088_mz015.htm.
14 See (1) above.
15 Mathews, Tom, "Does Speculation Make Energy Prices More Volatile? Academic Research and CFTC Data Suggest the Opposite," *Energy Pulse*, December 28, 2004, www.energypulse.net/centers/article/article_display.cfm?a_id=894.
16 *Monthly Oil Market Report*, July, 2005, OPEC.

CHAPTER 4

The Energy Complex and Investment Opportunities

O ne of the issues about investing in the energy complex is in under-standing exactly what you are investing in and the potential and complex risks associated with that investment. The energy industry is extremely complex and very volatile in terms of business change as a result of regulations, rules and market trends, and it is different for each commodity and each geographic market. In this chapter we will look at the energy complex; however, we will only give a brief introduction.

ENERGY INDUSTRY VALUE CHAINS

One way to look at the energy industry is as a set of overlapping value chains. It is overlapping because each energy commodity has a value chain of its own, and each energy commodity value chain bears some dependence on that of the other energy commodities. For example, natural gas, crude oil, coal, and other commodities may be used as fuel to generate electricity, and crude oil is used as an input into the refining of products such as gasoline and jet fuel. It is these interrelationships that are often difficult to understand and yet these very interrelationships provide for a number of excellent investment opportunities.

Figure 4.1 shows a simplified view of the energy value chain from exploration and production to end use. However, it should be noted that each energy commodity requires somewhat different processes, assets, and transportation methods as a result of its physical properties. Further, all of these processes are subject to rules and regulations at various levels, including national, regional, local, and even at the individual operating company level.

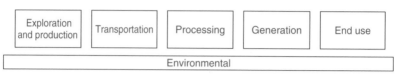

The Exploration and Production Segment

Crude oil and natural gas have to be first discovered through the processes of exploration. The exploration activity, of course, relies upon a whole other subset of the energy industry known as the oilfield services industry that provides services and equipment to the explorers. Oilfield service firms include well-known companies such as Halliburton and Pioneer Drilling, for example, as well as a whole host of smaller public and private companies. Oilfield services will include activities such as seismic acquisition and processing, drilling services, mud logging, electric logging and other geological services, offshore supply, and more.

Once oil and gas is discovered, it has to be proven to be an economic find due to the size of the reservoir and the quality of the oil. If the oil or gas discovery is economic, and that can depend on a number of factors outside of the forward price of oil or gas such as the proximity of existing industry infrastructure and the technical feasibility and cost of extraction, a development plan is created. Again, this phase uses an array of other engineering, design, construction, and technical expertise from service firms. At this stage, if the development plans meet with approval, the project can proceed. Note that the time gap between initial discovery of oil or gas and first production can be decades or many years.

Once the production equipment is in place, oil can flow but the reservoir needs to be managed over the course of the life of the field. Again, this will involve many different skills and services from the operator, partners, and service firms. In essence, the operator, usually an oil company, simply acts as the project manager throughout the process. As the oil is produced, it needs to be accounted for and extensive reporting is required from the operator to a variety of other parties, including government agencies, partners, interest owners, and more. Good reservoir management will mean using a variety of techniques to maintain reservoir pressure and to enhance recovery of the oil. Even then, oil recovery rates may be less than 50% (on average between 20% and 60%, depending on reservoir and oil properties along with extraction methods) of the oil actually present in the reservoir.

With oil prices as high as they are now there is also a good deal of interest in reworking older oilfields and wells. Often, these are old wells and fields that have been plugged and abandoned as uneconomic. However, with better technologies for fracturing reservoirs and techniques like horizontal drilling, they are worthy of reconsideration. There are growing numbers of such projects today and these will add incremental production from wells and fields that were once uneconomic. Since these projects also rely on available equipment and skills, it will take longer to complete the projects while the extra spending will also spill over into the oilfield services side.

The produced oil often needs to be processed before it can be transported to remove water, sediments, various gases, and other impurities. It will then be transported through pipelines, tankers, barges, and rail cars, possibly being stored at a variety of locations prior to arriving at its final destination. Moving oil around requires that transportation is available and that it meets environmental and safety regulations. This past year has seen high freight rates reflecting demand for oil tankers, for example.

The oil business involves any number of highly specialized activities, including the management of assets such as reservoirs, production platforms, logistics around transportation, and extremely complex transaction management dealing with accounting for oil and revenues. Rules governing these processes vary by country, state, and county, and issues such as taxation accounting can be extremely difficult as a result.

In the case of natural gas the processes are somewhat similar to that of crude oil and the major differences are related to the physical properties of the two commodities. Being a gas, natural gas requires certain differences in handling, transportation, and measurement. While in the United States, for example, it is customary to measure and track gas volumes, in Europe and other areas, it is the energy value of the natural gas that is measured and tracked. This means more sophisticated metering and different methods of processing at the production site and beyond, including the removal of noxious and other gases such as SO_2, CO_2, H_2S, and others, and differences in modes of transportation. This segment of the industry is often referred to as "upstream."

Exploration and production can be extremely expensive. It involves time-consuming activities, particularly in relatively inaccessible regions of the world such as deep water regions or polar regions. Additionally, there are innumerable risks associated with successfully completing the cycle, including political risk, reservoir risk, production facility risk, economic risk, and more. Political risk comes into play in politically unstable areas, but also in the form of government change that may result in industry nationalization or a change in rules and regulations relating to oilfield ownership or royalty payments. As stated above, the process can take decades from initial prospecting to economic extraction. Also, it may indeed be iterative in the sense that a discovery is made that is deemed sub-economic and is then continually revisited as new technologies become available for extraction, or as oil prices change, or new geological understanding is developed, for example.

Inherent in the risk is that of actually finding something. Discovery rates vary according to the maturity of the province in which exploration takes place and as to how the term is defined. It can be as high as 50%, but it is generally significantly lower. All of these risks and costs have to be included in any assessment of the economies of a development project.

With a sustained, almost 20-year period of low oil prices, exploration activities had declined and today the world consumes four barrels of oil for every one barrel that is added through exploration activities. Worse still, few new large oilfields have been discovered over the last 20 years. It is this factor that has, in part, led to today's high and volatile oil price as demand has increased from areas such as China, Asia, and North America. The world has been drawing on oil discovered 20 or more years ago. It is this fact and the difficulty of obtaining accurate and well-defined reserve data that has resulted in the resurgence of the "peak oil" theory (see Chapter 3 for a discussion of peak oil).

Over 2005, exploration activities have seen a resurgence as a result of the higher price of oil and the opportunities that this provides. Much of the exploration activity is led by independent and smaller oil companies. In fact, drilling rates and rig utilization have reached new highs recently and the oilfield services side of the industry is currently booming. As a result of a combination of the current price of oil, new drilling and extraction methods, and new exploration tools, this activity incorporates not just new exploration activity, but also new ventures in very mature provinces and the re-entry of older wells with the design to extract more existing oil and gas.

While this section has looked briefly at the exploration and production segment of the industry, the future will also see non-conventional sources of oil and gas draw greater interest (see Chapter 3). Non-conventional sources include tar sands and oil shale, for example. The Canadian tar sands have already attracted considerable interest and production rates are set to increase dramatically, while work on oil shale has already attracted renewed interest. Already Shell Canada and Western oil Sands have divulged that their production costs are higher than expected. Escalating capital costs must be considered if the oil sands projects are to reach the three to five million barrel per day level. In both these instances, oil extraction is performed differently through mining and processing, for example.

Midstream Segment

The midstream segment of the industry is generally considered to include the transportation of oil and gas from the production facility to the point of end use. In that sense it includes largely the transportation segments such as pipelines, gathering systems, processing plants (but not refineries), and other transportation and storage mechanisms. Think of this segment of the industry as the operators of the assets and facilities used to move and store oil and gas.

Once again, the complexities of moving and storing oil and gas are vast. They are related to the physical properties of the commodities, rules, and regulations governing the operation of the facilities; and the accounting for physical volumes of product and associated revenues, including taxation.

The midstream segment has been particularly active in terms of asset sales since the collapse of the merchant segment. Pipelines, gathering systems, and processing facilities have been the assets primarily involved, since by selling these assets, the merchants were able to raise much-needed capital. Often, the procurers of the assets have been investment banks and hedge funds using the MLP structure, which is a tax-effective corporate structure originally created 20 years ago for exploration and production companies.

The midstream oil and gas business in North America is currently undergoing significant change. Over the past 24 months or so, there has been an increase in the pace of M&A of midstream assets such as gathering systems, gas processing plants, and pipelines. This flurry of activity can be attributed, at least in part, to the demise of the mega-merchants. The collapse of the merchant energy business has had a domino effect, causing many energy entities to divest significant and often attractive physical assets to generate urgently needed cash. Indeed, the collapse of the mega-merchants has created a ripple effect through the entire industry in the form of increased stakeholder scrutiny of corporate financials, new regulation, and an emphasis on credit management and credit risk. In turn, these pressures have forced many larger energy companies to seek to clean up their balance sheets. This industry introspection is often the basis for the sale of assets that are very attractive to others.

Similarly, a renewed focus on portfolio optimization, rationalization of business strategies, and a return to the concept of a core business among large E&P, utilities and integrated energy companies is also driving some of the acquisition and divestment activity. The continuing adjustment of asset portfolios and business models is resulting in physical midstream assets changing hands, as well as allowing new, non-traditional players (such as energy hedge funds, investment banks, and MLP vehicles) to enter the market by capitalizing upon attractive acquisition opportunities.

The acquired midstream and pipeline assets are generally of good quality. They are attractive cash generators and often they bring experienced staff with the expertise to manage the assets effectively. Overall, investors appear to be warming to the midstream sector, as it offers good assets at attractive prices and often includes effective asset managers. Funding is more readily available for this type of investment than it has been in the past.

One interesting aspect of this furious pace of transactions is the players involved. On the buy side, non-traditional players such as investment banks, private investment firms, financial and insurance firms, private equity, and hedge funds all have acquired midstream assets. For example, Hicks, Muse, Tate & Furst, a private investment firm, purchased Regency Gas Services. Warburg Pincus provided seed funding for Targa Resources, Inc., a midstream start-up; and Loews Corporation acquired Gulf South Pipeline, LP, from Entergy-Koch.

Over the last year, publicly traded MLPs have emerged as one of the leading vehicles of choice for many of these M&As. MLPs have two major advantages over other corporations. This makes them attractive in today's environment for two reasons:

1. MLP earnings are taxed only once at the unit-holder level. Most other publicly traded corporations are actually taxed twice – once at the corporate level and once at the shareholder level. Therefore, MLPs can pay out significantly more of their cash flow to unit-holders than an ordinary corporation.
2. The non-tax expenses of an MLP, such as depreciation, directly benefit the unit-holder since such expenses diminish the taxable income passed through to unit-holders.

Created by Congress in the 1980s to stimulate oil and gas exploration, the MLP corporate structure was designed to allow energy companies to spin off production and transportation assets into separately managed MLPs. By spinning off the MLP, the energy company raised cash to pay debt or invest in other businesses.

While midstream assets may be considered to be primarily a slow growth but steady cash-flow business, by packaging such assets into an MLP, the entity can pay out all earnings to unit-holders and pay no taxes on those earnings. Essentially, companies can sell such midstream assets to investors for a market price in return for a promise to pay out the cash flow after maintenance expenses, while maintaining control.

Recently, M&A activity has also occurred as a result of the expansion of MLP ownership of assets. By increasing the asset-base, the MLP can operate more efficiently and generate more income for unit-holders. So MLPs are now in acquisition mode, aggressively seeking to aggregate and consolidate similar assets. The issue that is arising with this particular play is that, with demand for more assets, the price paid for those assets is also rising. MLPs that overpay for assets are punished by stakeholders. MLPs are generating between 6 to 8% returns for investors, which is well above returns on more traditional investments. MLPs provide investors with a useful and attractive vehicle for the acquisition of assets in the midstream energy industry.

Marketing Segment

Although the marketing segment of the industry collapsed in the days following Enron, it has not altogether disappeared. There are still merchant energy companies and energy marketing or trading is again growing. The marketing function is best looked at independently from other industry segments, since all of those are asset-oriented; that is, their activities and business processes are largely about managing and optimizing assets. The marketing segment of the industry is an overlay and extension to the other segments that is all about the commercial activities of trading and managing risk.

Today's energy merchants, excluding Constellation Energy and Sempra Energy Trading, are more likely to be smaller entities often created expressly for the purpose of managing a number of smaller energy company's trading needs, such as, for example, The Energy Authority or ACES Power Marketing. Both these companies are owned by groups of regional utilities in North America, and take on the trading and risk management activities for those municipal and other smaller utilities. A small number of larger merchants such as Constellation and Sempra still exist, but energy trading is now dominated by a different group of entities in the form of investment banks, hedge funds, and multinational oil companies.

The marketing segments' business activities are essentially moving in two different directions, and the gap between the two is widening. The "speculators" in the form of banks, funds, and multinational oils tend to trade to make money, whereas the utilities, producers, and others trade to secure supplies of fuel and sell excess commodities. More and more the utilities are being marginalized to trading around their assets. This emerging dichotomy is important to understand, since it reflects a difference in business strategy and also in business complexity.

Merchants essentially buy and sell physical energy commodities, and engage in hedging and perhaps speculation in energy financial markets, too. More physically oriented companies such as utilities have a heavy transaction management burden since they need to take delivery or deliver the physical commodity. This requires tracking, volume accounting, and management of payments and receipts. Additionally, they may engage in hedging activities using various financial instruments to reduce exposure to price variations and risks. On the other hand, the "speculative" traders will trade more energy derivatives such as futures and options contracts, and may not play in physical energy markets at all. In the latter case, the emphasis will be on analytics, risk management, and sophisticated quantitative modeling. Unfortunately, the picture is not as simple as this might sound, since there is much overlap between the two types of activities.

Trading takes place in all energy commodities, including crude oil, natural gas, coal, electric power, and refined products, as well as energy-related commodities such as various forms of emissions, other green credits, weather, sugar (ethanol), and uranium, for example.

Refining and Petrochemicals Segment

The refining and petrochemical segment of the industry is that set of activities related to refining crude oil and the production of various chemical feeder stocks and fuels such as petroleum, jet fuel, heating oil, lubricants, ethane, propane, and other gases. These activities take place at refineries and other processing plants where both feedstock and finished products are stored. Additionally, these will need to be transported to and from the plant by a variety of mechanisms including rail, truck, barge, pipeline, and so on. This segment of the industry is commonly referred to as the "downstream" segment.

Again, the refining and petrochemical segment business processes are as much about effectively managing and maintaining assets as anything else. These facilities are governed by tight environmental, health, and safety rules and regulations, and are extremely dangerous. For that reason, business activities such as maintenance, preventative maintenance, work management, and health and safety procedures are just as important as the actual physical processes that are used to refine or process the feedstock. Additionally, the refiners can also be marketers, since they must obtain feedstock in wholesale markets and sell finished products in retail markets. Plainly, it is a very complex segment of the industry.

It is also a segment of the industry that is faced with constant change. Not only are there many different types and standards for the various products that they produce, those standards can vary on a seasonal basis. For example, there are more than 60 variations on gasoline in the United States, based on environmental regulations in different states and cities across the country. Not only do these formulations change by season, but they are also based on demand. This means that refineries can be constantly changing a variety of factors to produce the right products.

Added to that is product distribution. A particular specification of gasoline is the same, whichever company makes it and from whichever refinery it was produced. This product must be transported to distribution centers where it is stored and sold to retailers. It is during this part of the process that the various additives are added to the gasoline to make it a particular "brand." There is therefore a high degree of logistical planning, volume, and financial accounting involved in the business processes, as well as various taxation and local health, safety, and environment rules to comply with.

The lack of investment in new facilities over the last 20 years, particularly in North America (the last US refinery was built in 1976), combined with the closure of older refining facilities, has seen utilization rates go up accordingly. While investments have been made in upgrading refineries and adding capacity to existing facilities, the lack of new refineries is, in part, driving up the prices of refined products.

Utilities Segment

The utilities segment comprises the delivery of electric power, natural gas, and water to end-users of various types.

Electricity is a unique commodity because it is consumed the instant it is produced. Other commodities, such as natural gas, can be used to take advantage of storage to counter-market upswings or dips. Because electricity cannot economically be stored, it offers less flexibility in managing trading positions as well as physical delivery options. The lack of storage makes it especially difficult to manage unanticipated increases or decreases in load above or below planned levels. Because a customer's actual usage cannot be controlled to precise levels, a utility normally means granting customers an option to take more or less electricity as part of its contracting. The changes in consumption are normally weather driven, so many trading companies offer weather derivatives to help assume the weather-related risks for those who prefer not to.

Additionally, electricity is normally accounted for in hourly incre- ments of receipts and deliveries. Because of the hourly transactions, the sheer volume of components for each trade is significantly larger than in other commodities. Another complicating factor with electricity is that its feedstock comprises other energy commodities such as coal, gas, and oil.

The power value chain starts with generation from a variety of sources, such as crude oil, natural gas, nuclear, wind, tidal power, solar, and biomass, for example. The generation facilities are subject to health, safety, and environmental regulations and rules adding complexity. Generators may be owned by a variety of different types of company, including utilities, merchant power companies, and the state. Power also has to be distributed through transmission grids and then delivered to end-users that can be operated by a variety of different entities. It requires tracking, measurement, and accounting for both the energy delivered to various points and associated revenues. Each power market is different, both in terms of how it is operated and regulated, and with respect to the various rules for settlements and trading. In the United States there are multiple power markets covering particular regions of the country.

Local distribution companies take delivery of electric power and/or natural gas and then distribute it to end-users via a network of pipelines and/or power grids. These companies also need to handle customer service, including billing, new connections, maintenance, and a host of other functions. Many utilities/local distribution companies provide a variety of other services too, including but not limited to broadband Internet access. Once again, this is a very complex segment of the industry.

Oilfield Services Service Segment

The oilfield service segment has essentially been described above but it comprises companies that provide a variety of services to E&P companies. These include, for example, drilling, logging, geophysical, and even catering services. It is an important segment, however, since it is dependent upon spending and activity levels in the upstream segment of the industry.

End-user Segment

The end-user segment should also be considered here. It includes all consumers of the various forms of energy, but specific interest should be paid to various industries that rely on energy, such as the transportation sector and heavy industry. These industrial end-users may also engage in price risk hedging activities.

Other Segments of the Industry

There are many other segments in the energy industry that have not been described above, including, importantly, coal mining. Coal is an increasingly important fuel and its price has also dramatically increased in commodity markets over the last two years or so. Coal quality is an issue that affects pricing and also requires tracking. This adds significant complexity. Again, the industry is beset with increasing health, safety, and environmental issues and regulations, and has both an asset management component and a trading component.

THE ENVIRONMENTAL OVERLAY

As can be readily observed, increasing interest in the environment is adding a significant level of complexity across the entire energy industry and that is set to continue. Environmental rules impact on facility-siting and design, facility operation, commodity transportation, and the end use. But the environmental overlay to energy is more than just an added cost and process burden – it is also a growing opportunity.

As energy commodity price and volatilities rise, new sources of alternative energy start to look increasingly attractive, spurring a surge of investment in fuel cells, biomass, geothermal energy, wind, solar, and other forms of energy. These projects offer an increasing array of companies, products, and projects to invest in. Furthermore, new technologies aimed at increasing fuel usage efficiency are likewise now creating interest from hybrid engine technology to newly efficient building design.

Finally, as rules are introduced in various locations to reduce various types of pollutants in the form of cap and trade markets for CO_2, SO_2, and NOx, for example, there is also a commodity trading opportunity around these emissions (see Chapter 7). There is also an arbitrage opportunity between the energy commodities and the emissions.

Our thesis is that the environment becomes an increasing element in the energy puzzle and both will add complexity as well as opportunity over the coming years. We believe that the "wrinkle" added by environmental considerations rapidly becomes a factor that sustains the energy bull market longer than many might expect.

INTRA-ENERGY OPPORTUNITIES

Historically, the energy industry has demonstrated some interesting trends related to the overall energy value chain that should also be understood by potential investors. In periods when the upstream segment of the industry is benefiting from higher commodity prices and is very profitable, the downstream side of the business has performed poorly as the price of feedstock and the cost of processing rises. Similarly, the reverse has also been true, such that low-energy commodity prices have meant that the upstream sector of the industry has underperformed while the downstream segment has done quite well. To some extent, this historical sector correlation broke down during 2005. While energy commodity prices were high, both the upstream and downstream segments were very profitable (see Figure 4.2).

This break with historical trends is in part due to the tightness in refining capacity, shown by refining utilization rates (see Figure 4.3), which was particularly emphasized after the damage of the Gulf coast storms of 2005. For us, this is a persuasive example in support of our arguments that the past is no longer a prologue to the future and that there have been structural changes in energy markets this past year.

However, another sector correlation that has held true is that between profits in the upstream segment of the industry. This eventually had a positive impact on the oilfield services segment as well. High oil and gas

FIGURE 4.2   Historical refining margins

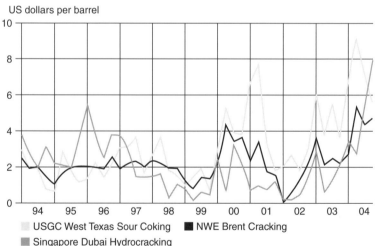

US dollars per barrel

USGC West Texas Sour Coking   ■ NWE Brent Cracking
Singapore Dubai Hydrocracking

Note: The refining margins presented are benchmark margins for three major global
     refining centers: US Gulf Coast (USGC), North West Europe (NWE) (Rotterdam), and
     Singapore. In each case they are based on a single crude oil appropriate for that region
     and have optimized product yields based on a generic refinery configuration (cracking,
     hydrocracking, or coking), again appropriate for that region. The margins are on a
     semi-variable basis; that is, the margin after all variable costs and fixed energy costs.

Source: BP, *Statistical Review of World Energy*, June 2005

FIGURE 4.3 Refinery utilization rates

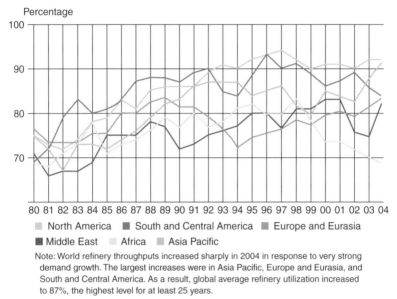

Note: World refinery throughputs increased sharply in 2004 in response to very strong demand growth. The largest increases were in Asia Pacific, Europe and Eurasia, and South and Central America. As a result, global average refinery utilization increased to 87%, the highest level for at least 25 years.

Source: BP, *Statistical Review of World Energy*, June 2005

prices encourage an upsurge in exploration and production activities that can have a knock-on effect on oilfield services firms as is currently the case. There are other correlations between the various industry segments, too, including between energy and end-users, where rising energy costs negatively impact such users such as airlines, for example. However, we believe that the single most important sector correlation in the future will be that between energy and the environment.

What is important to recognize is that the intra-energy value chain correlations give rise to a variety of investment opportunities and strategies that can be used for profit.

A BRIEF INTRODUCTION TO INVESTMENT OPPORTUNITIES

In reviewing the industry structure it is apparent there are really two broad sets of opportunities in energy:

- commodity trading
- industry asset-driven opportunities.

Commodity trading opportunities are not generally available to the average investor due to the extreme price risks of commodity markets, nevertheless there has been some discussion of an energy commodities-focused ETF in the press during the fall of 2005. However, hedge funds and CTAs can provide exposure to both financial and physical energy commodities, not just via exchange traded futures and options, but also through a wide variety of OTC transactions, too. The funds and CTAs follow a variety of strategies, including spread trading and directional trading, and arbitrage as well as exposure to different energy commodities and different commodity markets. Increasingly, funds are also trading emissions and renewable credits as well.

While some funds are focused on energy commodities, many others have a broader commodity focus, in which energy is only a component, providing exposure to softs, metals, and many other commodities. The funds may also provide exposure to commodities through a number of investible commodity indexes such as the Goldman Sach's Commodity Index. Buying on a commodity index allows the investor to profit on a rise in energy prices and other commodities without the risk of either financial futures or physical commodity trading. It is estimated that over $50 billion is tied up in index trading today.

The asset-driven opportunities include a whole host of investments from equities and other securities, through to debt and distressed assets. The average investor can gain exposure to the energy complex through publicly traded securities and sector-focused electronically traded funds, as well as a host of mutual funds, but many of the more attractive opportunities are unavailable. Hedge funds offer a variety of strategies and approaches to investing in energy that brings into focus equity holdings in private energy companies, sector-focused equity strategies, hybrid equity/commodity strategies, and others. There are funds that specialize in distressed energy assets, energy company debt, MLPs, Canadian royalty trusts, and even oil and gas in the ground.

Additionally, there are natural arbitrage opportunities across the energy industry that the funds exploit, including the "crack spread" (between refinery feedstock and refined products), the "spark spread" (between generation fuel and electric power), upstream against downstream, producers against end-users, and between the commodities themselves. These are sophisticated strategies that investors can only realistically access through a hedge fund.

Finally, with high energy prices there is growing interest in renewable forms of energy, alternative sources of energy, and energy efficiency technologies. The "green" area is now increasingly in focus for hedge funds and they are often essentially providing capital into this emerging sub-sector of the energy industry.

SUMMARY

The energy complex is ripe with investment and profit opportunities, but it is also extremely complex and very risky. By comparison with more traditional investment opportunities, the energy industry has far more risks, and for the non-energy expert these risks may be poorly understood. Today, the media and politicians have "dumbed down" rising energy prices and volatilities to a sound bite or two that often blame the speculators. The most insurmountable barrier to entry in energy hedge funds is the lack of knowledge of the world's largest and most complex business, which is rife with opportunity. You just need to know where to look. Energy is still the new kid on the block and still unfamiliar territory to many in the financial community. Yet the interest is there. Even the much-vaunted energy bill actually does very little to help today's energy situation because it is essentially a package of incentives that fails to address the fundamental issue in energy – under-investment in infrastructure.

Investing in energy requires that some basics about the industry are understood, such as the fact that electricity can't be stored, for example. Each commodity is different, each market or region is subject to different rules, regulations, and procedures, and business processes are extremely complex. However, if these things are understood, energy provides a tremendous wealth of investment opportunities and for investors seeking access to more sophisticated strategies, today's growing universe of energy hedge funds offer the possibility to do so.

CHAPTER 5

Energy Hedge Funds

O ver the last 18 months we have seen the number of hedge funds focused on energy literally explode in number and diversity, while many existing macro funds have also invested in the energy complex to some degree. Many of the new energy commodity funds were formed by ex-merchant energy traders who have now found another vehicle for their talents. Other funds have been formed by ex-bankers, consultants, and other people from the energy industry who see the hedge fund as the perfect vehicle to apply their skills and expertise to investing in the energy industry.

To some extent, this explosion in energy hedge funds owes its origins to the collapse of the energy merchant segment that released a large amount of energy trading talent on to the street and created a vacuum in energy markets. Existing macro funds like Citadel and Ritchie Capital of Chicago saw the opportunity to enter energy trading and immediately started seeking out the best talent among the unemployed or unhappy energy traders. For the next 12 months or so, it was largely existing macro funds with a focus on energy commodity trading that started the movement to energy, along with a small number of high-profile funds led by charismatic figures such as Boone Pickens of Dallas-based BP Capital.

By the beginning of 2004 the trend was well established and as a result of rising energy commodity prices and the excellent performance of some of the early energy funds, the hedge fund as a vehicle for investing in different parts of the energy complex became established. Today, we track 450 energy and environmental hedge funds and add at least 10–15 new funds a month to that number.

However, it hasn't been a one-way street. We know of a small number of energy funds that have closed their doors already and we expect more to come. In general, the funds that have closed have not done so because they lost all of their investor's money, but more as a result of understanding that their investment strategy would not work. Largely, they have been commodity funds with a high degree of exposure to the North American power markets, which are the riskiest of all commodity markets. (They are poorly developed with limited financial instruments and huge price volatility.) We have also seen a weather fund close shop recently and its founders return to trading weather for an energy merchant. Whether this was for lack of results or more of a return to a more comfortable work culture, we do not know. September and October of 2005 were ugly months for many energy hedge funds and investment banks in energy. It remains to be seen whether there were additional casualties arising out of those losses, but newly established energy funds that got caught in the energy retreat of October in particular may see investors looking to make early withdrawals.

It is clear to us that many energy funds will fold over the next year or so and for a variety of reasons. But it is also equally clear that for the foreseeable future, the number of new funds will exceed those closures.

THE UNIVERSE OF ENERGY HEDGE FUNDS

There are many alternative asset industry terms that describe hedge fund styles and strategies (see Chapter 2). The problem is that many of these terms don't readily apply to hedge funds playing in the energy industry. For that reason, we have created our own definition of fund styles and strategies (see Table 2.1 on page 24).

Of course, some of the traditional hedge fund strategies still apply to energy such as fixed income, arbitrage, and others, and these strategies can be deployed by any of the energy funds classified above. It's just that these terms don't really describe the energy specialist of the fund too well.

While most of the energy funds are based in North America – particularly in New York, New Jersey, and Connecticut; and to a lesser degree in Houston, Chicago, and Dallas – we have located significant numbers of energy funds in the United Kingdom, Scandinavia, and Switzerland as well. Recently, a number of new energy funds have emerged in Paris, France, and we have also detected a smaller number in Asia, mainly Singapore.

In that field of known energy funds, some 43% are energy-specialist funds – they are focused exclusively on some aspect of the energy industry (Figure 5.1). The remaining 57% are funds that have a substantial energy component to their strategy. Growth continues to occur in both segments as existing funds switch to a heavier investment in energy, and new energy-focused funds continue to be announced.

FIGURE 5.1   Distribution of energy hedge funds

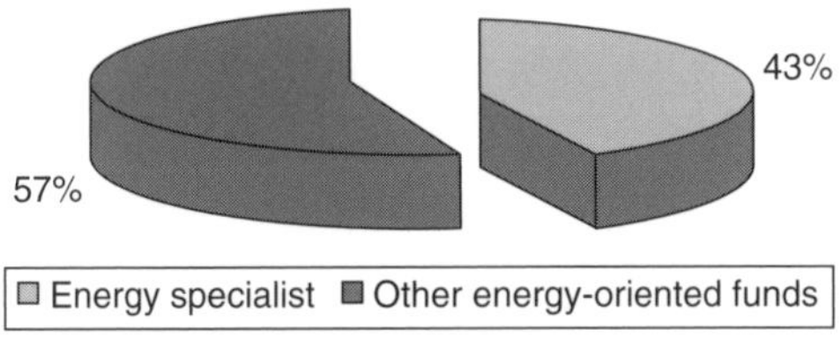

57%

43%

☐ Energy specialist   ■ Other energy-oriented funds

Source: Energy Hedge Fund Center, 2005

In terms of an overall energy fund strategy break out, commodity and equity strategies make up more than 50% of the universe of funds that we are tracking in about equal proportions.

Even as the price of crude oil has fallen to around the $55 barrel mark, and despite various individuals and institutions starting to try to talk down the price of crude, we expect to continue to see volatility in all energy commodity markets due to regional supply–demand issues. Indeed, many of the factors implicit in the rise and rise of energy prices have not gone away. The dollar is still fairly weak, China is still aggressively seeking new supply, and US demand remains strong. In short, not much has changed. On the equities side, whether oil is at $65 or $45 per barrel doesn't really make much difference in terms of the ability to make very large profits and produce good dividends. This is a view that is shared by others in the field.

Recent weather events have also created more interest in weather derivatives trading; drilling rates are very high; M&A activity in the industry is high, and may well get more active next year with the repeal of the US Public Utilities Holding Company Act (PUHCA) impacting on investment in utilities; and interest in alternative sources of energy remains high. All it takes is the weather or another event to precipitate a new round of price rises.

EQUITY FUNDS

Equity hedge funds made money shorting the merchant sector in 2001, and to some degree energy has always been in focus for equity funds as a part of a broader portfolio. We also know of a small number of equity-focused energy hedge funds that have been active for four to five years or more, however. It has been the sustained bull run in energy fueled by rising energy commodity prices that has sparked the surge in new energy equity funds over the last 18 months. We are now tracking some 125 energy equity funds.

Essentially, most energy equity funds are long/short with a long bias meaning they will both buy and short energy equities, but overall they will have a predominately long position. There are also a small number of long-only hedge funds specializing in energy. Some energy equity funds invest in only publicly traded equities and securities, while others will also invest in private equity or the somewhat illiquid "pink sheets" or equities floated on the AIM in the United Kingdom. We have also seen equity funds that use "pair" trades, seeking arbitrage opportunities between two related energy stocks to profit, and those that will utilize equity and ETF options, or invest more broadly in ETFs to gain exposure to a segment of the industry.

Most energy equity hedge funds charge a 1 to 2% management fee and a 20% performance fee, with or without a high watermark. Lock-up periods are generally less than 12 months but vary, and the minimum investment amount for qualified investors averages around $100,000.

While some energy equity funds are broadly based across the entire energy complex, many are seeking to exploit specific sectors of the industry such as exploration and production, utilities, refining, or petrochemicals. A smaller number are sector-oriented but migrate across sectors, or attempt to try to seek arbitrage between sectors of the industry. For example, we know of one fund that has progressively migrated from exploration and production equities into oilfield services during the fall of 2005. There has also been a lot of interest in Canadian Royalty or Income Trusts and Master Limited Partnerships on the part of equity hedge funds with a number of funds specializing in those segments of the industry.

There are multiple areas of the energy industry for equity funds to specialize in. For example, the ultraconservative Greek and Norwegian ship owners have been one of the hardest areas to breakthrough with new financial ideas in the energy complex. They will build a tanker on specification, but refuse to hedge their freight rate risks. Now, things are slowly changing in the shipping world. Clarksons, one of the world's largest shipbrokers, is launching the first hedge fund that will invest solely in shipping securities and derivatives. They are targeting 15 to 20% returns and will trade freight rate derivatives on dry bulk, tanker markets, and shipping equities. Shipping markets may be a good fit for a hedge fund, since they are highly volatile and go through boom and bust cycles. Tanker freight rates have gone up a factor of 10 in some markets in the past two years.

Returns have been very good over recent years for energy equity funds in general. In 2005 they have, as a class, performed better than commodity funds, although October 2005 was a bad month for many energy hedge fund returns. Even then a good number of energy equity funds didn't lose money (see Figure 5.2 below), they just saw their level of return contract in October. Of course, it should be noted that returns are also very variable across the different strategies pursued by energy equity funds, as is overall volatility.

Among the better known energy equity funds are the London-based RAB Energy fund and Boone Pickens' BP Capital. Essentially, these funds are reasonably broad-based energy equity funds and both have produced good returns of above 40% per year to date through to the end of September 2005. Energy sector-specific hedge fund examples would include London-based Ecofin, which has a utilities sector fund, including electric power, natural gas, and water utilities, and has performed within its target range since inception.

Today, all aspects of energy are booming. This means that the performance of energy equity funds *ought* to have been good. As energy stocks in the S&P gained 40% in 2005, most other sectors (except utilities and healthcare) were down. Without energy, the S&P would be down for the year and investors avoiding energy would have had a bad year. Can the market go further? A Merrill Lynch survey in Quarter 3, 2005, reportedly found that 60% of US mutual fund managers are still bullish on energy stocks. However, a few contrarians, hedge funds among them, are starting to bet against energy, or against certain of its segments.

Opportunities for 2006 and beyond continue to look good, although getting exceptional returns may be a little harder than it has been. E&P spending and activity levels are up (even some of the major oils have finally caught on and increased their budgets for next year). That activity will spill over into the oilfield services area and drive profits there, too. Even coal

FIGURE 5.2 Types of energy hedge fund by strategy/style

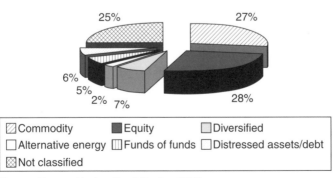

Source: Energy Hedge Fund Center, 2005

companies benefiting from much higher coal prices look promising. M&A activity will also periodically light up energy equities as larger oil companies seek to buy new reserves. They will acquire the smaller oil companies. There is also a lot of discussion and excitement regarding the potential for M&A activities in the utilities side of the industry in the United States, following the repeal of PUHCA. Here, the devil is in the details because, while PUHCA has gone, there are still many impediments to M&A activity. These include state variations of PUHCA, the energy bill (which extends FERC jurisdiction), and other regulatory issues in the sector that need to be clearly understood in an evolving regulatory situation. It is early days but everyone seems to agree that there will be an increase in M&A activity, though it might take longer to occur and be less significant than anticipated.

There is also increasing interest in "green" equity strategies. Over time, this will become an increasingly interesting investment area that is related to energy. There is also likely to be an increasing opportunity in technology companies associated with energy, as the industry seeks to mature and commercialize new technologies associated with oil exploration and exploitation, for example. Last, with high-energy prices, there is an opportunity to pursue a real energy long/short strategy by considering where increasing energy costs are likely to result in reduced profits. It is essentially a combination of being long in energy equities and short in various end-user equities.

On the downside is rising costs, in part, as a result of rising commodity prices generally – not just energy, but metals such as steel and platinum. The rising commodity costs will spill over eventually into more expensive services and operations, raising the price of projects in the industry and ultimately impacting on earnings. The other side of the cost equation is simply that so many skills and assets have already left the industry. What remains will attract premium prices.

COMMODITY FUNDS

Many in the industry will argue that energy commodity funds are not a new phenomena, since there has been a significant number of CTAs and CPOs around for quite some time. To some extent that's true, but the CTAs tend to be mechanistic trend followers and are often broadly diversified across commodities in general. What they are missing is the ex-merchant energy traders, whose talents became available after the collapse of the energy merchants, which have been snapped up by funds and investment banks over the last two years. Macro funds that got involved in energy trading early include Citadel, Amaranth, and Vega Asset Management. Many traders have now formed their own energy commodity trading funds to leverage at premium skill sets. Additionally, as the price of energy commodities has risen these past 18 months, others from the investment banking world have also spotted the opportunity and moved in to set up new energy commodity funds. The result is that today there are more than 120 energy commodity hedge funds, whereas just three years ago there were fewer than 20.

Typically, energy commodity hedge funds employ a more fundamental approach to their trading activities and increasingly have moved into spread trading and arbitrage. While many trade only derivatives, an increasing number also engage in the physical energy markets and some even have the capability to take physical delivery of the product. For most, the initial energy commodity was crude oil because it is an essentially global, liquid, and, for an energy commodity, it is fairly mature. However, energy commodity funds also trade natural gas, refined products, electric power, weather, coal, LNG, petrochemical feed stocks, and energy-related commodities such as uranium and sugar.

Again, there are really two groups of commodity funds. There are those that have energy commodities as a part of their overall portfolio, such as UK-based Armajaro, for example, and those that are focused on energy commodities exclusively. Among the latter group the specialist fund can extend further to commodities such as water, weather, and emissions. Weather risk is now becoming a very viable trading market with an explosion in both trading volume and open interest in 2005 (see Chapter 8, which is wholly concerned with weather derivatives). There has been tremendous interest, particularly following the big Chicago-based hedge fund, Ritchie Capital, and so there have been several new weather hedge funds launched at capitalizations of $10 to $20 million. There has also been some new interest and peddling of weather derivatives due to the impending Kyoto Accord as there is some semblance of linkage between weather and climate risk.

Over the last 18 months, energy commodity hedge funds have also been able to attract a premium in fees. Most command a 2% management fee but we have heard management fees as high as 3%, and many ask a 20% performance fee, but again many have got more than that. In part, their ability to command high fees has been related to past performance, where in 2004 particularly some funds exceeded 100% returns. This was not and is not sustainable. Energy trading is extremely risky, as many funds and even banks found out in September 2005, when they lost hundreds of millions of dollars. Needless to say, performance in 2005 has been much less impressive overall (see Figure 5.3 below).

Energy commodity funds will continue to trade and will expand their activities into other energy commodities. Coal, for example, fits their commodity diversification profile after many years of being ignored by investors. There is a rebirth in coal markets due to global energy supply tightness, as well as its lower (but rising) costs. Coal is still the cheapest form of fuel for power stations and half of the world's electricity (including in the United States) comes from coal-fired plants. Coal that is used for steel production is actually in short supply, due to Asian demand particularly as China has turned from a coal exporter into a coal importer. Increased pollution-control technologies are leading to cleaner burning of coal and more trading opportunities. Coal has become a global commodity. It has attracted investment banks such as Morgan Stanley and Goldman Sachs' J Aron, but also the funds such as Ospraie. One senior coal analyst told us that 25% of coal trading is institutional and fund driven in North America today.

An additional and growing area of interest is in emissions and other green trading. Much of the focus this year has been on Europe, where the Emission Trading Scheme began in earnest at the beginning of 2005, but there are viable markets for NOx and SO_2 in North America and elsewhere, too. Almost every European energy commodity fund we are aware of is either active in emissions trading or plans to be.

As we have discussed, much of what has happened in the energy industry is as a result of a lack of investment in infrastructure and supply–demand tightness. Increasingly, environmental issues are adding cost and complexity, too. Already, this has resulted in yet another opportunity for hedge funds – freight rates. We know of several funds active in these markets. Freight rates have gone up as environmental regulations led to the

FIGURE 5.3   2004 energy hedge fund performance distribution

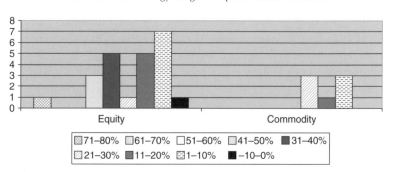

scrapping of single-hulled tankers and demand for tankers did not subside. New tanker builds now compete with LNG vessel builds at the world's shipyards and freight rates will continue to be high for some time.

In 2006 and beyond we expect to see some failures and an increasing number of start-ups and new entrants in energy commodities. We will continue to see increasing diversification into other energy and energy-related commodities, but we also think profits will be harder to come by. The increased volatility in commodity markets, combined with a slow but progressive increase in supply, signals more choppiness ahead. The funds will need to work harder and be more creative to obtain their alpha.

DEBT AND DISTRESSED ASSETS

There are many hedge funds that make money dealing in corporate debt and distressed assets, and a small number of specialist energy-focused funds such as the Kenmont Special Opportunities Fund. The big opportunity in the energy industry again really emerged after the collapse of the energy merchants, who had a tremendous debt burden to repay. In order to service that debt, many were forced to restructure the debt and sell off solid energy assets such as pipelines, gathering systems, and generation facilities. For example, with the energy merchants mostly gone who will now invest in new-generation projects? Hedge funds. The opportunities continue even today, although the easy pickings have already been had. However, the energy industry remains an opportunity-rich sector for funds specializing in this strategy.

Of particular note are two strategies. The first involves the MLP structure, a tax efficient vehicle in which to place assets. This has proved to be popular with all types of investors, including retail investors, mutual funds, pension funds, and hedge funds, since it typically generates between 6–8% returns, which is significantly above the much lower returns on more traditional investments, and moderate price appreciation. On the other side of the arrangement, the MLP represents a way to raise capital to pay down debt or for other purposes, and a way to accelerate revenues through flotation of the MLP. This has not gone unnoticed by the financial community and many investment banks have also created MLPs to hold the distressed and other assets that they have acquired. Additionally, since there are now mutual and other funds investing in this sector, there is more money available for MLPs looking to raise capital. Not only do the funds invest in the public securities of the MLPs, but also make private equity investments in them.

One issue surrounding MLPs is that the assets held by the entity are generally of diminishing value. For example, as an oilfield produces oil its reserves are progressively used up. As a result, one way for an MLP to maintain a healthy asset base is to acquire more assets. Over the last 24 months there have been numerous MLP-related acquisitions, particularly in the midstream sector of the industry. Of course, the price paid for the acquired assets may be of concern to the investor. In order to finance acquisitions, MLPs may issue debt and also utilize second-round equity offerings.

The second strategy is restructuring and variations on the theme. Here the hedge fund or funds purchase a significant amount of equity in a company that looks like it may be worth more after restructuring. In doing so the funds are able to seek board representation and convince management into a restructuring arrangement in which they profit. A notable example of this strategy is Massey Energy Co., a coal producer, who recently announced a plan to buy back $500 million worth of its own common shares and conduct a capital restructuring program that would remove another 6.8 million shares from the company's earnings calculation. Further, the company also announced that it would refinance some $220 million of 6.95% senior notes due in 2007; buy back $132 million in 4.75% convertible notes due in 2023; and offer to exchange $175 million in outstanding 2.25% convertible senior notes due in 2024. This in response to two hedge funds that had bought a combined 12.5% stake in the company and then placed pressure on management to buy back as many as 27 million shares.

The outlook for 2006 and beyond is to expect more of the restructuring strategy on the part of hedge funds in the energy and utilities industry. The increasing valuation of the various assets is now making the ability of MLPs to sustain themselves through acquiring more assets too expensive.

ALTERNATIVE ENERGY FUNDS

There has been noticeable interest in launching alternative energy or green hedge funds. These funds invest in long/short equities of fuel cell, flywheel, biomass, wind, and solar energy companies that are listed on US and European exchanges. One other fund that was launched on December 1, 2004, is also interested in trading REC credits. Other funds are talking about trading ethanol derivatives, although there is no market there yet. And some funds will be involved in renewable energy projects. It is a small part of the energy hedge fund universe, but it is of interest to both "fund of fund" macro investors and those who want to broaden their energy market exposure. (In Chapter 7 we will discuss green hedge funds in further detail).

HYBRID FUNDS

Energy equity long/short strategies with a long bias are common in the energy industry. But as more money is put to work in this strategy, fund managers are increasingly looking for an edge or an angle to differentiate themselves. We have observed increasing diversification away from just a general energy long/short with long bias approach. The diversification can be seen by sector focus; that is, managers focusing in on particular sectors of the energy industry; for example, E&P, oilfield services, and utilities. But the diversification goes even further than a sector focus. E&P-focused funds are getting involved in producing properties and have a direct exposure to the commodity through those investments. MLP-focused funds are getting involved in the creation of new MLPs and MLP debt financing for more asset acquisition. Some manager's focus more on pre-IPO opportunities and dabble in private equity.

Most recently, we have observed a trend to invest a small proportion of an equity funds' assets in commodities through exchange-traded futures and options, or in oil and gas reserves in the ground. This "hybrid" equity/commodity strategy is increasingly seen as a way to both differentiate and improve returns.

Diversification of the equity long/short strategy is good news for investors (providing the manager has sufficient expertise and risk controls in place). It ensures that money put to work in this strategy group has an increased chance of continuing to produce better than average returns. Even better news is that there are many additional vehicles still left open for diversification. There are still utilities and merchants with assets to sell at reasonable prices, there are innumerable opportunities to get involved in producing properties, and there is a surge in the formation of new independent and private E&P companies right now. In other sectors of the industry there are also potential opportunities. For example, there are bullish prospects for increased M&A in the utilities sector after the repeal of the US Public Utility Holding Company Act of 1935 (PUHCA). The repeal of this Act loosens US federal legislation on utility concentration and will now lead to further industry consolidation in this sector. Utility sector investment also led too exposure in the emerging water markets.

ENERGY HEDGE FUND PERFORMANCE

There has been much excitement over energy hedge fund returns. In 2004 some commodity-oriented funds were reported to have returned more than

Table 5.1 Comparative energy hedge fund returns (net)

	2004	Range	Sample size
Equity long/short strategies	21.96%	−7.68% to 74.47%	23
Commodity strategies	17.11%	−2.31% to 29.33%	7
All funds	20.55%	−7.68% to 74.47%	30
	First half 2005	**Range**	**Sample Size**
Equity long/short strategies	10.78%	−1.9% to 48.52%	26
Commodity strategies	−0.57%	−27.27% to 14.96%	8
All funds	8.2%	−27.27% to 48.52%	34

100% to investors. Recently, however, the tide has turned somewhat on the energy commodity funds, and we have seen some funds call it quits in 2005 and many others experience large losses. Of course, much of the focus in the media and elsewhere has been on energy commodity funds, but in reality many energy hedge funds are equity long/short and other strategies.

As of August 2005 the Vann US Hedge Fund Index was at 3.8% YTD for 2005 and for the whole of 2004 at 8.4%. Although there is no third party that we are aware of currently tracking energy hedge fund performance as a group, we do receive performance data for several funds in several strategies that can be used as a comparison. This can be viewed in Table 5.1.

Based on the results of our sample (which we recognize is somewhat limited by comparison to the Vann Index), it would suggest that in 2004, energy hedge fund performance exceeded the Vann US index by around 250%, and in 2005 it also exceeding the Vann index by about 215%. What is apparent in the data that we have is the drop off in performance in energy commodity-oriented funds from 2004 to 2005, while equity long/short strategies generally appear to be performing consistently. This can also be observed in Figure 5.3 on page 94 and Figure 5.4 on page 99.

The key question is why have commodity returns fallen off so dramatically in 2005? In part, the answer is related to some of the odd behavior

FIGURE 5.4   First half 2005 energy hedge fund performance distribution

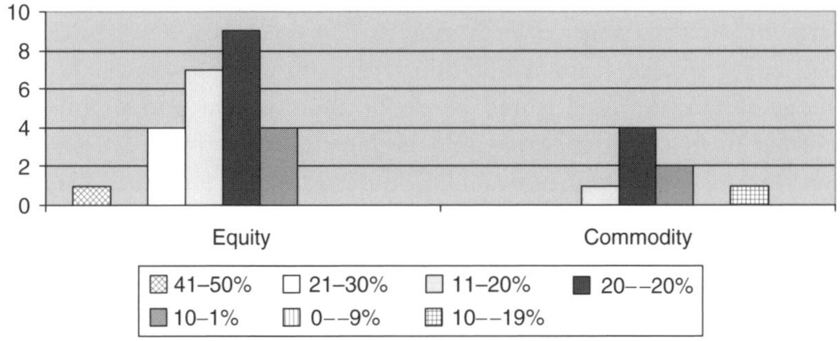

Source: The Energy Hedge Fund Center

observed in the energy commodity markets this year (a structural change has taken place in these markets and past trends may no longer be repeated). It may also point to attempts by the commodity funds to prematurely short energy commodities, something that has also been observed in trading data. Meanwhile, energy prices remain at high levels and this is feeding through into earnings and activity in the energy sector, which in turn has translated into a bull run on energy and energy-related stocks. In fact, the challenge for the equity-focused funds will be to correctly time shorting the market at some point in the future as the bull run inevitably ends.

But what is an investment in an energy hedge fund returning versus a more traditional investment? Throughout 2005, energy has been the hot sector (except for a few short spells when oil prices retreated) and this has not gone unnoticed by investors generally. Energy and natural resource stocks, mutual funds, and ETFs are all popular investment vehicles this year. As commodity prices have risen, so too have profits and dividends for energy and energy-related companies. It might be argued that the energy stock bubble has burst recently, with a retreat in oil prices and a drop in energy stocks across the board – but we don't think so. Certain sectors of the industry, such as oilfield services, for example, probably do not yet reflect increased activity and expenditures, and may still have some good upside potential. Additionally, the recent retreat in oil price has hit energy stocks hard. Why? The relative magnitude of the slip in oil price, as compared to the knock-on effect on energy stocks, seems unreasonable and an emotional reaction. In reality, with the oil price where it is, these energy companies will still make large profits and throw off good dividends.

Also, investing in energy these last 18 months has been the easy option. Oil- and gas-related stocks are the best performers this year in a stock market that is in danger of recording its first down year since 2002 amid high-energy prices, fears of inflation, and economic slowdown. Without energy stocks, the S&P would be down 2% this year and anyone who omitted to invest in energy would be having a very bad year. One has only to look at mutual fund and ETF performance to realize that. The energy sector Spyder has been heavily traded and is up 35.54% year to date. Likewise other ETFs and mutual funds (see Table 5.2). By comparison, energy hedge fund returns are, on average, only performing in the same range, and the question is – is this sufficient considering the additional risks and fees?

The answer to the last question in part is related to two issues. First, the range of returns by energy hedge funds demonstrates that if you invested in the "right fund" you did very well by comparison to mutual funds and ETFs. Although something of a motherhood statement, this shows that proper due diligence is required when selecting an energy hedge fund, since returns from energy equity funds in 2004 in our sample show a range of returns from around −7% to +75%. Second, and perhaps most importantly, one expects the energy hedge fund managers to do better when the markets move down, compared to ETFs and other traditional investment vehicles.

Table 5.2 Selected ETFs and average sector mutual fund returns as of September 2005

	YTD	3 months
ETFs		
Energy sector Spyder	35.54	5.79
Vangaurd Energy	34.71	6.44
iShares US Energy	30.50	4.42
iShares Natural Resources	28.51	6.06
iShares S&P Energy	27.76	3.65
Utilities sector Spyder	16.48	−0.17
iShares Utilities	15.37	−0.33
Mutual Funds		
Average natural resources	30.48	9.1
Average utilities	13.42	2.07

Source: Energy Hedge Fund Center (EHFC)

When equity markets move down, ETFs and to some extent mutual funds track down with the market, often moving disproportionately with respect to commodity prices. A hedge fund manager with a good strategy ought to minimize the losses at worst and, at best, profit from downward movements, too. The question for the future – just how well do energy hedge funds do when they have to work harder for those returns?

CHAPTER 6

Impacts and Evidence of Hedge Fund Activity in Energy

The ability to actually find out how much hedge fund activity there is in energy commodity trading is very limited, but some of the evidence is beginning to become more pronounced on the US Commodity Futures Trading Commission's (CFTC) Commitment of Trader report.[1] This is the only US government source for information on trading by energy hedge funds. The financial press rests usually on anecdotal information from brokers and trading floors. The CFTC report is usually quoted for all evidence on energy hedge fund activity; however, it is limited in monitoring energy hedge funds as it does not capture all the trading activity on the NYMEX, or any of the trading activity on OTC markets. However, it is a good indicator.

In early 2005, a NYMEX analytical report suggested that hedge funds actually lessened energy price volatility. CFTC staff expounded on the NYMEX report's merits.[2] However, the NYMEX report neglected to capture energy trading activity for the last four months of 2004, when energy hedge fund activity actually increased. We believe that CFTC's staff is actually not very cognizant of energy futures trading and the activity of energy hedge funds in particular. The good news is that the CFTC staff doesn't regulate the OTC energy markets and never will. We can be grateful for that.

Since it is the only public data available, we will examine the CFTC data in this chapter. It has shown a marked increase in "non-commercial" trading, which jives with the anecdotal evidence that the funds are now trading the futures contracts more than ever before.

THE "COMMITMENTS OF TRADERS" REPORT

The CFTC "Commitment of Traders" report for November 1, 2005, follows. Here we examine crude oil, unleaded gasoline, heating oil and Henry Hub natural gas futures and basis swaps data, and PJM electricity futures contracts for "non-commercial" market participants. The contract open interest data show 56.6% for crude oil, 57.7% for unleaded gasoline, 53.3% for home heating oil, 43.4% for the natural gas futures contract, and 50.8% for PJM electricity futures (see Table 6.1). These are a compilation of open interest data. Clearly, hedge fund participation has risen in 2005 to dominate energy futures trading for oil and gas.

While the CFTC data shows futures and options positions on the NYMEX, it does not reflect the OTC energy markets at all. This is still where most oil and gas trading takes place, particularly in longer date financial instruments. Futures dominate short-term trading, while the OTC markets dominate the long-term energy markets.

The CFTC provides monthly information on commercial and non-commercial holdings in the futures markets. The report shows the reportable positions. These reports are available in both a short and long format. The short report shows open interest separately by reportable and non-reportable positions. For reportable positions, additional data are provided for commercial and non-commercial holdings, spreading, percentages of open interest by category, and numbers of traders. The long report, in addition to the information in the short report, also groups the data by crop year, where appropriate, and shows the concentration of positions held by the largest four and eight traders. Current and historical *Commitments of Traders* data are available on the Internet at the Commission's website (www.cftc.gov). Also available at the site are historical commitment of traders (COT) data going back to 1986 for futures-only reports, and to 1995 for option-and-futures-combined reports.

Open interest is the total of all futures and/or option contracts entered into and not yet offset by a transaction, by delivery, by exercise, and so on. It is a better indicator of trading, since it reflects all the outstanding futures contracts. (A good rule of thumb for a successful futures contract is 10,000 to 20,000 contract lots of open interest, not daily trading volumes.) The aggregate of all long open interest is equal to the aggregate of all short open interest. Open interest held or controlled by a trader is referred to as that trader's position. For the *COT Futures & Options Combined* report for November, 1, 2005, option open interest and traders' option positions are computed on a futures-equivalent basis using delta factors supplied by the exchanges. Long-call and short-put open interest are converted to long

Table 6.1 Options and futures combined positions

NO. 2 HEATING OIL, N.Y. HARBOR – NEW YORK MERCANTILE EXCHANGE
OPTION AND FUTURES COMBINED POSITIONS AS OF **11/01/05**

NON-COMMERCIAL			COMMERCIAL		TOTAL		NONREPORTABLE POSITIONS	
Long	Short	Spreads	Long	Short	Long	Short	Long	Short

(CONTRACTS OF 42,000 U.S. GALLONS)   OPEN INTEREST: 215,426
COMMITMENTS

| 15,443 | 29,342 | 48,794 | 115,068 | 106,025 | 179,306 | 184,161 | 36,120 | 31,265 |

CHANGES FROM 10/25/05 (CHANGE IN OPEN INTEREST: −18,685)

| −2,340 | 2,782 | −10,317 | 184 | −8,083 | −12,474 | −15,619 | −6,211 | −3,066 |

PERCENT OF OPEN INTEREST FOR EACH CATEGORY OF TRADER

| 7.2 | 13.6 | 22.7 | 53.4 | 49.2 | 83.2 | 85.5 | 16.8 | 14.5 |

NUMBER OF TRADERS IN EACH CATEGORY (TOTAL TRADERS: 140)

| 32 | 31 | 42 | 70 | 69 | 121 | 125 | | |

NATURAL GAS – NEW YORK MERCANTILE EXCHANGE
OPTION AND FUTURES COMBINED POSITIONS AS OF **11/01/05**

NON-COMMERCIAL			COMMERCIAL		TOTAL		NONREPORTABLE POSITIONS	
Long	Short	Spreads	Long	Short	Long	Short	Long	Short

(10,000 MMBTU'S)   OPEN INTEREST: **850,834**
COMMITMENTS

| 38,440 | 80,321 | 368,327 | 369,465 | 367,225 | 776,232 | 815,873 | 74,602 | 34,960 |

CHANGES FROM 10/25/05 (CHANGE IN OPEN INTEREST: −75,381)

| −7,897 | −10,361 | −34,556 | −28,523 | −25,139 | −70,976 | −70,056 | −4,405 | −5,325 |

PERCENT OF OPEN INTEREST FOR EACH CATEGORY OF TRADER

| 4.5 | 9.4 | 43.3 | 43.4 | 43.2 | 91.2 | 95.9 | 8.8 | 4.1 |

NUMBER OF TRADERS IN EACH CATEGORY (TOTAL TRADERS: 197)

| 49 | 55 | 73 | 90 | 83 | 181 | 170 | | |

(continued overleaf)

Table 6.1 (*continued*)

HENRY HUB GAS SWAP – NEW YORK MERCANTILE EXCHANGE
OPTION AND FUTURES COMBINED POSITIONS AS OF **11/01/05**

NON-COMMERCIAL			COMMERCIAL		TOTAL		NONREPORTABLE POSITIONS	
Long	Short	Spreads	Long	Short	Long	Short	Long	Short

(2,500 MMBTU'S)   OPEN INTEREST: **1,343,590**

COMMITMENTS

345,957	87,974	246,376	731,247	997,742	1,323,580	1,332,092	20,010	11,498

CHANGES FROM 10/25/05 (CHANGE IN OPEN INTEREST: −50,897)

−8,232	−2,171	−2,215	−39,508	−46,682	−49,955	−51,068	−942	171

PERCENT OF OPEN INTEREST FOR EACH CATEGORY OF TRADER

25.7	6.5	18.3	54.4	74.3	98.5	99.1	1.5	0.9

NUMBER OF TRADERS IN EACH CATEGORY (TOTAL TRADERS: 131)

29	10	32	86	77	124	111		

PJM ELECTRICITY MONTHLY – NEW YORK MERCANTILE EXCHANGE
OPTION AND FUTURES COMBINED POSITIONS AS OF **11/01/05**

NON-COMMERCIAL			COMMERCIAL		TOTAL		NONREPORTABLE POSITIONS	
Long	Short	Spreads	Long	Short	Long	Short	Long	Short

(40 MEGAWATT HOURS PER PEAK DAY)   OPEN INTEREST: **84,273**

COMMITMENTS

25,886	8,873	15,459	42,800	59,839	84,145	84,171	128	102

CHANGES FROM 10/25/05 (CHANGE IN OPEN INTEREST: −4,035)

−714	−454	−611	−2,674	−3,017	−3,999	−4,082	−36	47

PERCENT OF OPEN INTEREST FOR EACH CATEGORY OF TRADER

30.7	10.5	18.3	50.8	71.0	99.8	99.9	0.2	0.1

NUMBER OF TRADERS IN EACH CATEGORY (TOTAL TRADERS: 53)

4	6	9	40	41	49	51		

Table 6.1 (*continued*)

CRUDE OIL, LIGHT SWEET – NEW YORK MERCANTILE EXCHANGE
OPTION AND FUTURES COMBINED POSITIONS AS OF **11/01/05**

NON-COMMERCIAL			COMMERCIAL		TOTAL		NONREPORTABLE POSITIONS	
Long	Short	Spreads	Long	Short	Long	Short	Long	Short

(CONTRACTS OF 1,000 BARRELS)   OPEN INTEREST: **1,536,361**

COMMITMENTS

119,650	91,243	484,180	869,391	880,961	1,473,221	1,456,384	63,140	79,977

CHANGES FROM 10/25/05 (CHANGE IN OPEN INTEREST: 38,167)

115	1,372	20,517	13,045	15,051	33,677	36,940	4,489	1,226

PERCENT OF OPEN INTEREST FOR EACH CATEGORY OF TRADER

7.8	5.9	31.5	56.6	57.3	95.9	94.8	4.1	5.2

NUMBER OF TRADERS IN EACH CATEGORY (TOTAL TRADERS: 280)

82	101	120	80	87	223	253		

UNLEADED GASOLINE, N.Y. HARBOR – NEW YORK MERCANTILE EXCHANGE
OPTION AND FUTURES COMBINED POSITIONS AS OF **11/01/05**

NON-COMMERCIAL			COMMERCIAL		TOTAL		NONREPORTABLE POSITIONS	
Long	Short	Spreads	Long	Short	Long	Short	Long	Short

(CONTRACTS OF 42,000 U.S. GALLONS)   OPEN INTEREST: **152,650**

COMMITMENTS

27,346	5,266	24,877	88,119	112,260	140,342	142,403	12,308	10,247

CHANGES FROM 10/25/05 (CHANGE IN OPEN INTEREST: −16,540)

48	978	−8,903	−6,738	−7,557	−15,592	−15,481	−948	−1,059

PERCENT OF OPEN INTEREST FOR EACH CATEGORY OF TRADER

17.9	3.4	16.3	57.7	73.5	91.9	93.3	8.1	6.7

NUMBER OF TRADERS IN EACH CATEGORY (TOTAL TRADERS: 151)

44	26	41	60	70	126	118		

Updated November 4, 2005
Source: ww.cftc.gov

futures-equivalent open interest. Likewise, short-call and long-put open interest are converted to short futures-equivalent open interest.

When an individual reportable trader is identified to the CFTC, the trader is classified either as "commercial" or "non-commercial." All of a trader's reported futures positions in a commodity are classified as commercial if the trader uses futures contracts in that particular commodity for hedging, as defined in the CFTC's regulations (1.3(z)). A trading entity generally gets classified as a "commercial" by filing a statement with the Commission (on CFTC Form 40) that it is commercially ". . . engaged in business activities hedged by the use of the futures or option markets." In order to ensure that traders are classified with accuracy and consistency, the CFTC staff may exercise judgment in re-classifying a trader if it has additional information about the trader's use of the markets.

A trader may be classified as a commercial in some commodities and as a non-commercial in other commodities. A single trading entity cannot be classified as both a commercial and non-commercial in the same commodity. Nonetheless, a multi-functional organization that has more than one trading entity may have each trading entity classified separately in a commodity. For example, a financial organization trading in financial futures may have a banking entity whose positions are classified as commercial and have a separate money-management entity whose positions are classified as non-commercial.

In Table 6.1 we show current trading volumes for the most successful energy futures contracts on the NYMEX. They all have robust open interest and daily trading volumes for both futures and options.

Let's look at these statistics in Figure 6.1. The difference in funds versus commercials has risen in the past few years, from an average of 118 in 2002 to 234 in 2005. The peak was 287 non-commercials. Commercials averaged 169 participants in 2005. This category has actually remained rather constant during the past few years.

Other CFTC Reports and Market Surveillance

To protect futures markets from excessive speculation that can cause unreasonable or unwarranted price fluctuations, the US Commodity Exchange Act (CEA) authorizes the CFTC (Commission) to impose limits on the size of speculative positions in futures markets. Furthermore, exchanges are required by CFTC rule 150.5 to adopt speculative limit rules for certain other contracts not subject to CFTC speculative limits. Unfortunately, in practice, the CFTC has been remiss. It has missed the MG violation of trading limits in old trading in 1993 and Enron's natural gas trading most recently.

FIGURE 6.1   Comparison of funds and commercial traders

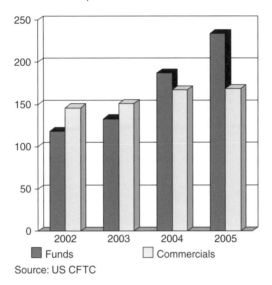

Source: US CFTC

There are three basic elements to the regulatory framework for speculative position limits. They are:

1. the size (or levels) of the limits themselves
2. the exemptions from the limits (for example, for hedge positions)
3. the policy on aggregating accounts for purposes of applying the limits.

The CEA, Section 4a(a), specifically holds that excessive speculation in a commodity traded for future delivery may cause "sudden or unreasonable fluctuations or unwarranted changes in the price of such commodity." This section provides that, for the purpose of diminishing, eliminating, or preventing such problems, the Commission may fix limits on the amount of speculative trading that may be done or speculative positions that may be held in contracts for future delivery. The NYMEX trades the following futures contracts and has specific speculative limits for each contract (see Table 6.2 on page 110).

Reportable Positions

Clearing members, futures commission merchants, and foreign brokers (collectively called "reporting firms") file daily reports with the Commission. Those reports show the futures and option positions of traders that hold positions above specific reporting levels set by CFTC regulations.

Table 6.2 NYMEX futures contracts

New York Mercantile Exchange (including COMEX Division)

Copper	**None**	**None**	**3,000 maximum, based on market conditions**
Silver (5000 oz.)	None	None	1,500
Gold (100 oz.)	None	None	3,000
Platinum	None	None	200
Palladium	None	None	225
Aluminum	None	None	750
No. 2 heating oil, NY (plus related contracts, see NYMEX rules)	None	None	1,000 for last 3 days
Heating oil crack spread calendar swap	None	None	None
Unleaded gas, NY (plus related contracts, See NYMEX rules)	None	None	1,000 for last 3 days
Crude oil, light sweet (plus related contracts, see NYMEX rules)	None	None	1,000 for last 3 days
Natural gas, Henry Hub (plus related contracts, see NYMEX rules)	None	None	1,000 for last 3 days
Natural gas basis swaps	None	None	500 to 2,500 depending on contract
PJM electricity monthly (plus weekly and daily)	None	None	3,000
NYISO LBMP swaps	None	None	1,000

Revised April 2004 (updated August 5, 2004)

Note: This table is only a general guide to speculative position limits and includes futures/option markets that had a combined open interest of approximately 10,000 contracts or greater recently. The limits are subject to change.
Source: CFTC website

(Current Commission reporting levels can also be found at the Commission's website noted above.)

If, at the daily market close, a reporting firm has a trader with a position at or above the Commission's reporting level in any single futures month or option expiration, it reports that trader's entire position in all futures and options expiration months in that commodity, regardless of size. The aggregate of all traders' positions reported to the Commission usually represents 70 to 90% of the total open interest in any given market.

From time to time, the Commission will raise or lower the reporting levels in specific markets to strike a balance between collecting sufficient information to oversee the markets and minimizing the reporting burden on the futures industry.

The most recent bank participation in futures markets' numbers shows that banks make up 12.4% of the open interest in the heating oil contracts, 14.0% for unleaded gasoline futures contracts, 20.5% of the open interest in the natural gas futures contracts, 9.5% for PJM electricity futures, and 28.9% of the crude oil futures contract participation. Their participation is similar for the NYMEX options contracts. The fact is that the hedge funds do not show up at all in this data, but they do trade through banks who act as their prime brokers. Table 6.3 shows the bank participation in the energy futures markets.

Table 6.3 Bank participation in futures markets' (in contracts)

Date	Commodity	Bank Type	Bank Count	Long Futures	%	Short Futures	%	Open Interest
11/01/05	NYMEX NO. 2	U.S	2	6,607	4.0	1,266	0.8	166,299
	HEATING OIL, N.Y.	NON U.S.	6	9,727	5.8	3,104	1.9	
			8	16,334	9.8	4,370	2.7	
11/01/05	NYMEX NATURAL	U.S.	6	28,104	5.3	24,401	4.6	527,674
	GAS	NON U.S.	11	28,487	5.4	37,953	7.2	
			17	56,591	10.7	62,354	11.8	
11/01/05	NYMEX PJM ELEC-	U.S.	2	280	0.4	3,330	4.5	73,701
	TRICITY MONTHLY	NON U.S.	3	1,652	2.2	1,764	2.4	
			5	1,932	2.6	5,094	6.9	
11/01/05	NYMEX CRUDE	U.S.	5	35,369	4.3	63,626	7.7	821,833
	OIL, LIGHT SWEET	NON U.S.	15	68,971	8.4	69,534	8.5	
			20	104,340	12.7	133,160	16.2	
11/01/05	NYMEX UNLEADED	U.S.	1	5,892	4.5	237	0.2	129,907
	GASOLINE, N.Y.H.	NON U.S.	7	9,928	7.6	2,154	1.7	
			8	15,820	12.2	2,391	1.9	

Updated November 4, 2005
Source: CFTC Website

IMPACT OF HEDGE FUNDS ON ENERGY TRADING FUTURES EXCHANGES

New York Mercantile Exchange (NYMEX)

The two energy futures exchanges, NYMEX and ICE Futures, are the clear beneficiaries of the increased activity of hedge funds and others in energy trading. They have seen a substantial rise is both daily trading volumes and contract open interest, particularly on the NYMEX. In fact, NYMEX continues to set daily volume records for total futures and options, energy futures, e–miNY energy futures^{sm}, and e–miNY^{sm} crude oil futures. The overall exchange volume of crossed one million contracts, and energy futures contracts, continue to set records.

Take a look at the e-mini contracts over the past few years. Oil now trades more than S&P futures. E-mini crude oil and gas futures are based on the New York Mercantile Exchange's light, sweet crude oil futures contract, and the Henry Hub natural gas futures contracts – these are the world's most actively traded futures contract on a physical commodity and the primary international pricing benchmark. But E-mini crude futures are just 50% of the size of a standard futures contract or 500 barrels of oil, and they trade fully electronically (not in open-outcry pits) nearly 24 hours per day. These contracts are a great way to play the crude oil market, but the smaller contract size means correspondingly less exposure to the market and less risk. This is perfect for those who want to experience the excitement of active energy markets, but have limited trading capital or are relatively new to futures trading. These Chicago Mercantile Exchange e-mini contracts have shown increased participation by hedge funds (see Figure 6.2).

The ICE Futures (Formerly International Petroleum Exchange or IPE)

ICE Futures did not initially show as much growth as the NYMEX, probably because most of the energy hedge funds are based in the United States, and because some oil market participants are not trading as much on the IPE due to increased intra-day trading. This change has made position-taking more complex for many oil traders. Brent crude oil futures have shown some growth in open interest on a year-to-year basis. The other ICE Futures contracts are gasoil and natural gas futures, and emissions futures contracts. The gasoil and emissions contracts have attracted more hedge fund interest than the natural gas futures contracts so far, but that should change as

FIGURE 6.2 E-mini futures

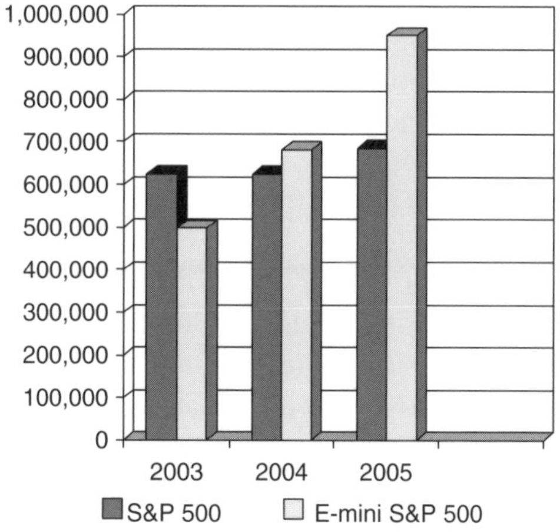

Source: Chicago Mercantile Exchange

the United Kingdom imports more gas and more price volatility enters European gas markets.

Anecdotally, we have heard that there has been similar growth on the electronic platform of the Intercontinental Exchange (ICE) in the United States. It makes sense. Hedge funds like electronical trading and most really don't understand the NYMEX floor trading operation. Additionally, inspection of ICE's list of users shows many energy hedge funds to be participating.

NYMEX'S CLEARPORT: POSITIONED FOR THE FUND BUSINESS

While the NYMEX is setting records on its trading floor, the OTC markets are also exploding in trading volume. The best indicator is the increased trading activity on NYMEX's Clearport, which continues to establish new trading records for clearing off-exchange contracts, although market participants continue to complain about high NYMEX exchange fees.

The New York Mercantile Exchange ClearPort[sm] technology network is a flexible, Internet-based system that provides a market gateway to trading and clearing services. The system lets market participants take advantage of the financial depth and security of the Exchange clearinghouse, along with round-the-clock access to more than 60 energy futures contracts, including natural gas location differentials; electricity, crude oil spreads and outright transactions; refined product crack and location spreads and outright transactions; and coal. Clearport is backed by the financial depth and integrity of an exchange clearinghouse. It is an open system, which allows trading firms to customize their front-end software to meet their particular trading requirements. The system lets commercial traders quote transactions in standard commercial units, such as barrels or British thermal units, while converting them to cleared contract equivalents. It uses enterprise-wide credit limits across both traded and cleared-only transactions to allow for prudent risk management. It also supports negatively priced contracts, allowing the trading of location, quality, and product differentials. All market participants desiring to execute transactions on NYMEX ClearPort^{sm} must first establish an account with an Exchange clearing member firm.

Since NYMEX still does not allow electronic trading during floor trading hours, it has opened up some arbitrage opportunities that were not intended. As we have seen with the floor in the Chicago Board of Trade (CBOT) and Globex, there is a mismatch between the trading floor and the electronic prices. This is also occurring with NYMEX and ACCESS. So, there can be some arbitrage between the trading floor and electronic platforms for price discrepancies.

Intercontinental Exchange and Trading

The direct competitor to NYMEX is the Intercontinental Exchange (www.theice.com), and it has picked up significant fund trading for OTC price swaps according to our sources. We were unable to get the level of fund participation on ICE, but it is rising. ICE, like NYMEX's Clearport, represents the preferred trading medium of hedge funds; that is, no trading floors. The ICE Exchange also offers the options of pure electronic futures trading for its exchange-traded futures contracts, as it eliminated floor trading during 2005. The ease of access and exit is clearly the preferred method of trading for the black box centric hedge funds.

Credit and counterparty risk are taken care of by the London Clearinghouse, which also clears for the IPE. OTC clearing on the Intercontinental Exchange provides traders and risk managers the best of both worlds; the safety and security offered by a central clearinghouse, along with the flexibility and accessibility of the fully electronic ICE platform.

With the addition of OTC clearing, traders see more "white" prices on the ICE screen, and risk managers have the opportunity to shift new and existing positions from bilateral to cleared trades through the use of the Block Trading facility. OTC clearing is an optional service on the

Intercontinental Exchange and is available to all ICE participants. OTC clearing is an evolutionary addition to the intercontinental model of bilateral trading. In a sense, OTC clearing trading occupies the niche between bilateral and futures trading. OTC clearing specifications correspond to bilateral products, and OTC clearing transactions occur on the same screen as bilateral trades. However, counterparties are not matched directly to each other, just as in futures clearing.

Participants benefit from the fact that OTC clearing trades are centrally cleared by the London Clearing House Limited (LCH), freeing the use of bilateral credit lines and allowing trade with a larger number of market participants. Additionally, efficiencies are gained as cross margining is allowed between intercontinental OTC clearing products and other futures. Finally, market liquidity is increased as more participants have greater access to more prices.

In a perfect world, there would be one seamless energy trading platform where new exchange-traded futures could clear on the existing floor or electronic trading platform of an exchange. What we have are two competing exchanges. We think that energy trading on the NYMEX floor will eventually change to a hybrid model of open outcry floor trading and electronic trading that will not cannibalize trading liquidity but grow the market. The future is totally electronic trading, particularly in the growing energy markets of Asia. As NYMEX moves toward IPO and is partially owned by a hedge fund, this seems inevitable. ICE has already completed a successful IPO on the New York Stock Exchange on November 16, 2005, and is now valued at over $2 billion. NYMEX will follow with an IPO sometime during 2006. It is now partially owned (10%) by the hedge fund, General Atlantic.

WHAT DOES THE EVIDENCE SHOW?

The structure of energy trading is now changing. The energy markets are seeing higher sustained daily price swings, as well as increased trading volumes in the outer month contracts for the more liquid crude oil market and North American gas markets. This increased intra-day price volatility while more frequent $1 price moves have presented fewer trading opportunities for more traditional oil and gas traders from the energy industry as the hedge funds move money in and out on a daily basis.

One fund that is known for doing significantly sized deals is Houston-based Centaurus, which is led by former Enron trader Jon Arnold. He was known to be doing gas storage swaps and trading large volumes on the OTC markets. Other funds known to be moving the markets are

New York-based D.E. Shaw, Chicago-based Ritchie Capital, Motherrock, and Citadel to name a few.

It seems that the fundamental attribute of the "new" energy traders is access to capital of up to $1 billion, stellar credit, and market models (many following the Goldman Sachs Commodity Index). The lack of energy trading expertise or knowledge of the physical oil, gas, or power markets does not bode well for long-term success, and we could see significant pullbacks. Many energy-trading debacles have been experienced by energy-trading companies in the past 15 years. This includes the squeezing of North Sea Brent in 1989; jet fuel hedging in Singapore in 1990 and in 2004 with China Aviation; the stacking and rolling strategy of MG in 1993; the power contract default of the City of Springfield in 1998; and the California energy crises with sleeving and phantom trading, which later led to more government intervention and oversight of the markets. Energy risk is pervasive, but hedge funds have the capability to take on much of that risk.

We also think that as hedge funds get more established in the energy complex, as they have during 2005 and will continue to do so in 2006, they will start to use more leverage. Many hedge funds in more traditional, established markets are leveraged three to four times. We have even heard of 20 times leverage used. In energy so far we have seen little. In the greater hedge fund universe, 30% of hedge funds use no leverage. While theoretically the use of leverage would not increase risk, that may not be true in the more volatile energy markets. The highly quantitative shops maybe more inclined to lever their portfolio. If they are also trend-following funds, which seems likely, then we can expect greater energy hedge fund trading disasters in commodity trading just like we have seen over the past 15 years in energy trading. The following on short and mid-term trends could lead to more problems on participation on large market moves in energy. Some funds shy away from a fundamental approach to energy trading, but a combination of both technical analysis and fundamental factors is usually how successful energy traders have functioned over the past 20 years. Commodity-based investment products and indices may be a better way for more passive investor participation in energy. (In Chapter 10 we will cover this area of hedge fund investment.) In this way, investors get exposure to price movement in energy futures contracts. There is now an increasing need for implementing energy alternative-based futures and options trading as an integrated part of traditional hedge fund portfolios. Energy futures and options products are just beginning to be considered as an addition to existing individual and institutional investor portfolios.

NOTES

1 "The Commitment of Traders Report," CFTC, www.cftc.gov.
2 "A Review of Recent Hedge Fund Participation in NYMEX Natural Gas and Crude Oil Futures Markets," NYMEX, March 1, 2005.

CHAPTER 7

Green Hedge Funds: Trading the Environment

WHY NOW?

Energy hedge funds have been mostly a North American phenomena until this year with the vast majority located in the New York metropolitan area. However, our continuing research into the secretive world of energy hedge funds is revealing evidence of a next wave of interest in Europe and Asia, as well as an extension of the commodity trading platform into green markets. Specifically, this involves carbon trading, renewable energy credit trading, ethanol trading, and emissions trading. The approach, like in all emerging markets with little price discovery, is to find arbitrage opportunities and a mismatch in pricing. This can be as simple as going long carbon in the hope that its value rises over time somewhere in the world, and as sophisticated as playing the "regulatory arbitrage" of shorting renewable energy credits in one state and buying long in another (20 US states have a renewal portfolio standards, or RPS). In the green hedge fund market, taking on the regulatory risk takes some degree of both government policy and market knowledge to be successful. Other green venues include biofuel trading such as ethanol or biodiesel, as well as other plays in biomass for power generation.

The market drivers for green hedge funds are many. Both global warming and environmental change are pushing investors to consider this sector for investment as air and water pollution rises as a corporate financial issue. Rising and sustained energy prices are making formerly risky investments more palatable as their return on investment (ROIs) increase. Concerns over homeland and national security considerations are also pushing capital into the alternative energy/clean technology sector. Finally, many countries are increasingly concerned about their dependence upon foreign energy sources, such as rising oil and gas imports, creating detrimental political and economic conditions. Another factor is that increased digitization/power quality and reliability issues due to both under-investment in transmission and distribution grids, as well as rapid economic development in emerging markets, is creating more investment and trading opportunities. Overriding many of these concerns is that fact that there is now an increased political awareness of environmental issues and a trend toward tighter environmental regulations. This is driving both energy efficiency and environmental benefits in new technologies.

The more traditional hedge fund approach has been in equities, and there is a play in green equities for alternative energy. Some of these funds include New Energy Fund LP, and Kurzman Clean Tech LP (which ironically are all in New York). They are pure alternative energy plays with investments in public companies in both the United States and Europe. The current high and sustained fossil fuels should start driving a move to alternative energy generation globally, and in the past year there has been much attention on the US venture capital sector on funding investment in alternative energy. Alternative energy includes not only wind and solar, but also biomass; ethanol; and distributed generation plays such as fuel cells, battery storage, and microturbines. One other emerging technology play is the rising interest in photovoltaic nanotechnology, which may make radical improvements in electricity generation from the traditional 8 to 10% efficiency to 15% and much higher, using solar technology. Other hedge funds that trade only long/short equities are dabbling in the alternative energy sector. As far as we know, the funds mentioned are the only pure alternative energy hedge funds.

There are others that have, or are considering, a portion of their energy portfolio in alternative energy. Some of these hedge funds are invested in electricity, gas, and water utilities, and are comfortable with green equity investments in alternative energy. Other energy hedge funds intend to be involved in renewable energy project finance on a very selected basis, as well where they may fly solo or club deals. Here the thinking is a bit more risky as they are also interested in monetizing credit streams for both emissions reductions and renewable energy. In fact, as the business model changes in the venture capital world for clean technology, we are seeing a blurring of the lines so that hedge funds are becoming investors in many of the new clean technology companies as both arbitrage plays but also for longer term returns. In effect, they are accepting longer lockdown periods of two to four years, and are starting to look like venture firms as they provide both seed capital and second stage investment to new technology firms and projects.

The reason for the new flurry of activity has been the low returns in traditional hedge fund investments. Thus, hedge fund investors demanded more and first invested into the energy arena. They have now entered the environmental energy play. Private investors such as high net worth individuals and family office as opposed to institutional investors are starting to invest in emerging environmental financial markets. While some energy hedge funds were up 40 to 50% during 2004 and 2005, and one is rumored to have been up 100%, environmental or green hedge funds have even shorter track records and there are fewer of them in which to invest at present. Other more conservative energy hedge funds are looking for 15% plus returns on a sustained basis. It's the more entrepreneurial funds seeking higher returns that are interested in the environmental or green trading arena. They also need to accept more risk and probably longer "up" periods, maybe as long as two to four years in some cases.

ENVIRONMENT BECOMING A BOARD ISSUE

Over the last several years, environmental issues and pressures have been growing and most corporations have created environment, health and safety departments, and managers to deal with them. Today, however, environmental risk management is increasingly – and rightly – being overseen by a company executive such as the CFO. There are several reasons for this elevation.

- The increasing importance of socially responsible investment groups that include mutual funds, hedge funds, and institutional investors, who screen their investment portfolios for several social and environmental criteria. According to the Social Investment Forum of Washington, DC, this now represents $2.2 trillion worth of assets.
- There is pressure from a variety of investor and other groups to change regulations and requirements around corporate environmental disclosure that are slowly gaining momentum with the SEC and other regulatory authorities.
- For North American corporations, the impact of Kyoto and subsidiary regulations and initiatives in many parts of Europe and elsewhere creates an additional issue: that of operating under different regulatory environments across the globe. It is easier and more effective for the corporation to apply a single standard across its global operations than to employ confusing standards applicable to each regulatory regime.
- There are existing regulations that now carry mandatory jail terms for C-level executives who misreport.

- There are additional auditing and insurance issues pertaining to environmental, health and safety processes, and reporting and environmental liabilities disclosure.

However, the most compelling reason for increased awareness and oversight of environmental risk is that this is an area of sustained historical under-investment that may now be used to both differentiate and compete more effectively in today's markets. Managing environmental risks as a component in an overall corporate risk structure makes not only financial sense, but it also allows optimization of management decision-making. While corporations that proactively manage environmental risk may perform well in the eyes of shareholders, they can also hone an additional competitive edge to increase profits. As an example, consider the evolving emissions trading environments in Europe and North America. Effective emissions monitoring allows proactive and better decisions to be made to maximize revenue generated from emission credits or to minimize exposure to the need to purchase credits. And this is just one example. There are many others. As a result, environmental risk management, like other aspects of corporate risk management, is finding a home with the CFO.

WHY GREEN TRADING MARKETS ARE RIPE FOR INVESTMENT NOW

The issues of environmental financial liabilities and the emergence of climate change risk have made companies extremely nervous on proceeding forward in market development with such near-term uncertainty. It has also highlighted the second as a new emerging financial market open for investment in equities and trading in commodities.

Green trading captures the triple convergence of capital markets and the environment into a mainstream corporate financial issue, which captures both the problem and the solution as a financial trading means to ameliorate pollution. Building on the successful 11-year program in sulfur dioxide (SO_2) emissions trading in the United States, green trading has become the bridge to reduce greenhouse gas (GHG) pollution, increase renewable energy credit trading, and to increase the use of energy efficiency or megawatt trading through the use of financial markets. The long-term impact would be to reduce pollution in a cost-effective manner and to accelerate the introduction of more environmentally benign technologies. This would cause minimal economic disruption to the capital-intensive energy industry, as well as other industrial sources of pollution. It would create new financial markets where "trading pollution" would actually create concrete and measurable emissions reductions for business. GHG trading has had an upsurge of interest and trading activity due to the EU Emissions Trading Scheme (EU ETS) on January 1, 2005, and the implementation of the Kyoto Protocol on February 16, 2005. Hedge funds are fueling some of that upsurge in trading.

While much of the financial press assumes that this all started in Europe in 2005, they are wrong. It must not be forgotten that the United States created emissions trading markets in 1995 for sulfur dioxide (SO_2) and in 1999 for nitrous oxide (NOx). It was also the US delegation that introduced emissions trading into the international climate change process. Today the United States, not Europe, has the most mature and advanced environmental financial markets in the world, and is actually way ahead on SO_2 and NOx reductions, and most probably mercury reductions soon. While it lags behind Europe in its trading greenhouse gas emissions, the United States does trade that commodity on the Chicago Climate Exchange (CCX) and on the bilateral OTC markets.

HOW THESE MARKETS WORK

Cap and trade systems have been proven to work effectively in reducing pollutants. But what is now needed are structurally sound emissions and renewable programs put in place in order to create global trading markets. These efforts are just starting now. Emissions trading markets are not true commodity markets, as they are "cap and trade," which means that emissions are ratcheted down over time. For the SO_2 markets, it is a 35-year regime of reductions and more stringent standards. For CO_2 and other greenhouse gas reductions, we will eventually recognize the need for a 50- to 100-year program that engages the entire world if it is going to be effective. It is finally being acknowledged that the short-term Kyoto Protocol compliance period of 2008 to 2012 is just a first step to global market development.

The Kyoto treaty was a watered-down politically expedient solution for the European Union, but what is needed is a much broader initiative to include the developing world with longer term targets that will last for decades. What was crafted was a "feel good" ineffective treaty that misses the obvious bigger picture – that greenhouse gas emissions continue to rise, particularly in the developing world where they are actually accelerating. The reality is, since CO_2 emissions disperse in the atmosphere on a global scale, the entire world is in this together for the long haul. There is no quick technological fix as long as the world is addicted to fossil fuels. That habit is not going to change quickly as it typically takes years to implement the alternatives required to put meaningful dents into CO_2 emissions.

Such emission reductions are now expanding throughout the world as one solution to reducing global carbon intensity. This needs to be expanded to reduce both stationary and mobile emission sources, which will begin in California in 2009. Then, we will see an acceleration of technology transfer, coupled with increased energy efficiency. The irony is that the technology exists today to get the job done. This is not the press hype of the non-existent hydrogen economy, but today's technologies such the highly efficient integrated gas combined cycle (IGCC) clean coal technology, and affordable hybrid vehicles that reduce tailpipe emissions and improve fuel economy now. We also have many energy efficiency devices that reduce building loads from both commercial and residential buildings. All these carbon reductions can be aggregated for future trading, and hedge funds are looking over these opportunities. We also have the controversial nuclear power option, which does not produce any carbon emissions. Once again, hedge funds are looking at all opportunities in nuclear power.

Environmental solutions exist but for many of them to become commercially viable in the near term we need a more concerted effort by the US government to set the rules that can bring a financial value to emissions reductions. The point is that both the SO_2 and NOx programs are mandated and have financial penalties for non-compliance. These real financial consequences have allowed technologies such as scrubbers and low-NOx burners to take hold. Voluntary CO_2 programs may be useful in practicing for future global trading of such credits, but hard limits will be needed to create a real market driver for change. Emissions trading is one mechanism to accomplish much of these goals. The ability to monitor and certify verifiable reductions is already in place through both third-party certification companies, and geopositioning satellites and remote sensing devices. Financial markets work. For the past few years, corporate America has been trying to figure out the business case for GHG reductions. The business case is fairly simple, either pay less now or pay more later. So we have companies beginning to analyze their risk and realize that there is a global issue here and that they have got to do something about it. One of the drivers behind the GHG market is that we now have institutional shareholders forcing corporations to acknowledge the environmental risk on their books. This has been done by pension funds mostly and is similar to the strategy that was taken in tobacco litigation.

Ironically, multinational corporations are beginning to see companies start to analyze their climate risks by inventorying them. They have realized that they have compliance issues at many locations throughout the world. Hedge funds are positioning themselves for this participation by US companies and some are aggregating carbon credits – buying them low to sell them at higher prices later.

HEDGE FUND TRADING

Hedge funds in the European Union have already stepped up to trade CO_2 emissions during 2005, and some funds in the United States are trading SO_2, NOx, and CO_2. Today, over a dozen European commodity-trading hedge funds trade carbon dioxides as part of their portfolio, and this is rising. The situation is different in the United States, with over 20 hedge funds trading SO_2 and NOx emissions in 35 regional markets. There are several trading renewable energy credits in 20 states. And a smaller number trade carbon dioxide, but that number is rising particularly with market maturation underway in Europe. Green hedge funds are also looking for global arbitrage opportunities in trading emissions or in aggregating carbon credits in China, India, Indonesia, or Brazil. These countries are hotbeds of greenhouse gas activities. They are also looking for cross-border opportunities in renewable energy trading, as these markets begin to form throughout the world. Today, renewable energy is traded in the United States, Canada, the United Kingdom, the Netherlands, Germany, Australia, and New Zealand, to name a few of the cross-border opportunities.

Energy projects and trades have begun. Much institutional money has flowed into project-based reductions. It is true that as for trades, there have been only a handful, but this will now accelerate. In the United States, we are getting a lift from the marriage of CO_2 injection for enhanced oil recovery and carbon sequestration. Ironically, a lot of this activity is centered in oil and gas production in Texas.

The CCX launched a GHG program in September 2003. We are now seeing over 140 companies sign up on a voluntary basis for the CCX, as well as many companies outside the CCX starting to look seriously at self-imposed caps. These markets are trading around $2 per ton. It's a start, and a noble effort, but its trading volumes are much lower than in the European Union, where there are six exchanges trading carbon dioxide emissions.

The overwhelmingly large program that is the EU ETS began on January 1, 2005. It covered over 12,000 facilities in the EU system. Companies are going to know whether they're buyers, sellers, or neutral. Multiple industries are covered in this program. We have seen increased trading activity by many investment banks in London during the past year. The

European Union traded 50 million tons of CO_2 from January 1 through June 30, 2005; however, it should be pointed out that the global carbon level is 24 billion tons and rising.

We are witnessing a market transformation. We are starting to see the risk manager in some major corporations handling the GHG issue, along with carbon finance playing a bigger role. We are now positioned for the beginning of a liquid spot market instead of one-off trades. To date, 2005 has become the breakthrough year with spot trading, high volumes, price indices, and advanced brokerage, similar to the power and gas markets. Also, we will see a growth in carbon finance.

The European program is a company-to-company cap and trade program, and the tradable unit is EU allowances. This is really the best hope for proving that we can have a successful GHG market globally. If the European Union succeeds, there will be a much smoother transition for GHG.

We are seeing REC trading moving from promise to reality – 20 states in the United States now have programs. Also, many other countries such as the United Kingdom, the Netherlands, Germany, Australia, and New Zealand have followed suit. Today, renewable energy is so popular for wind, solar, and geothermal that there is a temporary shortage of equipment. Turning back to the United States, as more states adopt renewable energy credit programs and renewable portfolio standards, many more trades will occur. There is also demand from commercial and industrial customers seeking green energy, with many active green power marketers meeting that market need. Today, the United States has over 600 green power programs, where consumers pay more for green energy. There are also state purchase mandates that include renewable energy procurement with some federal agencies also participating.

The evolving regulatory landscape is still an open issue. On the horizon, we expect more states to consider and enact RPSs and GHG reduction systems. We saw in the US SO_2 program something that we might see in GHG and something that we might see in renewables. That is, so many states started to put together their own regulations that companies operating in a multi-state environment finally said to the federal government that they wanted some consistency in the regulation. That's how the Clean Air Act amendments went forward and started the first successful emissions trading program in 1990 in SO_2. That action will happen in GHG. There are more than 28 states that already have GHG laws and proposals under consideration.

The GHG markets are beginning to start on a forward basis. It will take several years to come to fruition – from investment decisions, to operation of these projects, and implementation of their reduction plans. Companies have to act early. Here are two examples of timelines in terms of the creation of markets. The first example is the SO_2 market for acid rain reduction. In 1992, the first SO_2 transaction occurred and 1995 was the first year of compliance for it. The second example is the NOx market for the ozone transport region. June of 1998 was the first NOx trade and 1999 was the first year for NOx compliance.

The GHG markets are expected to take off in 2006 and follow a similar rate of acceleration as SO_2 and NOx experienced. This is because there is more at stake and because the European market can draw on the US experience. But they can also draw on the experience and the talented pool of people that are available in the financial community and the energy trading community. Moreover, US multinational companies active in Europe are now in the vice of dual environmental standards – one for Europe and one for the United States. This is an untenable position for corporate America.

Green trading markets are now entering the hockey stick phase of market development. In 2005 we have seen the financial market acceleration that has been expected for many years. The United States is still well positioned to lead on environmental financial market development with its entrepreneurial culture, risk capital, and knowledge base in trading.

WHY ARE THE HEDGE FUNDS HERE?

The more developed environmental financial markets for sulfur dioxide (SO_2) and nitrous oxide (NOx) trading have also attracted some hedge fund interest, as well as Wall Street interest in the recent past. It is not well known, but commodity powerhouse Morgan Stanley is now the largest emissions trader in the SO_2 markets since this is the most developed and the largest in the world. Wall Street firms have told us that they will wait for more liquidity in carbon markets before jumping in, but their purchase of generation assets has already given them both a "carbon footprint," as well as an "emissions footprint." Highly successful Houston-based energy hedge fund Centaurus has been known to trade both SO_2 and NOx markets, and are making good profits. NOx emissions traded as high as $40,000 per ton in the Houston/Galveston NOx markets during the summer of 2004, and recent forward prices have approached that again. NOx trading is used to reduce urban ozone emissions.

The more mature SO_2 markets for acid rain reduction got a boost of adrenaline in North America last year when coal burning went up due to the high cost and under-supply of the more environmentally friendly natural gas. With recent trades staying at the $1,000 per ton level for SO_2

allowances, the market has now indicated that gasification technologies for coal called IGCC may now be economic. With a carbon reduction regime a certainty in the United States, despite the present stance of the Bush administration, IGCC projects have proliferated in the past several months so that there are about 20 such projects in the pipeline. In the spring of 2004 there were none.

Hedge funds are known to trade the California RECLAIM market for SO_2 and NOx reductions. They are highly successful due to confusion over the rules and a proposed tightening of air quality standards in Southern California. In fact, there are said to be 35 regional emissions markets in the United States and the hedge funds trade most of them as the operable word is arbitrage.

Despite the lack of the Kyoto stamp on US carbon markets, there are developing carbon markets in the United States, as well as Europe. Trades of over one million tons have taken place with Gulf Coast utility Entergy in December 2004. More CO_2 trades are in the pipeline with a link to carbon sequestration and enhanced oil production that uses "commodity" CO_2 for oil field projection through CO_2 injection. There is also increased activity and higher prices on the CCX due to market changes in Europe.

The beginning of a global carbon market is now emerging, with all the attendant risks of emerging markets; that is, little price discovery, low liquidity, and wide arbitrage opportunities. It's the trading arbitrage mindset of the funds that is driving this change. This is a pure trading mentality, not an altruistic value of saving the world. That's what traders do – seek arbitrage opportunities and exploit. They have found them in the global carbon markets.

WHAT'S AHEAD?

Investors in green trading markets want diversification for their fund portfolios. They like the opaque prices and high returns that the green markets presently provide. The downside risk is that the knowledge base of fund traders is limited in these emerging commodity markets, since it requires both an industrial knowledge of trading, but also a regulatory policy knowledge of government. These are not true commodity markets, but hybrid markets where government sets the standard and industry reduces their emissions over time. In the US SO_2 market, the federal government has set up a 35-year regime for SO_2 emissions reductions through to the year 2030. And contrary to popular opinion in Europe, in which the United States is doing nothing because of its opposition to the Kyoto Protocol, in actuality the United States is moving to more stringent standards on SO_2 and NOx (it already has the most stringent in the world). Also, it will be controlling mercury using market-based trading solutions. Furthermore, every manager of a US power plant, industrial facility, or other stationary source of pollution knows that a carbon regime is forming. In fact, 28 states in the United States have some sort of GHG initiative underway. The funds, being pure traders, will also exploit the carbon rules between states as they are doing in renewable energy markets.

More recently, two more "green hedge fund" plays are underway. One is to trade sugar as a surrogate for ethanol trading, as these markets are more developed. This will bring in soft commodity giants such as Cargill and Louis Dreyfus. The other new interest that is following carbon market development, which is still nascent, is water hedge funds. Here they trade long-dated water rights in the western United States to start, as water is now becoming a commodity, 10 years after Enron's ill-fated foray into water trading through Azurix – but that was not a pure commodity play incidentally.

The interesting thing is that the interest in green hedge funds is great from all quarters, including Asia. Investors want returns and are now focusing beyond the energy complex in year 2 of the energy and environmental hedge fund play. All we can say is "buyer beware," since emerging markets have attendant risks.

We are witnessing a major market transformation throughout the world. Generally, the market drivers for RECs are the same as for renewable energy or green power. These drivers include utility green pricing programs, competitive green power marketing, state renewable portfolio standards and purchase mandates, and electricity information disclosure. In some instances, REC trading is given added impetus by a requirement that RECs be used for compliance with certain programs. Further, particularly in carbon markets, RECs may be used to claim greenhouse gas reductions.

Since carbon dioxide is about 80% of greenhouse gas emissions, most of the focus on market development has been focused on carbon trading, with the goal to reduce CO_2 emissions. Carbon markets today are only about a $5 billion market, but estimates are that this will be over $100 billion or higher by 2010. That makes for real money and real financial trading. The United States actually stepped in first with the launch of the CCX in September 2003.

Today, many states are presently following innovative and diverse approaches to greenhouse gas reductions; however, it seems likely that collaborative state GHG registries are in the offing and have been proposed. The issues for companies are that multi-jurisdictional registries create multiple reporting requirements, multiple registries, and multiple trading regimes. This situation is a disincentive for business to take early action. The need for harmonious standards will be more cost effective for many companies and encourage voluntary reporting. It will accelerate the fungibility of CO_2, as a commodity that will trade globally just like the oil markets.

Registries help companies deal with state, regional, national, and international GHG trading schemes. Industries need standardization for measurement methodologies to facilitate trading as well as transparency. The integrity function of registries allows GHG credits to become commodities with certifiable rules, measurement auditing, and reporting requirements. They are the precursor for commodity markets, but not markets in themselves. Markets will address performance, delivery, and price risks and hedging needs as they mature.

Hedge funds are looking over the globe for market opportunities in carbon trading, renewable energy trading, and also SO_2 and NOx trading. China has begun SO_2 trading to reduce its acid rain footprint by allowing its utilities to trade credits. The shift in technology to alternative energy is also providing the impetus in both equity investment and trading. Hedge funds are becoming providers of venture capital for new alternative energy technology, as well as environmental remediation technologies as their role shifts to that of pools of capital for new technology investment and trading. Some funds are both investing in new clean energy projects and trading the stream of carbon and renewable credits.

As the business model shifts, there is also another factor to consider – that the environment becomes the next disruptive factor in energy markets. While the primary focus is on emissions and renewable energy trading, what is really happening is a global movement to environmental protection as we are running out of environmental capacity. Thus, environment is primed to be the next disruptive factor in energy markets as the energy value chain is now overlaid with an environmental value chain. Hedge funds will be positioned to benefit from these new risk factors and should profit handsomely by being the first movers into these new markets where risk is endemic and reward very visible.

CHAPTER 8

Weather Hedge Funds

WHY WEATHER DERIVATIVES NOW?

Weather derivatives trading markets are now accelerating with trading volumes going through the roof in 2005 and more hedge funds venturing into that space. It is hard to ascertain why it is occurring this year, but it is. Weather trading actually started in August 1997 with Enron and Koch, was set back by the demise of energy merchants in the United States in 2001 through 2003, gravitated to Europe and Japan, and is now exploding on the Chicago Mercantile Exchange (CME). It now seems that 2005 was a breakthrough year for both weather trading and the entrance of weather risk management participation by hedge funds. In this chapter we provide a background to these innovative products and some perspective and scope on the future of weather derivatives.

The CME futures contracts have exploded in both open interest and trading volumes during 2005. In 1999 the CME created a weather derivative market to enable businesses to transfer risk that could be adversely affected by unanticipated temperature swings. CME heating degree day (HDD) and cooling degree day (CDD) futures and options on futures are the first exchange-traded, temperature-related weather derivatives. These contracts were designed to help businesses protect their revenues during times of depressed demand or excessive costs because of unexpected or unfavorable weather conditions. The CME contracts trade on both the exchange floor and use the GLOBEX electronic platform.

The CME is the largest US futures exchange, and during the summer of 2005, the exchange expanded its weather futures' offerings with seven more futures and options contracts, three in the United States (Baltimore, Detroit, and Salt Lake City) and four in Europe (Barcelona, Essen, Madrid, and Rome). Today the CME offers a total of 22 cities, which are listed on the exchange, for trading (15 in the United States, five in Europe and two in Japan). For the newest CME contracts, the US listings will include HDD and CDD on both monthly and seasonal futures, and options and the new European listings will include HDD and cumulative average temperature (CAT) on both monthly and seasonal futures and options. Product specifications are identical to the existing US and European cities. Cities in the United States will be priced in US dollars and cities in Europe will be priced in British pounds. (More information on the weather contracts and weather risk management is available on www.cme.com, or the excellent Weather Risk Management Association (WRMA) website: www.wrma.org.)

Weather is obviously one of the largest variables impacting on economic activity and corporate performance, and it now seems that the CME has established itself as the "Weather Exchange" after initial hiccups and setbacks. Weather is also the largest unknown variable for energy and agricultural commodity markets to manage, as evidenced not only by hurricanes but heating and cooling needs. The CME contracts and the more established bilateral markets are getting much momentum (CME trading interest surpassed all of 2004 in April 2005). Funds known to be trading weather are Ritchie Capital, Citadel, Parthelion, and Hudson Seven in the United States, and Coriolis and Cumulus Weather Fund in London. There are probably many others already in the market or considering entering the markets. Since weather is a global market, there are many paired trades that can be made based on heating and cooling degree days. There is also a great investor risk appetite to trade weather as it is "sexy to hedge the weather." We know of Japanese money behind some of these funds, and the slow-moving Japanese financial markets are now breaking out from the one-off weather swaps between Tokyo Gas and Tokyo Electric Power of several years ago.

We expect more hedge funds to extend their offerings in weather risk management as they expand their activity into the energy markets. We expect more esoteric weather swaps such as snow and precipitation plays to move beyond only heating and cooling degree days, and more activity in precipitation risk management (read rain and snow). We also expect an additional uptick in investment interest and trading activity from climate change risk management in carbon markets that is just starting to take root. The timing is now for weather derivatives to finally take hold, despite some earlier fits and starts. Expect more hedge fund trading in these markets as more data are standardized globally, enabling more weather trades.

Weather drives much of the price action in the energy markets from the demand side and in the agricultural markets from the supply side. All three markets (weather, energy, and agriculture) are growing rapidly and are complementary, due to their weather component. The weather risk management market almost doubled in the last financial year, according to the latest survey by the WRMA. The notional value of weather risk management contracts transacted between April 2004 and March 2005 reached $8.4 billion, up from $4.6 billion in 2003–04 – an 83% rise.

Strong growth looks set to continue, with volumes of the weather contracts on the CME – which accounted for a large percentage of the market growth – up by a factor of six this year compared to last. The growing impact of weather on the energy and agriculture sectors are contributing to the growth of weather derivatives.

The WRMA survey, which was conducted by consultants Pricewater-houseCoopers, and which involved 17 leading weather derivatives dealers reporting details of their trades, looks at both privately negotiated OTC transactions, and those on the CME. While the OTC market saw more modest growth than the market overall, up by around one-quarter, volumes on the CME have exploded. The growth in CME volume can be explained by the entrance of more hedge funds trading weather and due to the transparency and liquidity needs of more traditional market participants according to WRMA.

The CME weather contracts alone could hit $25 billion during 2005 according to the WRMA. At the onset of the 2004–2005 winter season in November 2005 – when weather trading has traditionally been heaviest – the year's volumes already stood at 720,000 contracts traded, compared to 122,000 in 2004. Interestingly, there was a temporary contraction of approximately 25% in the size of the European market. This was due, at least in part, to the preoccupation of many in Europe's energy sector with the EU carbon dioxide ETS, which began operating in January. Ironically, many market observers think that climate risk factors will bring much more trading to the weather derivatives market as the obvious link of emissions trading and weather establishes itself more evidently in coming years. Thus, interest in weather risk management should be rebounding in Europe in 2006 and beyond.

WHAT IS WEATHER DERIVATIVES TRADING?

Weather derivatives are the first financial tool available to risk managers to stabilize earnings volatility caused by the unpredictability of the weather. These financially settled products are structured as temperature swaps and options, and are used to hedge volume-related risks caused by extreme weather conditions. While traditional weather damage insurance has been available to businesses for years, protection in the form of a derivative designed specifically for non-catastrophic weather conditions has only recently become available. When used together with traditional price hedges, properly structured weather derivatives can reduce cash flow volatility, lower financing costs, and stabilize revenues.

The market started during the summer of 1997 when two US power companies, realizing that they had opposite weather exposure, entered into the first weather derivative swap contract for the winter season. Since then, the market in the United States has grown rapidly. It collapsed and has been rebuilt with active hedge fund trading. Markets have also developed in Europe, East Asia, and Australia.

A weather derivative's most distinctive property is its ability to address volume risk, as opposed to other traditional risk management tools that address price risk. For example, an electric utility can utilize a weather derivative that generates payments when extreme summer weather requires the ramping up of high-cost generators. Conversely, this same electric utility can benefit from a different weather derivative that generates payments when mild summer conditions result in a decreased load. Revenues are a function of price and volume. Price and volume affect revenue and profitability. A hedge program that combines weather and traditional price hedges enables risk managers to address both components that affect the bottom line. This will result in more efficient cash flow management leading to an overall improved corporate financial position.

Companies in a variety of industries have previously either absorbed or sought to manage risks with potentially less than efficient tools. The ability to hedge price risk for many financial and commodity products is well developed and widely used; however, for many buyers and sellers of these products, unit volume variance can be as detrimental to the bottom line as unit price variation. Managing energy risk introduces a class of risk management tools that potentially hedges volume-related risks caused specifically by variations in average temperatures over defined future time periods. When combined with price risk management tools, these volume-related hedges increase the potential to provide superior risk management capabilities.

The basic trade inherent in weather-related risk management products is indexed to the HDD, a widely used measure for the relative "coolness" of the weather in a given region during a specified period of time. HDDs are calculated using temperature data provided by the US National Weather Service (NWS). For any given day they are calculated as the greater of (1) zero or (2) 65 degrees Fahrenheit less the midnight-to-midnight average of the high and low temperatures for the day.

The weather risk management product class includes caps. Floors, collar, and swaps with pay-outs are defined as a specified dollar sum multiplied by differences between the HDD level specified in the contract (that is, the "Strike") and the actual HDD level that occurred during the contract period.

In a wide variety of industries, from property management to natural gas retailing, weather creates volatility in expenses and revenues. For example, in order to meet customer demand, a heating oil wholesaler must purchase adequate inventory to cover an expected heating season. If the season is warmer than normal, sales volume will decrease, leaving the wholesaler with excess inventory and associated storage expenses. Conversely, if the winter is colder than normal, the wholesaler will not have enough inventory to cover demand and will be forced to pay relatively expensive spot prices.

Weather is ever-changing and unpredictable. How can anyone protect themselves against something as random as it? The answer is simpler than you may think. It is not necessary to accurately predict the weather to protect your business from weather risk. The key is to find counterparties who are better able to absorb weather-related risks such as insurance and reinsurance companies and hedge funds.

SPECIFICS OF WEATHER OPTIONS

A key feature of the weather derivative market is that there is no underlying instrument as, obviously, there is no physical market in the weather. (You can't buy rain in New York for January, although you can count on its occurrence.) Derivative products are used to hedge exposures built up in underlying physical markets. As there is no such underlying in this market, weather derivatives are used to hedge against the risks that are affected by the weather; for example, the risk that energy demand decreases.

With the absence of an underlying instrument traded, the market's best estimate of the weather will be its swap level, or futures price if such a contract exists on an exchange such as the CME. The swap and futures level will change as the market's estimate of the weather changes, taking into account the information contained within short- and long-term meteorological forecasts.

Unlike many commonly traded derivative instruments, weather options will settle on an accumulated index, such as HDDs and CDDs. By definition then, these options will always be European in style and not be exercised until the end of the contract period.

Weather derivatives, like insurance policies, almost always have a maximum pay-out – not only because most participants, particularly from the insurance–reinsurance industry, require knowledge of their maximum risk exposure, but also as the weather is finite. We know that temperatures cannot exceed 65 degrees Fahrenheit for an entire month in New York, so we know that there will be a natural boundary to the value of which a cumulative temperature index will reach.

The two principal benefits of a weather derivative over traditional insurance are:

- There is no need to prove a financial loss to receive a payment from a weather derivative. An insurance policy will not only require a specific weather event to occur, but also to demonstrate that a financial loss was incurred as a result of this weather event before the insurance company pays out. A weather derivative will pay out simply if the weather event occurs. For example, a Florida citrus farmer who makes a claim against an insurance policy because frost has damaged his crop will have to wait until the end of the growing season to demonstrate that his crop is ruined before he is compensated. If he instead chooses protection with a weather derivative and there is a frost, not only will he be compensated by the derivative, he can save a portion of his crop by harvesting early before it is entirely ruined and sell it for concentrate.
- Derivative contracts are generally more efficiently priced than insurance policies, with weather derivatives often trading at, or near, their fair value (that is, where net expected returns to the counterparts is zero).

Finally, insurance products are better suited to protecting against extreme one-off weather events, catastrophes such as hurricanes, whereas weather derivatives are most often used to protect against milder movements in weather conditions over a season.

COMPONENTS OF A SUCCESSFUL WEATHER MARKET

As in all markets, there are several conditions that need to be met in order to promote market liquidity. Although the weather market is illiquid when compared to, for example, interest rate derivatives, it does satisfy many of these conditions with the rest to follow in the near future. And as we stated before, liquidity is growing as evidenced by the CME futures contracts trading volumes and open interest. Some of those components are a large number of market participants, reliable data in which to produced indices, and an attraction to both hedgers and risk-takers (different views on the market).

With the large number of market participants, the potential for this market was first realized by the energy sector. It is not surprising to find that the most active participants in weather derivative trading are power marketers/utilities, hedge funds, and banks engaged in this sector. Many end-user deals have also been within the energy industry and should continue to remain so. There are also new market participants, such as ski resorts protecting against a lack of snowfall and supermarkets protecting against a fall in shoppers caused by bad weather.

There has also been rapid growth in financial institutions participating, most noticeably within the reinsurance industry. Reinsurance companies are in the business of taking on risk. They are able to do this by building a very large portfolio of diversified risks and since weather patterns are unlikely to be correlated with the traditional risks that they have on their books, taking on positions in weather derivatives is a natural for their business. They are able to take very large exposures and will lend capacity to the market that the current energy participants cannot. There are a fairly wide variety of players in the market now and it is diversifying rapidly, and more deals will be transacted in the non-energy sectors. These are positive signs for future liquidity as well as the active engagement of hedge funds.

Reliable data for indices has been an important issue hindering market development in some areas of the world. Reliable data is not only important for establishing indices that participants will trust and actively trade, especially in the weather market where historical data are essential for the pricing of structures, it is essential for market development. In the United States, highly reliable and unbiased data are published by the NWS. It is generally possible to obtain at least 50 years of historical data for over 300 primary automated sites and 2,000 secondary "cooperative" sites nationwide at an extremely reasonable cost. All this helps to provide transparency to all those wishing to enter the market, increasing confidence, the result of which is elevated participation.

We have seen the result that opaque data sources have had on the development of European weather derivatives in their initial phase of market development, where data quality was high but so was the cost. Originally the UK Meteorological Office had intended to sell 50 years of data for eight UK locations for around $30,000. This had the immediate effect of preventing all but the largest companies from getting involved in weather derivatives – if you are an end-user looking to put in place a one-season protection. The cost fell eventually, which helped to boost UK market development. Data transparency and quality are improving throughout the world. This will further add to market liquidity.

Regarding market manipulation, there can be little confidence, leading to diminished liquidity, if there is the feeling that the market can be manipulated. With weather derivatives, this is virtually impossible. No one can corner the market for CDDs in Philadelphia for the summer, or try to squeeze HDDs in Boston in December. The weather cannot be controlled, stored, or transferred from place to place. Mother nature provides a level-playing field for everyone.

Weather is also attractive to both natural hedgers and risk-takers. It is important for liquidity that we see increasing participation from natural hedgers, or end-users, in order to provide a basis for a secondary, or re-traded market. Potential natural hedgers are in abundant supply with approximately 20% of a country's GDP being at the mercy of the weather. Fortunately, there is a growing contingent of risk-takers, helped by the fact that volatility, driven by frequently released weather forecasts, exists in the market. Volatility is essential as it increases the value of options and swaps to risk-takers in any market. As mentioned above, reinsurance companies, investment banks, and some power companies participate in the market as risk-takers, and we are now seeing more and more hedge funds taking advantage of the uncorrelated risks that weather derivatives offer.

TYPES OF INDICES FOR WEATHER CONTRACTS

Generally, as long as there is a reliable source of data, it is possible to base a weather derivative contract on any kind of weather activity. Listed below is a sample of the most commonly traded and talked about indices on which weather derivatives are based on:

- heating degree days (HDDs)
- cooling degree days (CDDs)
- absolute temperature, such as daily maximum temperature (Tmax) and daily minimum temperature (Tmin)
- precipitation, such as actual rainfall, snow pack, and snow fall
- dual commodity structures; for example, a weather contract that is linked to a gas, or electricity contract
- wind speed, which could be used for offshore storm protection
- the distance of a hurricane from a specific location
- misery, a combination of temperature and humidity
- growing degree days (GDDs).

HDDs AND CDDs ARE THE MOST ACTIVELY TRADED PRODUCTS

Most weather derivatives traded are swaps and slightly out of the money options that settle against cumulative degree day indices. These products are customized to cover individual cities, or baskets of cities, with risk periods ranging from a few months to several years. These types of contract have proved to be very popular with the US energy industry. The vast majority of deals traded since the market's inception have been of this kind, with most providing seasonal winter or summer coverage.

Degree days are the number of degrees the midnight-to-midnight daily average temperature deviates from a base of 65 degrees Fahrenheit. CDDs reflect the "cooling" requirements during summer months and HDDs reflect the "heating" requirement during winter months. The degree days for a single day cannot be a negative number, and are calculated as the greater of zero, or 65 minus the midnight-to-midnight average of the high and low temperature for the day. CDDs are calculated as the greater of zero, or the midnight-to-midnight average of the high and low temperature for the day minus 65. For example, if the average temperature for a summer day is 85 degrees, then the number of CDDs for this day would be 20. If the average temperature for a summer day is 62 degrees, then the number of CDDs for this day would be zero.

Degree days contracts are settled against the cumulative degree days over the contract period. To calculate the value of the degree days index, you would measure the degree days for each day within the contract period and sum them up. By definition then, you will have to wait until the end of the contract period to know the full value of the cumulative degree days index on which to settle (unlike options in many other markets where it is possible to exercise them before the expiration date).

The rationale behind using a base temperature of 65 degrees Fahrenheit in the degree days calculation is that homeowners will turn on their air conditioning above this temperature, hence CDDs, and turn their heating on below it, hence HDDs. It is unreasonable to assume that 65 is the magic number in all locations across the United States, let alone across the globe. It is, however, convenient that all participants have agreed to use 65 degrees Fahrenheit for the United States in order to standardize as much of the contract as possible. Outside the United States, it is widely accepted that 18 degrees Celsius will be used as the base temperature for the degree days contracts.

GDDs lend themselves naturally to the agricultural industry. They function in a similar way to HDDs and CDDs, and are used to estimate the growth and development of plants and insects during the growing season. The basic concept is that development will only occur if the temperature exceeds some minimum developmental threshold, or base temperature (Tbase). The base temperatures are determined experimentally and are different for each organism.

GDDs cannot be negative and are calculated as the greater of zero, or the average of the midnight-to-midnight temperature minus Tbase. For example, if we wish to calculate the GDDs for wheat on a day where the average temperature is 65 degrees Fahrenheit, the GDDs will equal 25 ($65 - $ Tbase $= 65 - 40 = 25$). As before, a weather derivative structure would settle against the cumulative GDDs over the contract period.

Often when temperatures rise to high values, the benefits on the growth rate of an organism will be diminished and sometimes reversed. Modified GDDs will take into consideration this effect. If the daily maximum temperature is above 86 degrees Fahrenheit, it is reset to 86 degrees Fahrenheit. If the daily minimum is below 50 degrees Fahrenheit, it is reset to 50 degrees Fahrenheit. Once the maximum and minimum temperatures have been modified, if needed, the average for the day is computed and compared with the base temperature (usually 50 degrees Fahrenheit). Modified GDDs are typically used to monitor the development of corn, the assumption being that development is limited once the temperature exceeds 86 degrees Fahrenheit.

WEATHER DERIVATIVE STRUCTURES

Weather derivatives are very flexible and can be tailor made to hedge very specific risks. Consequently, there are numerous types of contract that are commonly talked about, and a number that are actively dealt. Commonly traded structures include the following:

- Caps – A call option on a weather index where the buyer of the option receives a payment if the defined weather index exceeds the strike level at the end of the contract period. The amount of the pay-out is generally related to by how much the index exceeds the strike level. The buyer pays the seller a one-off premium for this contract.
- Floors – A put option on a weather index where the buyer of the option receives a payment if the defined weather index falls below the strike level at the end of the contract period. The buyer pays the seller a one-off premium for this contract. For example, the buyer is looking to protect against a drop in earnings from a mild winter, while allowing for the increased earnings from favorable weather conditions. The pay-out increases the below the strike price upon the index settlement. The floor buyer receives payments from the floor seller if the HDDs are below the strike level.
- Swaps – A financial contract that has the effect of "swapping" cash flows between the counterparties, depending on which side of the

agreed swap level the defined weather index settles at the end of the contract period. The buyer of the swap receives payments from the seller if the index settles above the swap level. Conversely, the buyer makes payments to the seller if the index settles below the swap level. There is no exchange of premium for this contract, as both the buyer and seller have the potential to make or lose money equally on the swap contract. For example, in extreme summers the utility sells more electricity, increasing volume-related revenues. To protect against a mild summer, the utility can sell a swap, giving away some upside profit for downside protection. The result is earnings stability.

- Collars (cost-less, or low cost) – This is similar to the other options described above. A collar allows a business to protect against adverse weather conditions at little or no cost by giving away some upside potential. The buyer of collar essentially buys a call option, cap, and funds this by selling a put option floor. Naturally, the strike of the call will be greater than the strike of the put, and if the collar is cost-less, then the average of the strikes should be equivalent to the swap level. The energy company can buy or sell the collar.

CUSTOMIZED DERIVATIVE STRUCTURES

There are other financial transactions that can take place in the weather derivatives markets. These include:

- Baskets – If a business has its weather exposure spread across multiple locations, then it is possible to enter into a derivative that pays out depending on the weather on each of these locations. This is called a basket. For example, if you want to protect against low HDDs over the winter in Boston, New York, and Washington DC, and that you have twice the exposure in Washington DC than you have in the other two cities, then consider the following. First, construct an HDD index that is equal to 20% of the HDDs in Boston over the winter contract period, plus 20% of the HDDs in New York, plus 40% of the HDDs in Washington DC. Finally, enter into an HDD floor contract based on this index, which will pay out for a mild winter, with greater emphasis on the actual weather in Washington.
- Digitals – Whereas HDD and CDD caps, floors, and swaps tend to have fluid pay-out structures – that is, the amount paid depends on how far the index deviates from the strike – a digital structure will make a single fixed lump-sum payment, simply if the strike level is breached. Because the nature of the pay-out is all or nothing,

these structures are also referred to as binary derivatives. In the example below, the power producer knows that there is a fixed cost of bringing a peaking facility on line when temperatures exceed 95 degrees Fahrenheit. The company buys a digital call option that will compensate for this one-off fixed cost when the daily maximum temperature exceeds 95 degrees Fahrenheit. Of course, the buyer will pay the seller an up-front premium for this contract.

- Compound options – This is an option on an option. If a business is unsure about taking up weather risk protection, it can purchase a contract that gives it the right, but not the obligation, to buy a specific weather option at a predetermined price before a certain date. For example, a business will know if a winter season (November to March) HDD floor option will best suit its risk-hedging needs one month into the contract period. It can buy a compound option on this structure, which expires on December 31. So, if the regular floor costs $300,000, the company may expect to pay $75,000 for the compound. Should it wish to exercise and take up the full November to March option on December 31, it will pay an additional $275,000. It is reasonable to expect that the full cost of the exercised compound option be more expensive than the regular floor because of the greater flexibility it gives the buyer.

- Trigger options – Also known as barrier options, these structures either come into existence or cease to exist if the weather index breaches some predetermined level. Knock-ins are options that come into existence when this level is breached; knock-outs will cease to exist when this level is breached. Knock-outs have been more common to date. An example would be a November to March HDD call option with a strike of 5150. The option pays $10,000 for every HDD the index settles above the strike, up to a maximum of $4 million or 400 HDDs above the strike. If the option knocks out at 5550 and if the index settles above this level, then instead of the buyer receiving the maximum $4 million the option will expire worthless. Naturally these types of option will be less expensive than their non-trigger equivalents.

- Dual commodity – A weather option that pays out in the form of another physical or derivative commodity contract. For example, a power distributor who wishes to receive a call option on electricity when temperatures are extremely high during the summer, in order to protect against price spikes, will consider a dual commodity structure.

THE HEDGE FUND OPPORTUNITY

Since weather risk is a large part of the operating cost of many businesses, there are many end-users that would like to participate in this market. But the loss of market-making during the demise of merchant energy trading in the United States led to a liquidity vacuum. Just like the entrance of energy hedge funds into oil and natural gas trading in North America, we are now seeing an uptick of weather derivatives hedge funds due to the market opportunity to provide liquidity. Many of these funds are using their weather expertise and marrying that to proprietary technical trading models in the commodities markets. Therefore, it makes a lot of sense for hedge funds to trade not only weather derivatives on the bilateral OTC markets and the exchange-traded futures of the CME, but also to trade the energy and agricultural markets on futures exchanges such as NYMEX and CBOT and bilateral OTC markets.

It is the hedge fund's trading acumen and risk management knowledge that is attracting this participation in the weather markets. Their proprietary global weather databases and ability to measure correlations between commodity prices and weather conditions make them a natural participant in these markets. They can build on their technical trading platform, as well as make markets with end-users. By leveraging trades in commodity markets, there is also less risk to weather market fluctuations. It must be remembered that the mantra of hedge funds is the return of alpha, management of diversified correlation risk, leverage, and lessened volatility to bring forth consistent returns.

NOTE

1 Some of the information on weather derivatives was reproduced from the book *Energy Derivatives: Trading Emerging Markets* (Energy Publishing Enterprises, 2000), whose copyright is owned by Peter C. Fusaro.

CHAPTER 9

Energy and Natural Resources Fund
of Hedge Funds

Our research into the world of energy-oriented hedge funds has detected another important trend in the energy hedge fund sector that highlights the maturation process for hedge funds in energy. In recent months we have identified the emergence of funds of hedge funds in the natural resources segment. The strategy of fund of hedge funds is to invest in other hedge funds. In this way, they are able to capture some of the upside appreciation, while not having to develop a team of traders and bear the attendant overhead costs. Fund of hedge funds signal energy and, for that matter, green hedge funds, which are now in vogue for investors.

The increasingly volatile and higher priced energy markets for oil, gas, and coal have brought a new religion to investors. They want in. This can be observed in the activities of hedge funds and investment banks, and also in the record amounts of investment coming into energy-focused mutual funds and exchange traded funds (ETFs) such as SPYDER Energy (XLE).

As we have previously argued, lower energy prices are not coming back. There will be no mean price reversion in energy markets. This time it's different, and we expect to see continued higher prices for energy commodities despite recent price drops from previous highs. However, the issue for investors will become one of capacity. Just how many new hedge funds can realistically come into this sector?

Energy is only a $2.2 trillion financial market in notional value, compared to a $200 plus trillion for the much more developed and mature foreign exchange and interest rate derivatives markets. The physical energy markets are over $4 trillion and growing. The second question is how well will all these new funds perform. We have found over 450 energy hedge funds and predict that there will be more this year and next, and that may be an underestimate. Fund of hedge funds solves some of those issues as they find the winners among all the noise.

FUND OF HEDGE FUNDS

A fund of hedge funds is an investment company that invests in other hedge funds rather than investing in individual securities. Some funds of hedge funds register their securities with the SEC and these funds of hedge funds must provide investors with a prospectus and file certain reports quarterly with the SEC. However, not all fund of hedge funds are registered. Many funds of hedge funds also have much lower investment minimums (for example, $25,000) than individual hedge funds. Thus, some investors that would be unable to invest in a hedge fund directly may be able to purchase shares of funds of hedge funds.

Observers of the hedge fund industry have noted a significant rise in the number of funds of hedge funds over recent years as their popularity has exploded. According to Vann Hedge Fund Advisors,[1] there were less than 50 fund of hedge funds in 1990, and that has grown to an estimated 3,000 worldwide, with about 40% of the industry's assets under management. The May 2005 Hedge Fund Manager/CorrectNet fund administrator survey[2] suggests that global hedge fund assets are at $1,920 million only a year after first breaking the $1,000 million mark. Of this, 65.1% ($1,260 million) represents single hedge funds and the remaining assets are in funds of hedge funds ($660 million). The same survey suggests that fund of hedge funds actually enjoyed a higher rate of asset growth over the past 12 months at 27.3%, compared with 22.6% growth in single hedge fund assets.

Celent projected the growth of the fund of hedge funds industry in 2002 (see Figure 9.1), based on their growth over the period from 1999 to 2001.[3] Figure 9.1 shows that the fund of hedge funds' growth has not been steady in the past and that the forecast was a little optimistic as compared to the May 2005 Hedge Fund Manager/CorrectNet survey results. However, the figure demonstrates that despite occasional periods in which net inflows slowed down their overall growth continues. It is likely that the slower growth periods corresponded with times when other investment opportunities were making better returns for less cost.

The growth of the funds of hedge funds sector has been remarkable over the last few years, but recent figures show that asset inflows have been slowing down. Disappointing returns and high fees for this type of investment vehicle have meant that these funds have come under closer scrutiny from investors. According to data from Chicago-based Hedge Fund Research,[4] inflows into fund of hedge funds fell almost 40% during

FIGURE 9.1   Growth of fund of hedge funds to 2002 and projected to 2006

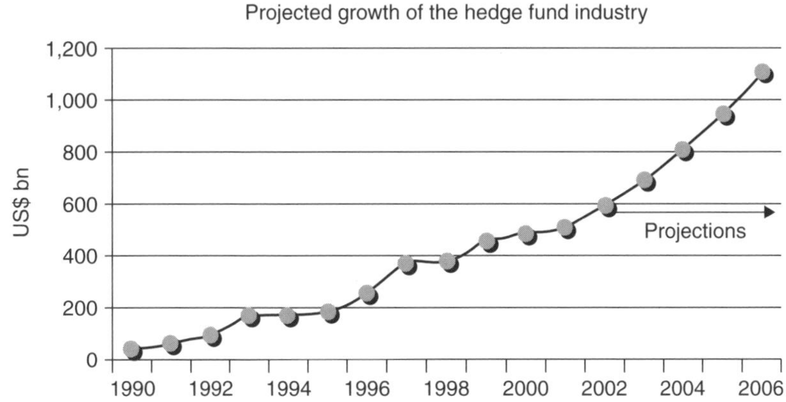

Projected growth of the hedge fund industry

Source: The Fund of Hedge Funds Industry, *Celent Report*, 2002
(www.celent.com)

the first half of 2005, compared to figures for the same period of 2004. However, while capital inflows have declined, the total of assets invested in funds of hedge funds has not declined. Disappointing performance has been an issue, as returns in the sector are now lower than they were a couple of years ago. The Hedge Fund Research Fund of hedge funds composite index,[5] for example, returned 11.61% in 2003, 6.8% in 2004, and, as of the end of the third quarter of 2005, just 3.58%.

This, combined with the relatively high fees for an investment in a fund of hedge funds, has caused investors to look at other ways of obtaining a return. Additionally, as the markets become more crowded, return opportunities decrease. Hence, the pressure to reduce fees will be greater in the near future. So just as investors in single-manager hedge funds have seen returns decline and sought alternative investment opportunities in energy, will the same be true for energy fund of hedge funds?

BENEFITS OF FUNDS OF HEDGE FUNDS

The fund of hedge funds approach provides a number of potentially significant benefits for investors. First, it can provide them with access to a professionally managed and diversified portfolio of generally uncorrelated hedge funds and, in so doing, reduce overall risk levels. Risks are believed to be reduced, since the investment is spread over a number of hedge funds such that the overall returns should be less volatile and more stable over time. By diversifying exposure across a number of funds, poor performance of a single fund has less overall impact. Further, since it is actually quite difficult to track and find individual hedge funds, a fund of hedge funds approach means that investors can obtain exposure to funds and managers that otherwise they may not have been aware. Due diligence on the fund is performed for the investor by a professional fund of hedge funds manager. Another benefit of a fund of hedge funds approach is that investors often have access to funds that would otherwise be closed to them, or where the initial investment amount would be much greater. Typically, a minimum investment amount for a single fund might be $100,000 or more, but a fund of hedge funds minimum investment can be much lower, perhaps as little as $25,000.

The benefits associated with a fund of hedge funds approach are that they:

- provide an investment portfolio with lower levels of risk and can deliver returns uncorrelated with the performance of the stock market
- deliver more stable returns under most market conditions due to the fund of fund manager's ability and understanding of the various hedge strategies
- significantly reduce individual fund and manager risk
- eliminate the need for time-consuming due diligence required for making hedge fund investment decisions
- allow for easier administration of widely diversified investments across a large variety of hedge funds
- allow access to a broader spectrum of leading hedge funds that may otherwise be unavailable due to high minimum investment requirements
- give access to a wide variety of hedge fund strategies, managed by many of the world's premier investment professionals, for a relatively modest investment.

A fund of hedge fund manager will usually be looking for a portfolio of relatively uncorrelated hedge funds to invest in, and as such performs the necessary fund monitoring and constant due diligence of funds on behalf of the investor. It is this latter point that causes difficulties for fund of hedge funds that desire access to the relatively high returns currently being obtained by energy hedge funds. The issue is that many energy hedge funds have little track record and only a few have more than a 12-month track record by which to gauge the funds' success. As a result, the fund of hedge funds manager will need to take a view on the individual fund manager and style that is not necessarily supported by historical success.

However, the fund of hedge fund is also often a popular vehicle for institutional investors as a result of its more stable and supposedly lower risk approach. Our research suggests that the vast majority of energy specialist funds currently being started are backed by private wealthy or family investor money. The emergence of fund of hedge fund activity in energy would also suggest, by inference, that more institutional money is now finding its way into the sector or at least looking to invest in it. It's what institutional investors are comfortable with. Once again, this would point to an issue in terms of track record and due diligence, since institutional investors often demand greater assurances of quality of investment.

Recently, fund of hedge funds fees have seen pressure from investors, too. Typically, a fund of hedge funds will charge a 1% management fee (sometimes 1.5%) and 10% performance fees, while the investor also has to bear the costs of the underlying hedge funds, too. With so many funds of hedge funds available, and with little to differentiate them, fund of hedge funds fees have been criticized as being too high. Interestingly, however, natural resource and/or energy fund of hedge funds, because they are different and as a result of good underlying returns, may be able to attract premium fees. Because fund of hedge funds' fees can be high, investors need to believe that their chosen fund of hedge funds can more than offset the extra layer of fees by superior manager and strategy selection.

THE EMERGENCE OF NATURAL RESOURCE FUND OF HEDGE FUNDS

We observed evidence for this new trend, both directly from hedge fund announcements and indirectly from interest created by our energyhedge-funds.com website and speaking engagements. In the latter case, during 2005, we observed a large number of inquisitive fund of hedge funds professionals attending our speaking engagements and approaching us for intelligence and information on the state of energy hedge funds. In the former case, in the two months between September and November 2005, the number of fund of hedge funds reported in the Energy Hedge Fund Directory has increased from less than five to around 25. As might be expected, their strategies are quite diversified and include managed futures; commodity-focused fund of funds; energy, including both equity and commodity foci; and more general fund of hedge funds that have diversified into a small number of energy hedge funds trading natural gas, crude oil, and other commodities. One of the funds of hedge funds invests in other funds, trading power futures in the Scandinavian NordPool market, for example.

However, the emergence of broader based "natural resources" fund of hedge funds represents a significant maturation point in the rush to energy. It brings institutional money and more conservative investors looking to benefit from the upsurge in energy prices and current interest in everything energy and/or environment. It will force greater rigor on the part of the new energy hedge funds via more intense due diligence; and will help with the "rooting out" of weaker plays, managers, strategies, and funds as well. What is very apparent is that the more conservative investors want to cash in on the strength of the energy sector as a whole and that is good news for the industry.

The issue for fund of hedge funds managers remains the relative youth and immaturity of the hedge funds focused on the energy industry and their lack of a track record. On the other hand, there are a small number of energy specialist funds with greater than 12-month (and highly positive) track records, as well as a larger number of more established macro or broader based hedge funds that have exposed more of their assets under management to energy for them to chose between. In the longer term the rush to invest in energy, both through traditional investments and via the alternative universe, begs a question about capacity. How much money can come into the sector and still deliver a better than average return? While the answer to that question may not become obvious for a while, it is readily apparent that natural resources fund of hedge funds will be a winner for more conservative investors wishing to diversify their investments into the extremely volatile energy complex.

Generally, fund of hedge funds appeal to institutional investors; however, the lack of a track record for energy fund managers means that the profile of an energy fund of hedge funds doesn't quite fit the normal mold of a fund of hedge funds for institutional investors. Currently, it appears that energy fund of hedge funds will be funded by HNW investors and only limited institutional investor funds, at least until more underlying energy managers develop the longer track records that institutions prefer. Despite that, family office and individual investors do seem to have an appetite for the energy fund of hedge funds concept. Another potential problem is volatility. The traditional fund of hedge funds has low volatility, while energy funds are quite volatile, and even what seems like a very low volatility of 10% for an energy fund of hedge funds can be considered to be too high by more conservative investors.

In reality, institutional money is finding its way into energy through more general fund of hedge funds vehicles that include one or two energy managers. These funds are not at all energy focused, but have seen the good returns from the energy sector and then sought out energy managers that fit their investment criteria and overall strategy. However, it is difficult to know how widespread this practice is among the 3,000 fund of hedge funds in existence, and our assessment is based purely on what we have heard from fund managers.

The energy funds of hedge funds are today largely focused on energy and other commodities. We know of one fund of hedge funds in Scandinavia that invests only in other energy commodity hedge funds that trade in the more mature NordPool electric power market, but most of the others are either managed futures focused or very broadly natural resources. This means that they invest in managers across the commodity space and their actual energy component may not be very high. A more diversified approach across the energy segment that includes broader energy exposure to equities, debt, distressed assets, and commodities has yet to emerge. There are, however, two Canadian funds of hedge funds in formation that appear to be targeting this more diversified approach.

FUND OF HEDGE FUND PORTFOLIO CONSTRUCTION

Constructing a fund of hedge funds involves selecting the right hedge funds, managers, and strategies. This actually requires a large database of hedge funds and good knowledge of investment strategies. An individual investor is unlikely to know which are the best funds, or even if they have seen the best funds among the ones that they are aware of. Very few individual investors have the deep knowledge of strategies and investing to properly evaluate the funds and perform the necessary due diligence. However, a professional hedge fund manager has that access and knowledge, theoretically anyway, and should be able to build a strong and diversified fund of hedge funds.

Fund of hedge fund managers build portfolios designed to produce an array of returns, from very conservative to quite aggressive. They do this by selecting non-correlated funds and by performing proper due diligence on each manager and strategy. As stated above, quite often a professional fund of hedge funds manager can also invest in individual funds that are closed to other investors. Again, the idea is to generate consistent returns with lower risk and lower volatility. Over time, the manager may actively manage the fund by weeding out investments in under-performing funds, while introducing new funds to the portfolio. While there are some limitations to this based on individual fund lock-up periods, an active manager can consistently rebalance the portfolio. This requires ongoing due diligence work on the part of the manager. Fund manager's track records are an important part of that due diligence process.

ISSUES WITH ENERGY FUND OF FUNDS

We have discovered that a strictly energy portfolio can be problematic for some fund of hedge funds managers and more conservative investors. In the first instance, they may not have a good understanding of the energy industry and may not be able to understand how to create a portfolio of relatively non-correlated energy managers. Not understanding that there are some natural relationships in the energy value chain and between certain commodities, for example, it is difficult to understand how a portfolio can be 100% energy without all of the funds in the portfolio being highly correlated.

This is related to a second issue – that of volatility. By selecting relatively non-correlated funds the overall impact is not only to reduce risk, but also to reduce volatility to theoretically give consistent returns. At first sight, an energy fund of hedge funds will almost certainly have high volatility and be quite risky. However, we have developed an approach that utilizes the natural correlations between parts of the energy value chain, different commodities, and different geographies to come up with portfolios that, on a historical basis, have a volatility of less than 10%. To us, the issue here is related to the lack of detailed knowledge about the energy industry, rather than the idea that energy does not fit the model.

There is a third issue – we have mentioned the lack of history of many energy hedge funds several times in this chapter. However, there are enough funds with at least a 24-month track record to build a reasonable energy portfolio. Furthermore, even though some managers don't have a track record as a hedge fund manager *per se*, they do have testable track records as energy traders on the commodity side. It's a small industry and everyone knows who the performers are and who they have been. Finally, we are told by fund of hedge funds managers that the best returns are to be found from the newer managers and strategies. Energy certainly fits that bill!

This latter issue becomes most concentrated in the environmental sector. There are now a growing number of environmental or green energy hedge funds, but they are all relatively new with little or no track record. Additionally, the environmental space is probably less generally understood than energy. Furthermore, there has been some disappointment after the initial excitement around socially responsible investments and mutual funds that have just not performed in the past. This has carried over into energy. However, we see that the intersection of energy and environment will simply continue to grow through 2006 and beyond. It is a matter of time.

Despite the fact that there are some issues around energy-focused fund of hedge funds, we think that these issues can be overcome. Watch this space as the move to energy commodity and natural resource fund of hedge funds stampedes into the broader energy sector during 2006. At the end of the day, it is down to the risk reward appetite of the various groups of investors. The interest in energy is growing across all investors and the fund of hedge funds approach still represents a good way to gain exposure to energy while reducing overall risk and volatility through diversification.

WHAT'S UP NEXT?

Our view is that, given the interest in energy on the part of all investors and the opportunities for energy fund of hedge funds to produce better than average fund of hedge fund returns, the trend toward energy fund of hedge funds will become strongly established in 2006. While energy may not fit the traditional profile for fund of hedge funds, the attractiveness of strong returns with a lower risk profile will likely prove too strong. Additionally, as more time goes by, more new energy managers will develop a track record of sufficient length to fit the criteria. Further, despite the lack of maturity of many energy hedge funds, there is a general view that the best returns are produced early in the pursuit of a particular strategy by a particular manager. If the same is true for energy and environmental hedge funds, then the best returns are being made now.

As the overall performance of fund of hedge funds declines, the hunt will be on for new opportunities to make money in less-crowded markets and strategies. We believe that this will signal a surge in interest in energy, both as a diversification for generic fund of funds, as well as a slightly more high-risk, higher return energy fund of hedge funds play.

Today, the funds of hedge funds in the sector are largely commodity oriented, either as managed futures, broader natural resource commodity funds, or energy commodity funds. Two new funds of hedge funds in formation are planning to target the energy complex, specifically through both commodities and equities. The more diversified approach makes sense since it provides more relatively non-correlated strategies and managers that can help reduce overall portfolio volatility. We expect to see more diversified energy fund of hedge funds emerge in 2006, and a growing environmental component to these funds later in 2006 and 2007.

The important thing about the emergence of energy fund of hedge funds is that they stand to bring increasing amounts of institutional money into energy hedge funds. They represent another source of assets for this emerging class of funds in the future and psychologically signal the maturation of the sector as an alternative asset class.

NOTES

1 "Hedge Fund Demand and Capacity 2005–2015," Vann Hedge Fund Advisors, 2005.
2 "May 2005 Hedge Fund Manager/CorrectNet Fund Administrator Survey," *Hedge Fund Manager Magazine*, May 2005.
3 "The Fund of Hedge Funds Industry," *Celent Report*, 2002 (www.celent. com).
4 "Hedge Fund Research," www.hedgefundresearch.com.
5 "Hedge Fund Research Fund of Hedge Funds Composite index," www.hedgefundresearch.com.

CHAPTER 10

Energy Indexes

Commodities trade on many futures exchanges, so it was a natural evolution of commodity markets to credit indices with futures contracts to allow more investors to trade commodities in a more passive way. Brokerage firms are increasingly looking to offer ETFs, since investors seek lower expenses and portfolio diversification. In this chapter we examine more passive and less risky ways for investors to invest in energy and environmental hedge funds.

COMMODITY TRADING INDEXES

Direct commodity investment has been a minor part of an investor's asset allocation; however, with high energy price volatility and investable commodity indices, there are more opportunities to participate in energy markets. The principal argument for investing in commodities in the past has been that they are a natural hedge against losses in equity and debt holdings that lose values during periods of inflation.

Commodity indexes are a source of information on cash commodity and futures commodity markets that can be used as performance benchmarks and as a good indicator for developing asset allocation strategies. Commodity indexes usually provide returns comparable with passive long positions in listed futures contracts and can be invested. Commodity indexes attempt to replicate the returns available to holding long and short positions in energy and other commodities. Price return derives from changes in commodity futures prices. Futures prices are used as a surrogate for cash market performance.

The Goldman Sachs commodity index (GSCI®) is denominated in dollars, nearby futures contracts using five-year moving averages. It is well traded by hedge funds who follow the index. JP Morgan Chase has estimated that commodity index money has increased from $2 billion to as much as $50 billion in the past several years. Most of that money trades the GSCI® with minor investment in the other indices, although the Dow Jones AIG index is gaining in market participation. JP Morgan Chase estimates that passive long positions in crude and natural gas may translate into significant positions on NYMEX oil and gas futures contracts.

Buying on a commodity index is another popular strategy for hedge funds. The reason is that it allows the investor to profit on a rise in energy prices and other commodities without the risk of either financial futures or physical commodity trading. It is estimated that over $50 billion is tied up in index trading today.

The importance of commodity trading indexes cannot be understated. While many funds of hedge funds have struggled to raise assets in other sectors besides energy, indices have taken in tremendous amounts of money recently. The energy sector appears to be no different, with four major commodity indices ready for trading. We also learned over the course of this study that a commodity-specific hedge fund index has been under development in Switzerland for the past 18 months, and will be sold to investment banks and funds as a stand-alone investment product. This section of the report will explain what these indices are and their added importance in energy trading.

The indices are comprised of the underlying commodities. The four major indices are:

- Goldman Sachs commodity index (GSCI®)
- Dow Jones-AIG Index
- CRB Reuters Index
- Deutsche Bank index

The indices have been further commoditized as futures contracts traded on the two Chicago commodity futures exchanges, the CBOT and the CME. The popularity of trading indices is that this is a more passive approach than trading commodity futures contracts or OTC energy derivative products. They are gaining in popularity as they are perceived as less risky investments. They seem to be a natural investment for pension fund investment. Further evolution of this product will be the investable hedge funds indexes that are attracting much capital in other hedge fund markets. They began in 2002. The success of these indices is their simplicity and transparency. They appear to the opposite of the typical hedge fund approach. The commodity indices are different and are more volatile, reflecting the price movements of the underlying commodities.

GOLDMAN SACHS COMMODITY INDEX (GSCI®)

Goldman Sachs is an investment bank that covers virtually all commodity-related exposures, including oil, natural gas, electric power, coal, metals, weather, and forest products throughout the world. The company developed the GSCI® as an investment vehicle by which investors can gain global exposure to the commodities markets and hedge against risk. The GSCI® is designed to provide investors with a reliable and publicly available benchmark for investment performance in the commodity markets comparable to the S&P 500 or FT equity indices. The GSCI® is a composite index of commodity sector returns, representing an unleveraged, long-only investment in commodity futures that is broadly diversified across the spectrum of commodities. The returns are calculated on a fully collateralized basis with full reinvestment. The combination of these attributes provides investors with a representative and realistic picture of realizable returns attainable in the commodities markets. The GSCI® tracks real economic activity, as well as measuring the level of world commodity prices. GSCI® futures and options contracts were launched in 1992, and open outcry and electronic trading on the CME on February 19, 2002. Goldman Sachs saw the commodity index as a good way for investors to hedge against risk and decrease overall portfolio risk while obtaining relatively high returns. There was an opportunity to present a diversified portfolio of commodities that the average investor may not have had the resources to construct. Goldman can earn fees on derivative securities from this index, similar to those provided to Swedish Export Credit Corp. The cost includes management, administrative, and transaction costs. Today, the GSCI® has become the premier global commodity benchmark for measuring investment performance in the commodity markets for hedge fund trading. It is also the most actively traded by hedge funds active in the energy sector. As holding actual commodities entails the holding, storage, transportation, and insurance costs, it would be prohibitive to most investors, except for those who actually consume those commodities. As a result, an index futures is a very useful tool to gain exposure to commodity markets without all the physical aspects of the underlying commodities.

Currently, 24 commodities meet the eligibility requirement for the GSCI®. A list of these components and their dollar weights in the GSCI®, organized by sub-sector, is presented in Table 10.1 on page 158.

The GSCI® was constructed to be similar to that of a capitalization-weighted stock market index that reflected the relative impact each individual stock had on the overall market. Commodity futures in the GSCI® were weighted according to the dollar value of their physical

Table 10.1 GSCI® components and weights (%)(November 10, 2005)

Energy	76.64	Industrial metals	6.60	Precious metals	1.82	Agriculture	9.88	Livestock	5.06
Crude oil	27.81	Aluminum	2.68	Gold	1.63			Live cattle	2.76
Brent crude oil	13.53	Copper	2.53	Silver	0.19	Wheat	2.21	Feeder cattle	0.69
Unleaded gas	7.56	Lead	0.26			Red wheat	0.91	Lean hogs	1.60
Heating oil	8.84	Nickel	0.54			Corn	2.07		
Gasoil	4.68	Zinc	0.58			Soybeans	1.47		
Natural gas	14.22					Cotton	0.94		
						Sugar	1.41		
						Coffee	0.69		
						Cocoa	0.18		

Source: www.gs.com/gsci/#economic

quantity of worldwide production. It is predominantly weighted to energy more than any other index. It has 24 commodities represented in the index. As of November 10, 2005, its composition included 76.64% energy, 9.88% agricultural and livestock, 6.6% industrial metals, 5.9% livestock, and 1.82% precious metal. (The composition changes every week.) The index is heavily fuel sensitive. The GSCI® was normalized to a value of 100 on January 2, 1970. The October 1, 2004, index is 339.95 for open outcry and 339.08 for Globex, the electronic trading platform (see the CME website). Goldman Sachs chose this design because it believed that the weights reflect the relative impact each commodity has on the worldwide economy.

The GSCI® was calculated from the total returns of futures contracts, rather than from the spot prices for each commodity. Each contract was rolled over into the next nearest contract. Total returns consisted of yield from the collateral Treasury bills, and the return from the futures that consist of the spot return and the roll yield. An investor would post collateral consisting of US Treasury bills and obtain its yield. The investor would roll the contract to the next nearest contract and obtain the roll and spot yield. These returns are what an investor can get if he or she replicates the index.

The GSCI® is rolled each month by selling 20% of the prompt contract on each of the fifth through ninth business days of the calendar month, and buying the next contract on the schedule. These index rolls temporarily distort the share of the futures curve that has recently been exacerbated by the funds following the index. This has led to a temporary contango between the front two contracts of the NYMEX WTI contracts, the most heavily traded energy contracts, during 2004 and much of 2005. Energy markets are usually backwardated.

The index is world-production weighted. The quantity of each commodity in the index is determined by the average quantity of production in the last five years of available data. Individual components qualify for inclusion in the GSCI® on the basis of liquidity and are weighted by their respective world production quantities. The principles behind the construction of the index are public and designed to allow easy and cost-efficient investment implementation. Possible means of implementation include the purchase of GSCI®-related instruments, such as the GSCI® futures contracts traded on the CME or OTC derivatives, or the direct purchase of the underlying futures contracts.

While in equity markets representative measurement of investment performance can be accomplished through weighting indices by market capitalization, there is no direct counterpart to market capitalization for commodities. The problem is that commodities, and the related price risks, are held in a variety of ways; that is, long futures positions, OTC investments, long-term fixed-price purchasing contracts, or physical inventory at the producer, making a complete accounting of capital dedicated to holding commodities from the time they are produced to the time they are consumed. A simple way to achieve a close analogue to true market capitalization, abstracting from differences in inventory patterns, is to note that the net long position of the economy is proportional to the quantity produced; hence, production weighting.

The GSCI® contains as many commodities as possible, with the rules excluding commodities only to retain liquidity and investability in the underlying futures markets. Currently, the GSCI® contains 24 commodities from all commodity sectors: six energy products, seven metals, and 11 agricultural products. Energy futures contracts include NYMEX's West Texas intermediate (WTI), heating oil, unleaded gasoline and natural gas contracts, the Ice Exchange (formerly IPE), Brent crude oil, and gas/oil futures contracts. The broad range of constituent commodities provides the GSCI® with a high level of diversification, both across sub-sectors and within each sub-sector. This diversity minimizes the effects of highly idiosyncratic events, which have large implications for the individual commodity markets, but are muted when aggregated to the level of the GSCI®.

Three GSCI® indices are published: excess return, total return, and spot. The excess return index measures the returns accrued from investing in uncollateralized nearby commodity futures, the total return index measures the returns accrued from investing in fully collateralized nearby commodity futures, and the spot index measures the level of nearby commodity prices. Thus, the excess return and total return indices provide useful representations of returns available to investors from investing in the GSCI®. In fact, the total return (that is, the return on the GSCI® total return index) is the measure of commodity returns that are completely comparable to returns from a regular investment in the S&P 500 (with dividend reinvestment) or a government bond, while the return on the excess return index is comparable to the return on the S&P 500 above cash.

Passive Portfolios

By design the GSCI® reflects a passive portfolio of long positions in futures. However, unlike a passive equity portfolio, a passive futures portfolio requires regular transactions, for the simple reason that futures expire. Thus, the futures portfolio represented by the GSCI® is, in this way, comparable to a bond portfolio of a specific duration.

In the GSCI's® case, the maturity of choice is the nearby futures contract (that is, the contract nearest to expiration). Futures contracts near to expiration are rolled forward (that is, exchanged for futures contracts with the next applicable expiration date) at the beginning of their expiration months.

Many commodities, like those in the energy and industrial metals sectors, have liquid futures contracts that expire every month. Therefore, these commodities are rolled forward each month. Other commodities, most notably agricultural and livestock products, only have a few contract months each year that trade with sufficient liquidity. Thus, these commodities, with futures that expire less frequently, roll forward less frequently than every month.

Rolls and Holding Periods

All of the rolls occur at the end of the business day. Therefore, on the first through to the fourth business days, and throughout the day, until the end of the day, on the fifth business day, the GSCI® portfolio consists of a single basket – the first nearby basket. Hence, even though the fifth business day is the first day of the roll, the portfolio return for the fifth business day is based on the portfolio construction of the evening before (that is, the first nearby basket).

On the sixth business day, the returns are generated by the portfolio constructed at the end of the fifth business day (that is, 80% first nearby basket and 20% second nearby basket). The roll continues, until the tenth business day (the last roll occurring at the end of the ninth business day). The returns are generated by 100% of the new first nearby basket, which is held until the beginning of the following month's roll period. Note that the period from the end of the fifth business day to the end of the ninth business day is the only period during which the GSCI® consists of a mixture of the two baskets and hence it may contain more than one futures maturity per commodity.

As the baskets contain futures with different maturities for some of the commodities, the prices are generally close but not exactly the same. Hence, the percentage of the portfolio value (that is, dollar weight) held in each basket is generally close to, but not exactly equal to, the 80%/20% split specified for the quantities. This has led to interesting arbitrage opportunities recently as the hedge fund actively follows this contract when trading energy.

The GSCI® total return index is constructed to be comparable to simple investing in traditional assets. Uncollateralized futures investments, such as those represented by the returns in the GSCI® excess return index, can be thought of as fully levered transactions, while fully collateralized futures investments are unlevered.

To make futures investing comparable to typical long positions in equities and bonds, the futures need to be fully collateralized. In a fully collateralized futures purchase, the investor pays the face value of the futures as collateral at the time that the futures position is opened. Hence, the investor receives the Treasury bill rate on this collateral, as well as the return for holding the futures contract.

DOW JONES – AIG COMMODITY INDEX (DJ-AIGCI®)

The primary goal of the DJ-AIGCI® is to provide a diversified commodities index with weightings based on the economic significance of individual components, while maintaining low volatility and sufficient liquidity.

Employing both liquidity and dollar-adjusted production data to determine its individual component weightings, the DJ-AIGCI® index differs from other commodities indexes, such as the GSCI®, as it allows for varying component weightings, but maintains restrictions such as maximum and minimum component weightings to ensure adequate diversification. The DJ-AIGCI® is re-weighted and re-balanced each year in January on a price percentage basis.

The DJ-AIGCI® is designed to be a highly liquid and diversified benchmark for commodities as an asset class. It was developed by Dow Jones and the AIG Trading Group Commodities to trade on the CBOT. The index was created in 1998 and launched as the CBOT® DJ-AIGCI® futures contract on November 16, 2001. The index trades on the CBOT's electronic trading platform as futures and options contracts. It is still a thinly traded contract. The DJ-AIGCI® is composed of futures contracts on 19 physical commodities and is less weighted toward energy. As of November 10, 2005, the energy commodities include crude oil (12.81%), heating oil (4.05%), unleaded gasoline (3.85%), and natural gas (10.28%). Other commodities in the index include aluminum, cattle, cocoa, coffee, copper, corn, cotton, gold, hogs, nickel, silver, soybean oil, sugar, wheat, and zinc. No one sector can have more than 33% of the index. Its total return for 2004 through September 30 has been 8.91%.

Unlike equities, which entitle the holder to a continuing stake in a corporation, commodity futures contracts specify a delivery date for the underlying physical commodity. In order to avoid delivery and maintain a long futures position, nearby contracts must be sold, and contracts that have not yet reached the delivery period must be purchased. This process is known as "rolling" a futures position. The DJ-AIGCI® is a "rolling index."

The DJ-AIGCI® is composed of commodities traded on US exchanges, with the exception of aluminum, nickel, and zinc, which trade on the London Metals Exchange (LME).

The DJ-AIGCI® family of indexes includes both the DJ-AIGCI® (which is calculated on an excess return basis) and a total return index based on the DJ-AIGCI® (the DJ-AIGCITR). While the former reflects the return of its underlying commodity price movements only, the latter reflects the return on a fully collateralized investment in the index. In addition, there will be seven sub-indexes, representing the major commodity sectors within the index: energy (including petroleum and natural gas), petroleum (including crude oil, heating oil, and unleaded gasoline), precious metals, industrial metals, grains, livestock, and softs (coffee, sugar, and cocoa).

To determine its component weightings, the DJ-AIGCI® relies primarily on liquidity data, or the relative amount of trading activity of a particular commodity. Liquidity is an important indicator of the value placed on a commodity by financial and physical market participants. The index also relies to a lesser extent on dollar-adjusted production data. The index thus relies on data that are endogenous to the futures markets (liquidity) and exogenous to the futures markets (production) in determining relative weightings. All data used in both the liquidity and production calculations are averaged over a five-year period.

The component weightings are also determined by several rules designed to insure diversified commodity exposure. Disproportionate weighting of any particular commodity or sector may increase volatility and negate the concept of a broad-based commodity index, unduly subjecting the investor to micro-economic shocks in one commodity or sector. To help insure diversified commodity exposure, the DJ-AIGCI® relies on several diversification rules. Among these are the following:

- No related group of commodities (for example, energy, precious metals, livestock, and grains) may constitute more than 33% of the index.
- No single commodity may constitute less than 2% of the index.

An Oversight Committee meets annually to determine the composition of the index in accordance with the rules established in the DJ-AIGCI® handbook.

Table 10.2 DJ-AIGCI®

2005 Commodity index percentages	
Item	%
Natural gas	12.282992
Crude oil	12.810567
Unleaded gas	4.051497
Heating oil	3.854944
Live cattle	6.152719
Lean hogs	4.388980
Wheat	4.869456
Corn	5.937836
Soybeans	7.595688
Soybean oil	2.665386
Aluminum	7.055306
Copper	5.887357
Zinc	2.673422
Nickel	2.606530
Gold	5.978087
Silver	2.000000
Sugar	2.933043
Cotton	3.231786
Coffee	3.024406

Note: These target weights have taken effect from January 2005.
Source: www.djindexes.com

REUTERS-CRB® TOTAL RETURN INDEX

The Reuters-CRB® futures price index, developed in 1956, is the most well-known indicator of overall commodity prices in the world. Its original design had weighted the index heavily toward agricultural commodities. Over the past 10 years, changes have been made so that the Reuters-CRB® today is more equally representative of a broad range of commodity prices. But it is still heavily weighted toward agricultural commodities, and thus it is not an attractive index for hedge funds trading energy. Currently, the index is geometrically weighted evenly among 17 arithmetically averaged component commodities. Reuters-CRB® future and option contracts have been traded on the New York Futures Exchange (a division of the New York Board of Trade) since June 1986. The Reuters-CRB® futures contract has six expiration months per year (Jan–Feb–Apr–Jun–Aug–Nov). All futures and options expire to cash on the same date. One Reuters-CRB® contract is worth $500 times the price of the index.

As the recognized benchmark for commodity prices, the Reuters-CRB® plays an important role in the investment strategies of funds, both large and small. In the past, fund managers based their commodity allocation investment decisions on commodity index prices instead of actual realized returns. It would be hard to fault them on this, since overall commodity return information was practically non-existent. The very nature of commodity future contracts requires them to regularly expire. When this occurs, an existing position needs to be continually rolled forward. This is rarely done at the same price. Storage, interest charges, and short-term supply/demand anomalies are some (certainly not all) of the factors attributing to the difference in price between the near-term futures price and a more deferred one.

The Commodity Research Bureau index (Reuters-CRB®), listed on the New York Board of Trade (NYBOT), in conjunction with Bridge Data and RTM Management, has recently produced a total return calculation based upon the Reuters-CRB® cash index and is directly related to the New York-listed Reuters-CRB® futures contract. This calculation is referred to as the Reuters-CRB® total return index (Reuters-CRB-TR). Previously, any analysis of the Reuters-CRB® index could only be done on the level of commodity prices. The information now available will allow investors to analyze the *return* characteristics of the Reuters-CRB® index, which may make it particularly attractive to some risk-averse hedge funds that want a more passive investment but exposure to commodity price movements.

FIGURE 10.1   Reuters-CRB® futures index

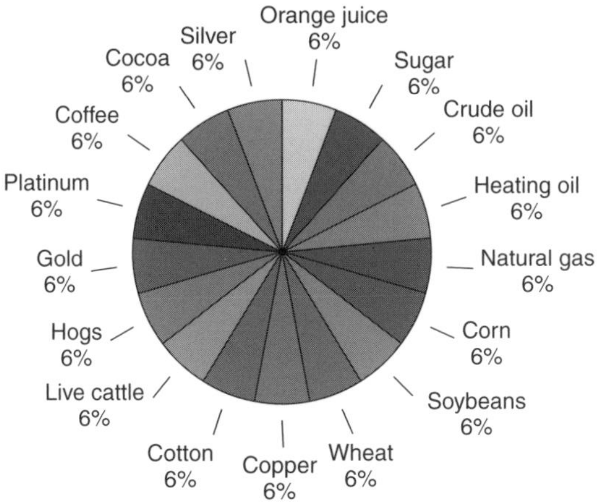

'Reuters-CRB Futures Index is a trademark of
Reuters-Commodity Research Bureau
Source: djindexes.com

The Reuters-CRB® futures price index is based on the average price of individual commodities over a six-month period. When a commodity expired it was simply deleted from the index. Whatever effect this may have had on it was simply reflected in the price the following day. This is why, many times, the index may be seen to be moving significantly from its closing price the day before to the next day before any of its components have opened for trading. This is the effect of actual component future contracts being added or deleted to the index. This properly reflects price levels for its component commodities and is therefore useful in gauging commodity price strength or weakness against historical periods. What it does not show are the returns that would have been achieved by a passively held investment using the Reuters-CRB® index. By calculating this return characteristic, investment professionals are now able to accurately assess the usability of commodities in their overall investment program. A total return index allows commodities to be examined on an even-playing field with other traditional asset classes.

According to the Moore Research Center Inc., the composition of the index is 17.6% for energy (crude oil, heating oil, and natural gas). The remainder of its composition is grains at 17.6%, precious metals 17%, cotton 11.8%, orange juice 23.5%, and 11.8% for softs. This has not changed since December 1995. The contracts also have comparatively low volatility.

DEUTSCHE BANK LIQUID COMMODITY INDICES (DBLCI)

To meet the growing demand for such products, Deutsche has developed two commodities indices (described below). In August 2003 it launched the first note linked to performance (the second index): a seven-year, principal-protected note, that was targeted to private banking clients. This was because many investors are still not fluent with the asset class and are also looking for hybrid products – again playing straight to the strength of the all-service banks. But there is growing demand for structured notes or structured deposits that are based on commodities mixed in with fixed income and equities. In effect, combining commodities with other assets with which investors are already familiar is a good way to introduce investors to this new asset class, commodities.

Deutsche Bank provides the Deutsche Bank liquid commodity index (DBLCI) and the Deutsche Bank liquid commodity index – mean reversion (DBLCI-MR), which are two indices that track the performance of investments in a small set of liquid commodities. Their strategy is that commodities tend to trade within wide but defined ranges due to the simple economic principles of supply and demand, and therefore the net effect is that commodity prices are bound by their long-run average price. As prices rise, supply is increased through new production capacity, the use of alternative sources, and circumventing quota systems. At the same time there is a reduction in demand. The opposite forces come into play when prices fall below their long-term averages. The net effect is to keep commodity prices bound around their long-run average price. The DBLCI-MR capitalizes on this recurring characteristic of commodities and applies these in a rule-based methodology.

The DBLCI is made up of six commodities: sweet light crude, heating oil, aluminum, gold, wheat, and corn. Each commodity has a constant weighting, which reflects world production and inventory changes. The DBLCI-MR explicitly uses variable weights for its constituent assets to capture the mean-reverting properties of commodities. The weights depend on price deviations from long-term averages. The result is extra returns from holding a diverse portfolio of assets while lowering volatility of returns.

THE GARDNER MACROINDEX® (GEMI®)

Another new index that was launched on April 1, 2005, is Swiss-based Gardner Finance's Gardner Energy MacroIndex® (www.macroindex.com). This is a forward-looking index that unites all relevant developments within the international energy industry. With the ever-rising need to a proper exposure in the global energy industry, the Gardner Energy MacroIndex® (GEMI®) provides a broad exposure into all energy sectors. The purpose of the index is to present a macro view on global energy markets by looking at the performance of selected investment vehicles belonging to the investment class, "Energy Funds." Objective criteria, arranged in a proprietary selection matrix, are applied in selecting the energy funds to be included in the index as components. The performance of the components forms the index performance and is used as a basis for monthly calculations of the index value.

The index components represent a careful hypothetical investment in the investment class, "Energy Funds," to make it suitable for use as a benchmark by investors in international energy markets. Prior to inclusion in the index, all potential index components must undergo a standardized quantitative and qualitative analysis, which also serves to achieve a high level of consistency of the index composition through continuity of included index components.

These index criteria include the following components:

Components	Minimum 20 components.
Sector components	Minimum three per sector, whereby one component may belong to more than one sector.
Volume	90% or more of components must manage at least US$10 million (based on index value).
Audit	90% or more of components must have an annual audit (based on index value).
Redemptions	80% or more of components must allow redemptions at least on a quarterly basis.
Notice period	75% or more of components must offer a maximum notice period of 90 days.
Reporting (e)	Estimated monthly net asset value must be reported within 10 business days.
Reporting (c)	Confirmed monthly net asset value must be reported within 20 business days.
Quantitative	Measurement of average gain, standard deviation (ann.), downside deviation, Sharpe ratio, skewness and Kurtosis.

Quantitative	Assessment of personnel and organization, security, conflicts, execution, administration, research and data, and IT.
Transparency	Assessment of process, valuation, risk, position, operational, liquidity, fees, and expenses.

Any component must reach a minimum rating of category 3, out of a scale of 1 to 6, or above at the time of evaluation and inclusion in the index. Category evaluation is based on the quantitative and qualitative drivers of the index criteria.

The suitability of a component for inclusion in the index is assessed on the basis of both strategy-inherent risk and market-inherent risk. At any time, at least 90% of the total index value must consist of components that fall into strategy- and market-inherent risk, categories 1 and 2. Strategy-inherent risk is the risk level a component is prepared to assume by choosing a certain strategy (investment behavior, average and maximum leverage, liquidity of underlying investments and securities, and risk tolerance). Market-inherent risk is the level of future-oriented risk of the market environment in light of the investment behavior of any component (volatility within the investment universe, structure of market participants, market correlation, and future development scenarios).

The index categories includes energy exploration and development (Sector 1); refining, processing mining, and chemicals (Sector 2); pipeline and transportation (Sector 3); generation and storage (Sector 4); and utilities and energy products trading (Sector 5).

ROGERS INTERNATIONAL COMMODITY INDEX

An additional commodity index worth mentioning because of its tie to a particular hedge fund is the Rogers International commodity index (RICI). This index represents the value of a compendium (or "basket") of commodities employed in the global economy, ranging from agricultural products (such as wheat, corn, and cotton) and energy products (including crude oil, gasoline, and natural gas), to metals and minerals (including gold, silver, aluminum, and lead). The value of each component is based on monthly closing prices of the corresponding futures and/or forward contracts, each of which is valued as part of a fixed-weight portfolio. Near-month contracts on international commodity markets are employed to the best extent possible. The selection and weighting of the portfolio is reviewed not less than annually, and weights are assigned in the December preceding the start of each New Year.

The index was developed by Jim Rogers to be an effective measure of the price action of raw materials on a worldwide basis. The broad-based representation of commodities contracts is intended to provide two important characteristics: the large number of contracts and underlying raw materials represents "diversification," and the global coverage of those contracts reflects the current state of international trade and commerce. Accordingly, in many cases, allocation of a portion of an investment portfolio in a product based on the RICI may reduce overall volatility while providing the opportunity to profit, assuming the continued growth of the global economy and that such growth translates into higher prices for those commodities.

RICI is based on monthly closing prices of a fixed-weight portfolio of the nearby futures and forwards contract month of international commodity markets. The selection and weighting of the portfolio is reviewed annually and weights assigned in the December preceding the start of a new year. If a commodity is traded on more than one exchange, the most liquid, in terms of volume and open interest combined, it is included in the RICI. For example, silver is traded at the New York Commodity Exchange, the CBOT and the Mid-America Commodity Exchange. The largest volume and open interest is consistently transacted at the New York Commodity Exchange; consequently, this contract represents silver in the RICI at the exclusion of the contracts at the CBOT and the Mid-America Commodity Exchange.

In March 2004, Rogers announced a new hedge fund devoted to commodity futures. The Diapason Rogers commodity index fund is a joint venture with Switzerland-based hedge fund manager Equinoxe Partners, and it will be based on the Roger's commodity.

INDICES' RELATIONSHIP TO HEDGE FUND TRADING

Commodities as an Asset Class

As the world markets continue their evolution toward one global market-place, the advent of financial futures trading has had much to do with that unification. The popularity of financial futures has removed some of the stigmas and fears that were associated with the perceived rough and tumble world of commodities. Previously, commodity futures were considered too risky for investors looking for the stability associated with a traditionally diversified portfolio. But now, with money managers searching the globe for additional investment opportunities, commodities have fallen under the spotlight. The advantages of asset diversification have uncovered this area of investment as the newest tool that will enable investors to better evaluate their long-term exposure to the up and down movements inherent in today's markets. By allocating a portion of their investment dollars to commodities, investors are better able to obtain desirable long-term results while at the same time lowering the volatility of their portfolio. This asset diversification play is very popular with energy hedge funds.

Diversification into commodities allows the portfolio to attain a more balanced inventory of assets. Whether or not high levels of inflation resurface, the allocation of a percentage of investable funds into an asset that will successfully lower the overall volatility of a portfolio, while improving the annual performance, is every investor's goal. The counter-cyclic nature of commodities to financial assets makes commodities an ideal asset class to incorporate into a portfolio to achieve a more desirable return scenario. Should inflation remain under control, the commodity portion of a properly allocated portfolio may lag behind other asset classes, but that lag normally indicates that the other non-commodity assets performed well. This is historically true because low to moderate inflationary periods allow for the stable environment in which traditional financial assets have performed well. In such a case, the commodity allocation would have served its purpose as a counter-cyclic asset to the rest of the portfolio. It also provides a hedge against political instability and natural disasters that may adversely affect existing supply–demand alliances.

Many investors looking to commodities as a hedge against other held assets are not so much concerned with commodity prices rising, but with commodity prices rising quickly. Large upward spikes in commodity prices may send investors scrambling to insulate their portfolio against the possible inflationary ramifications associated with such a move. Trading indexes are a natural way to diversify risk.

The "idea" of indexes for managed futures began with Commodity Research Bureau's commodity index and now the GSCI®. The index idea for managed futures was originated by Mount Lucas Investment Management in the 1980s, which created the MLM index. It was the first index that included both long and short positions in commodities. Their intention was to emulate an investment in managed futures and to teach institutional investors the value of adding managed futures to their portfolios. The presentation proved that managed futures were an excellent inclusion in a traditional portfolio. Rightfully so, the MLM index was not presented or used as a benchmark.

As the managed futures industry grew, various sectors and style indexes grew. Sector indexes include energy, stock index, diversified, and grain traders. Style indexes might be systematic or fundamental traders. These indexes include the past performance data of traders in a database, which are categorized. The indexes are "erroneously believed" to be valuable benchmarks for determining CTA performance.

Commodities have demonstrated a low historic correlation with stocks, bonds, and positive returns over time. Including commodities in a traditional investment portfolio may increase diversification and reduce overall portfolio risk. During the 1990s, they had fallen out of favor with investors as stocks and bonds offered more attractive returns and less risk.

Since commodities lack a straightforward measure of valuation, they often give investors a pause to consider investments in this sector. Commodity consumers and producers can make assumptions and estimate returns from an integrated business plan, but commodities investors ideally desire some indication of value. How can a value metric be derived from a commodity price?

In effect, the futures markets connect investors to the commodity business, serving as a clearing house for risk. Futures investors can earn returns from backwardation (a phenomenon whereby the spot price is greater than the futures price), which has, over time, contributed 1.9% to the annualized return of the GSCI®. But backwardation does not have a one-to-one association with price, as does the yield on stocks or bonds, and its magnitude provides little guidance to spot-price cheapness. Instead, commodity prices lend themselves to more conceptual valuation tools.

Commodity-linked derivative instruments, including structured notes and swap agreements linked to a commodity index, are designed to provide investors with exposure to the investment returns of real assets that trade in the commodities market without direct investment in physical commodities. Commodity-linked investments can provide portfolio diversification and a hedge against inflation because commodities and commodity-linked investments have historically demonstrated a negative correlation to stocks and bonds and a positive correlation to inflation.

Today, commodities are back in favor. Since the second half of 2004, we have seen more dedicated commodities funds being established, which has continued to the present and is now ramping up globally. We have also seen more macro, broader funds allocating risk capital to the commodity sector. While commodities tend to follow economic cycles, as well as long boom and bust cycles, the cycle is now on the upswing with energy dominating as more money can be absorbed into the sector than metals or agricultural commodities.

Goldman's futures-oriented index is the primary commodity index used to trade the energy complex, and is definitely the primary vehicle for investment as it heavily follows the futures markets. New products are also being introduced, such as more and smaller managed futures accounts for small investors and institutions to invest in commodities. It is estimated that $20 billion is invested in the index, not including hedge fund money.

EXCHANGE TRADED FUNDS (ETFs)

ETFs are becoming increasingly popular as investment vehicles. Many firms have filed applications for active ETFs with the US SEC, but don't expect these to trade on exchange anytime soon, due to regulatory review, money manager scrutiny. In the four years since the SEC has sought comments on actively managed ETFs, nothing has been launched. However, the market activity is there as index fund tracking also continues to grow. We expect actively managed ETFs to gain market acceptance for both the energy and environmental sectors in coming years, as the investment appetite in this sector appears insatiable.

There is some confusion that ETFs look like conventional index funds, but there are differences. An ETF is an investment vehicle that typically trades a stock market or other index and trades on an exchange. Indexes don't trade on exchanges. ETFs usually have lower expenses than actively managed funds and traditional index funds. A commission is paid to buy or sell an ETF, as an ETF can be bought and sold daily on an exchange. Index funds are bought and sold on NAV, which is usually calculated daily after the close of trading. For energy, we foresee many more ETFs and some more indexes launched in the coming years, including green or environmental indexes and ETFs.

WHAT'S COMING UP

Investors interested in participating in the emerging and environment hedge fund play should consider indexes. Besides the ones mentioned in this chapter, we foresee green financial indexes becoming increasingly popular in coming years, as well as green MLPs for biomass energy, and green and more energy ETFs. As the funds become more established in this sector, we will see a plethora of energy and environmental financial products to capture investor interest in both passive and active ways.

CHAPTER 11

A Five-year Bull Market in Energy?

In October 2005 we saw a general retreat in oil prices and energy equities. As might be expected, that brought out the bears in droves, anxious to explain why the bull market in energy was over. The problem is that so many of these voices speak with a lack of knowledge about energy and/or they have their own axe to grind. We, on the other hand, expect the bull market in energy to continue for some time to come, simply because *nothing significant* has fundamentally changed in the energy arena at all! As we have demonstrated in this book, the current hot energy market is about a long-term lack of investment in the industries' infrastructure that has resulted in supply–demand tightness in energy markets. At the time of writing, nothing has occurred to significantly change that dynamic.

For the last two decades, with the exception of short Middle Eastern wars, energy prices have moved sideways within a relatively predictable range. Because of this, many were lulled into a false sense of security, and both the analysts and experts got lazy as well. People who have a memory of energy markets before the "sideways drift" are today in their forties or older; and many have simply left the industry altogether. There are very few of us around that can recall anything but cheap energy and fairly predicable price movements. There is still a comfort zone issue at play here – there is a desire for energy markets to exhibit mean reversion and for all the issues to simply disappear again. Unfortunately, that isn't going to happen and, in this chapter, we will show why and demonstrate that energy will remain a hot investment sector for some time to come.

THE FUTURE OF ENERGY SUPPLY AND DEMAND

There are numerous good sources of information for the interested investor regarding energy supply and demand, including the *BP Statistical Review of World Energy*,[1] published annually and the statistics available on websites such as the International Energy Agency (IEA), and the US Energy Information Administration (EIA), among others. There are always inaccuracies in the absolute data, but, in general, the trends in the data reported by the various agencies and institutions are all the same. They all show that there is supply–demand tightness in almost all energy commodity markets.

According to the BP (2005) review, last published in June 2005 for the year 2004, primary energy consumption increased globally by 4.3% in 2004, led by an 8.9% rise in the Asia Pacific region.[2] But what is more interesting is that the growth in consumption impacted on all sources of energy, including oil (up 3.4%), coal (up 6.3%), natural gas (up 3.3%), and electric power (up around 5%). Data from the IEA from a report issued in April 2005 was forecasting world oil demand to increase by 2.1% over 2004.[3] Other forecasts call for growth rates of around 2.5% through 2005 and 2006, and, since that IEA report was issued, Chinese economic growth has again increased.

Crude Oil

Worldwide oil demand is projected to grow at an annual average of 2.1 million barrels per day in 2005 and 2006, representing a 2.5% annual average growth rate, compared with a 3.2% growth in 2004. Chinese demand growth, which averaged about one million barrels per day in 2004, is projected to be slower, but still strong at an annual average of 600,000 barrels per day in 2005 and 2006. In 2004 Chinese oil consumption rose 15.8% year over year, consuming 8.2% of annual world crude output. Only the United States ranks higher, using up a 25% share of world output, but US demand growth in 2004 was a more moderate 2.8%.[4]

As a result of the increasingly high prices seen for crude oil these last two years, there has been much talk of demand destruction having a downward impact on these forecasts. The reality is that, to date, there has been little or no demand destruction – even as gasoline prices peaked at around $3 per gallon after the hurricanes of 2005 in the United States, gasoline demand only slightly dipped off of demand for the same period the year before. Why? One of the reasons is the relative weakness of the US dollar in which oil is priced. The real price of oil has not risen as dramatically for many in the world because of US dollar weakness. But perhaps the most significant reasons are twofold. First, the price of oil (and for that matter energy in general), when allowing for inflation, is still relatively cheap and has still not approached its historical highs (see Figure 11.1); and second, the surge in demand throughout Asia in particular is driving global competition for supply.

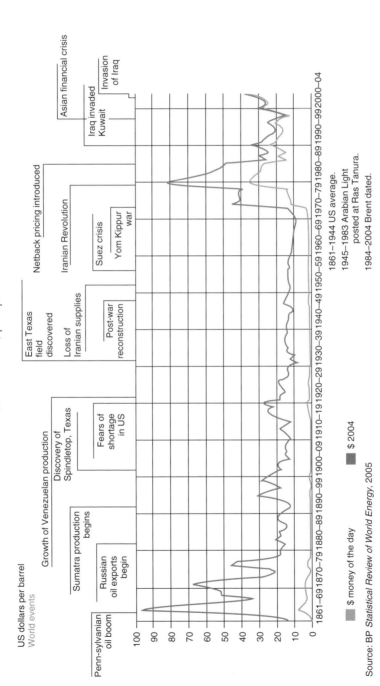

FIGURE 11.1   US$ price per barrel of oil

Source: BP *Statistical Review of World Energy*, 2005

Talk of demand destruction to date is just talk. That is not to suggest that some demand destruction will not occur over the next few years – just that demand destruction is already being overestimated by those who wish for a return to the past where everything was orderly and history was a predictor of things to come. Over time, we will see fuel replacement and increased efficiency as a natural response to higher prices. However, at the rate that China and India are growing, and will continue to grow (particularly in terms of fuel-users like automobiles), much of that demand destruction in the Western world will be more than compensated for through increased demand from Asia, which accounted for 49% of global demand growth in 2004 according to the IEA.[5]

So what is happening on the supply side of the equation for oil? During late 2004 and progressively through 2005, we have seen an acceleration of exploration activities in all regions of the world. While it is true that very few giant fields have been discovered in the last two decades and that the oil majors have dramatically failed to replace reserves on an annual basis, the honest assessment is that they haven't really been looking to do so. Besides, it is the independent side of the E&P business that most often leads the surge in terms of new exploration, and that has certainly proven to be true this time around. Recently, of course, the oil majors have finally woken up and they have announced extensions to exploration budgets for 2006. One thing that most analysts agree on is that OPEC currently has little spare capacity to bring to the market and it is only Saudi Arabia that has spare capacity (see Figures 11.2 and 11.3). Consistent levels of Iraqi oil supply still seem to be problematic, too.

So far this year, there has been a steady stream of new discoveries, discovery extensions, and projects to extract more oil from existing reservoirs. This will continue.

FIGURE 11.2   World oil spare production capacity according to the EIA

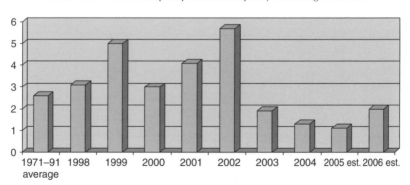

Source: Short-term Outlook, November 2005, EIA

FIGURE 11.3 OPEC spare capacity trends

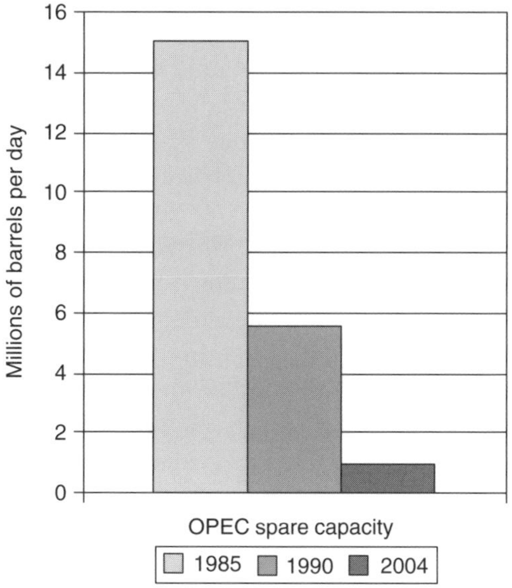

OPEC spare capacity

☐ 1985 ☐ 1990 ■ 2004

Source: Rice University/*The Economist*

As pointed out in November of 2005 in a speech by Lord John Browne, CEO of BP, "there remain plenty of new opportunities for exploration and production, pointing to recently discovered oil and gas deposits in the Caspian Sea, Angola, Russia, and here in the US from the deepwater of the Gulf of Mexico." He added, "Across the industry, investment which has gone in over a period of years is leading to new production. And beyond those projects which are already under way there is more to come – not least here in the US, the development of gas in the Rockies, where we announced a $2 billion investment plan a few weeks ago, and the major long-term development of the 35 trillion cubic feet (tcf) of natural gas in Alaska, which will add a whole new source of supply to the US market."[6]

There are new conventional reserves being discovered at a more rapid pace because we are now looking harder for that oil and gas. Oil companies have woken up to their renewed opportunity after 15 years of drawing down their reserves and handing earnings back to shareholders to appease Wall St., the latest being ChevronTexaco, which announced in December 2005 that it would hand back several billion dollars. Of course, this will disappoint hard core "peak oil" theorists, who are right about energy prices but for the wrong reason! Peak oil is yet some distance off and the truth of the matter is that there is still plenty of oil. In fact, BP reports that the world's reserves to production ratio for crude oil fell to 40.5 years in 2004, down from 43.3 years in 2002, although reserves have continued to increase and are 17% higher than 1994, while production is 20% higher.[7]

Additional sources of non-conventional oil supply are also attracting interest and action. Canadian tar sands now produce a growing proportion of Canada's oil. The Athabasca oil sands of northern Alberta are thought to hold about 870 billion to 1.3 trillion barrels of oil (an amount equal to or greater than all of the conventional oil extracted to date). Also, recent improvements in mining and extraction techniques have cut heavy oil production costs nearly in half since the 1980s, to about $10 per barrel. Shell and ChevronTexaco jointly opened the $5.7 billion Athabasca Oil Sands Project in Alberta recently, and pump out 155,000 barrels per day. Last year, Suncor shipped 77 million barrels of its Syncrude Sweet Blend out of Canada, too. Production of the tar sands is over one million barrels per day now and may rise to three to five million barrels per day in the coming years. Meanwhile, Venezuela's Orinoco Belt (which has similar heavy crude reserves of 272 billion barrels) yields 500,000 barrels daily, and that number should spike when a new ChevronTexaco plant goes online.

Further in the future are the oil shale deposits. Such shales occur in many parts of the world and total world resources of oil shale are conservatively estimated at 2.6 trillion barrels. However, oil shale production is expensive because of the additional costs of mining and extracting the energy. Even worse, it has tremendous environmental issues associated with it. Because of these higher costs, only a few deposits of oil shale are currently being exploited in China, Brazil, and Estonia. With oil prices at high levels and declining crude oil production in most areas, some investors are taking another look at the huge volume of potentially recoverable hydrocarbons in vast oil shale deposits (particularly in the western United States); however, any significant production is a long way off.

At issue with respect to oil supply–demand is that early in 2005 there was considerable supply tightness. We have heard from our sources that excess supply might have been as little as 500,000 barrels per day, although the EIA suggests higher than that (see Figure 11.2). Through 2005, that excess supply has been steadily, but slowly, growing, and we believe that there will continue to be a slow but steady growth in excess oil supply over the next few years. Certainly, any larger discoveries that are made now will take several years to work their way through into the supply side. Furthermore, while we are observing high rig utilization rates and other indicators of higher exploration activities, there is still a skills and equipment shortage issue that will act as a short-term cap on activity levels. As a result, we expect to see no mean reversion in oil prices and sustained higher prices for several years to come. Because of that supply–demand tightness in oil markets, especially when combined with tightness in transportation capacity such as tankers, oil markets will also continue to be very volatile. Any unexpected event that disrupts supply and/or any move in oil stocks will be interpreted by the market and will effect price movements.

Natural Gas

Natural gas is a somewhat similar story, but one must also consider that natural gas markets are quite regional. New pipeline developments and the prospect for LNG transportation is gradually changing natural gas into a more global market; nonetheless, it is still about regional supply–demand issues. By far the largest natural gas reserves are located in the Middle East and Eurasia, while some of the largest markets for gas are in Western Europe and North America.

The issue of regional supply–demand tightness is best exemplified by the United Kingdom. For many years the North Sea had meant that it was self-sufficient, but gas production has since peaked and fallen off very rapidly. Despite a rush to build new pipelines and LNG terminals, the United Kingdom faces natural gas shortages again during the winter of 2005–2006. Ironically, analysts predict that in just a few years, the United Kingdom could once again be awash in natural gas as the infrastructure gets put in place. Similarly, from 1986 to 2001 Canada's natural gas production more than doubled, and much of that natural gas was exported to the United States. But since 2001, Canada's natural gas production has flattened and begun to decline, with the result that natural gas prices in the United States have reached high levels each winter. The regional nature of natural gas can be even more complex, due to pipeline capacity issues and swift weather changes causing demand to spike and supply to lag in various locations during the winter.

Again, exploration activities have picked up over the last 18 months, led by the independents and, more recently, some of the major oil companies, who have announced substantial exploration programs targeting natural gas reserves in North America. For example, BP has committed $2.2 billion to double production from its acreage in Wyoming, which will include drilling 2,000 wells over the next 15 years. According to EIA, the United States replaced 118% of dry gas production in 2004, but mainly through existing field extensions, not through new discoveries.[8] The problem is that the cost of finding new natural gas reserves has increased considerably as it has become harder to find new deposits. The Ziff Energy Group recently reported that the cost of exploiting natural gas jumped 34% from 1999 to 2002 in the Permian basin.[9] Past exploration activities in the United States have actually not had much impact on natural gas production either (see Figure 11.4). So, if new natural gas reserves in the United States are becoming harder and more costly to find, where will its future supplies come from?

Many in the industry believe that it will be imported in the form of LNG. While there will be LNG imports into the United States, there are a number of issues that we think will mean that the LNG supply will be much less and much later than many like to believe. First, LNG is not new and there has been lots of excitement about it in the past that resulted in very little, largely due to environmental and siting issues. We think that environmentalism is still a large and underestimated factor and that NIMBYism (not in my backyard) will effectively stop any real LNG facility development almost anywhere except the US Gulf Coast. It will certainly delay the process indefinitely. Second, the global market for LNG cargoes is competitive and more LNG vessels will have to be built. The impact is that LNG may prove to be more costly than thought in the near-term and not as easy to import either. LNG may or may not be the answer to the US natural gas issue, and it certainly won't help significantly supplement supply in the next few years.

Other potential sources of natural gas include coal bed methane and coal gasification. There are thought to be tremendous reserves of coal bed methane around the world and the United States produced 1.72 TCF in 2004 of coal bed methane.[10] China is also looking to exploit its huge coal reserves for the gas, and a significant project is underway

FIGURE 11.4   US natural gas production and exploration activity

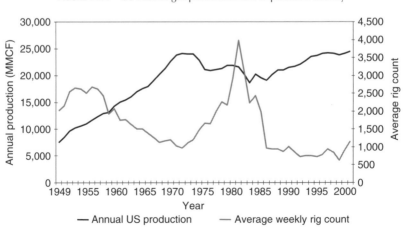

between Texaco and a Chinese company to extract 60 billion cubic meters of methane resources in east China's Anhui Province. Coal gasification is a process for converting coal partially or completely to combustible gases. After purification, these gases – carbon monoxide, carbon dioxide, hydrogen, methane, and nitrogen – can be used as fuels or as raw materials for chemical or fertilizer manufacture. New coal gasification technologies are highly efficient and use less coal to produce the same amount of energy. Since the CO_2 can also be scrubbed from the gas before its use, the technology also has some potential environmental benefits, including carbon sequestration efforts that are now underway to reduce carbon dioxide emissions.

We expect to see continuing supply–demand tightness in regional natural gas markets over the next few years, related to local supply, transportation capacity, and weather trends. Demand for natural gas has recently been substantially driven by its use to generate electricity, since only a few years ago it was a relatively clean and cheap fuel. BP[11] estimated the world reserves to production ratio for natural gas at 66.7 years in 2004, but production rates are 28% higher since 1994 as compared to a 26% increase in reserves over the same period.

Coal

Like other commodities, the price of coal has soared in the last two years and so has price volatility. Over this period, China has turned from exporter to importer of coal (in 2004, China accounted for 75% of global consumption growth according to BP[12]), and coal has remained cheaper and more efficient in power generation than other fuels. This demand has resulted in supply–demand tightness in the world's coal markets. Yet there are tremendous reserves of coal and the United States has often been labeled the "Saudi Arabia" of coal! Unfortunately, not all coal is created equal. It comes in various qualities, and quality is important both from an energy conversion perspective, as well as from an environmental point of view. The fact is that, in the United States, high-quality coal (low sulfur, high btu content) is becoming scarcer, and it is found only in certain regions, meaning it has to be transported elsewhere. Quality issues cannot be underestimated as a complexity factor in global coal markets. Nevertheless, prices for high btu, low-sulfur eastern United States coals doubled in 2004.

Issues impacting on coal prices outside of quality include growing electricity demand, declining coal stockpiles, rising natural gas prices, new coal-fired generation construction, and increased costs of transport. However, new coal reserves can be brought to market faster than other commodities, and supply constraints may ease a little through 2006 and beyond. More importantly, much of this coal supply will need to be gasified in coming years as higher coal burning by US utilities during 2004 and 2005 has caused emissions credit prices to reach an all-time high of $1,600 per ton. It is also an area of increased hedge fund activity as we discussed in Chapter 7.

Electric Power

By their very nature, electric power markets are regional. Electricity is real-time and has to be produced to meet demand as it happens, and moving electricity through lengthy grids is inefficient and wasteful. Demand is increasing worldwide for electric power related to population growth, increased urbanization, and increasing industrial output and mechanization. Today, much of the world still does not have access to reliable power supplies. As that portion of the population increasingly gains access to the devices that the West has increasingly come to rely on – such as TVs, computers, cell phones, and household appliances – the demand for electricity will grow. Since electric power is invariably produced using fossil fuels, China and Asia are again in the spotlight (see Figure 11.5) and, in part, it is this demand that is contributing to the demand for those fossil fuels.[13]

Once again, a significant reason behind the supply–demand tightness in regional markets for electric power is simply a lack of historical investment.

FIGURE 11.5   Electric power industry plant-level expenditures for China ($ billion)

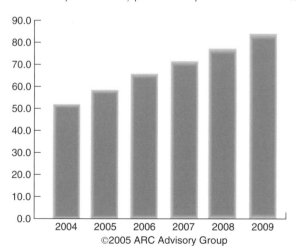

©2005 ARC Advisory Group

The August 2003 US black out, more than anything else, has focused attention on supply reliability and on the lack of investment in the North American power infrastructure.

There are, however, other renewable sources of electricity, including hydroelectric generation, wind, solar, tidal, geothermal, and biomass. About $30 billion was invested worldwide in renewable energy, excluding hydroelectricity. Renewable power capacity is now 160 gigawatts, or about 4% of the global power sector capacity according to the Renewable Energy Policy Network,[14] while large hydropower is around 16%. Many of these technologies are becoming more efficient, more affordable, and they are increasingly being adopted. Today, electric utilities have oversubscribed green power programs, and most recently, we now have global equipment shortages for wind turbines, silicon for photovoltaic energy, and heat exchangers for geothermal energy. Investors and hedge funds have become increasingly interested in trading the environmental attributes of renewal energy. It also has an additional benefit of less carbon dioxide emissions through the new technology used to generate green power. We think that the conservative estimates for renewable energy issued by large institutions such as the IEA, EIA, and the World Bank underestimate the global nature of the new demand for green power throughout the world. In fact, consumers will pay more for green energy. Finally, increased interest in nuclear generation is also apparent, although it has significant environmental and other dangers associated with it. But, this is having a knock-on effect on uranium prices.

As environmental issues translate into more public policy and demand for "green" energy, we expect to see an upsurge in investment in these areas. Energy and environment are inescapably interlinked, and the environment is the next phase of the bull market in energy. We think that environment actually will become a more disruptive factor in energy markets in coming years, as it impacts on costs along the entire energy value chain. Today, only a small number of green hedge funds have entered the markets, but institutional investors, family office, and social responsible investors are becoming very interested in investing in this sector.

Refined Products

Nowhere is the lack of investment in energy over the last two decades or so more readily apparent than in the refining segment of the industry. No new refinery has been built in the United States since 1976, and the over-concentration of refining capacity on the Gulf Coast became apparent to everyone after the hurricanes of 2005 severely damaged some refineries.

Refineries are complex and dangerous, requiring preventative, periodic maintenance, and constant upgrading, as well as seasonal configuration. They are subject to all kinds of environmental, health and safety regulation, and in the past margins have been thin. No one wants a new refinery sited near them.

Over the last 18 months, however, something has changed in the downstream segment of the industry, especially in the United States, as demand has reached levels close to capacity. This can be seen in refinery utilization rates, which at times in this last year have been operating at levels close to the maximum (see Figure 11.6), and also in the profitability of downstream operations, which has gone up significantly in line with crack spreads.

From a gasoline perspective the complexity of different grades and formulations, both geographic and seasonal, means that there is some truth in OPEC and others' views that the refining bottlenecks are partly responsible for higher oil and products prices. What good is producing more oil if that oil cannot be turned into usable products? Refineries are mostly sited close to markets, as opposed to the source of oil requiring a constant stream of supply to be brought to the facility. In the United States particularly, the industry is running close to capacity without much

FIGURE 11.6 Refining utilization rates

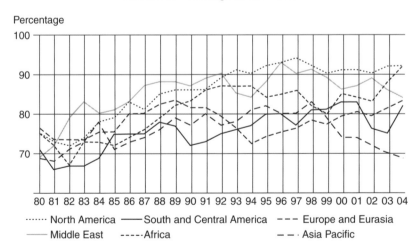

Note: World refinery throughputs increased sharply in 2004 in response to very strong demand growth. The largest increases were in the Asia Pacific. Europe, and Eurasia, and South and Central America. As a result, global average refinery utilization increased to 87%, the highest level for at least 25 years.

Source: BP *Statistical Review of World Energy*, 2005

prospect of significant new capacity being added in the future. The ever-increasing demand for gasoline in the United States (consumption rose 2.1% according to BP in 2004[15]) means that gasoline prices will likely remain higher and more volatile, but China's gasoline consumption was only about one-tenth of that of the United States in 2004. As Chinese consumers increasingly seek to buy automobiles, that consumption is set to rise aggressively, too.

In the refining segment, we expect regional supply–demand tightness to continue. This drove up European fuel oil prices earlier this year and US gasoline prices, as discussed above. Without new refining capacity in the United States, nothing will change in the fundamentals unless the price of oil recedes. Refiners should continue to do better from a profitability standpoint than they have done historically. From the US standpoint, relief from the current tight capacity situation might only be brought about by new CAFÉ (Corporate Fuel Economy) standards for automobile fuel consumption rates, along with a move on the part of consumers away from SUVs toward more gasoline-efficient vehicles. Recent announcements of US capacity upgrades will not be sufficient to meet rising demand in this area.

Other Energy-related Commodities

The bull market in energy and commodities has also extended to a variety of other commodities, including uranium; steel; sugar; and emissions such as CO_2, NOx, and SO_2. Uranium in particular has become a recent hedge fund play as nuclear power plant requirements have outstripped current mining production without a single new reactor being built. Current worldwide production is more than 80 million pounds, but demand is running at an annual deficit of 60 million pounds.[16] As a result, prices have gone up. The driving force behind that demand is nuclear power generation and as electric power demand goes up (two billion people still have no access to electric power), it will continue to grow. Furthermore, nuclear power is again in focus as a source of relatively clean electric power. At least 30 new reactors are planned in various countries, and the International Atomic Energy Agency predicts that some 60 new reactors will be built over the next 15 years.

Steel prices have also risen over the last several years, and may continue to do so, reflecting increased energy costs. Sugar used to make ethanol as a gasoline substitute is another energy-related commodity that will increasingly be impacted on by the current energy issues.

ENVIRONMENT – THE NEXT WRINKLE IN ENERGY MARKETS

It is our thesis that the confluence of energy and environment will potentially prolong the energy bull market and eventually the environment will become the next primary opportunity for investors. There are a number of reasons for this. First, as we have stated, increasing environmental regulations and concerns on the part of consumers are driving increased costs and complexity. Moreover, it also makes it increasingly difficult to site energy facilities and in some cases to undertake exploration activities. We think that these environmental issues will also impact on the United States' ability to build LNG terminals, impacting on natural gas supplies. In fact, the environment will rise as the dominant factor, driving energy markets over the next 10 years. It will influence price formation and already it is in electric power markets to a degree it never was before with SO_2 emissions credits reaching $1,600 per ton when they normally traded at most $225 per ton. Once again, no expected mean price reversion here.

We have also seen the rise of global carbon dioxide markets during 2006, led by the European Union. Carbon is the new gold, and there have been predictions that it may be the largest commodity market ever, reaching $3 trillion in notional value in 20 years. But more obviously, we see that carbon market developments emulate oil market developments. Oil today is a fungible global commodity. Carbon is becoming one, as a metric ton of carbon can be traded anywhere. Price arbitrage opportunities are also rising everywhere; not only Europe, but Canada, Japan, the United States, Australia, and recently China are developing carbon trading markets as well. Hedge funds are instrumental in many of these efforts, particularly in the European Union, where they both trade and finance carbon funds.

Turning to green finance, there are now efforts to monetize streams of carbon credits, as well as renewable energy credits in project finance for renewable energy. A renewable power project will last 20 to 40 years and thus a stream of credits is created that can be monetized and also traded in the markets. Hedge funds have stepped up activities in these markets, not only for renewable power but also for ethanol and biofuels. These two new cleaner fuels also have credit trading dimensions to them.

Finally, we are seeing the beginning of alternative energy hedge funds that are focused on the over-325 market caps in the alternative energy space. Several new funds have formed during 2005 to trade long/short equities for the wind, solar, battery, fuel cell, flywheel, and biomass companies listed on stock exchanges.

The next market play for many of these hedge funds will be in trading water equities and water as a commodity. We have learned that several funds are in formation to trade water rights in the United States and Israel.

WHAT DOES THIS ALL MEAN FOR INVESTORS?

The bull market for energy will continue for some time to come. We don't know how long it will last, but the industry fundamentals have not changed, and when one factors in the environmental issues and opportunities, we see the tremendous investment opportunities lasting longer than many might expect. To us, this means that if you think you are late in energy as an investment opportunity, you are probably wrong. However, that doesn't mean that some of the early returns can be repeated, just that energy and environment can still provide superior returns, as compared to other more traditional opportunities. It also means looking and working a little harder for those returns.

What has been the hardest obstacle for many energy analysts and investors to comprehend is that it is different this time. Most energy companies and governments have continued to look backward and wait for the expected mean price reversion to lower energy prices. They saw that happen with the price crashes of 1986 and 1998, and expect it again. It has not occurred and it will not this time. There is no surplus supply cushion this time in these demand-driven markets. As the fourth quarter 2005 ends, the profit picture should close substantially higher for energy companies, and the perception may change to one of this being the greatest energy bull market of all time. Global energy demand continues to rise and global refining capacity surpluses are almost exhausted, leading to a summer of greater highs due to capacity tightness. While it may be buyer beware, savvy investors know a good thing when they see one. Energy is that new asset class.

Energy Commodities

There are many conflicting views on where energy commodity prices might be headed. Some are still looking for mean reversion, while others foresee extortionate highs in the near future as the production of oil peaks and will no longer keep up with demand. We look for sustained higher and more volatile energy commodity prices for several years as a result of global and regional supply–demand tightness. This means that simple trend-following strategies might not produce the returns that have been seen over the last two years as prices moved in one direction – up. Certainly, there will be directional opportunities in different commodities and markets, but not like the one we have just experienced. Instead, we expect to see an increase in various spread and arbitrage strategies to make money in energy commodities. The volatility that we have experienced in the commodity markets will remain for some time to come. To us, this also means that hedge funds will have to work harder to make profits and that their strategies will need to pay off in both up and down markets.

Today, the funds have arrived. Funds like to "move money in and move money out." However, what they are missing is that there are now fewer trading opportunities for that type of trading; and second, that there are greater risks in the market because they have arrived to trade. The funds often lack knowledge and experience in energy markets. Energy trading is the most volatile and complex of any commodities. These factors bode for more impending energy-trading disasters, and we saw some in 2005 in North American gas markets in the August–October 2005 period, as funds tried to short the market and lost hundreds of millions of dollars when prices spiked due to Hurricane Katrina.

While funds have lower costs of capital and lower overheads, the fear is that some funds are financially unstable due to their very short-term perspective. Hedge funds are primarily organized as private partnerships to provide maximum flexibility in constructing a portfolio. They can take both long and short positions, make concentrated investments, use leverage, use derivatives, and invest in many markets. This is in sharp contrast to mutual funds, which are highly regulated and do not have the same breadth of investment instruments at their disposal. In addition, most hedge fund managers commit a portion of their wealth to the funds in order to align their interest with that of other investors. Thus, the objectives of managers and investors are the same, and the nature of the relationship is one of true partnership. This is quite a bit different from energy traders on the trading desks of banks or energy companies.

This drive for profits in energy trading is also altering the nature of taking risks. Banks are feeling more confident that they can place longer term bets on which way oil and gas prices will go. For example, in the past, power traders have felt comfortable going out only about 18 months into the future. Yet, the longer the contract, the greater the chance to earn revenues on a well-chosen trade. Armed with sophisticated risk management and modeling systems that have been honed in the derivatives markets, banks are pushing out the futures market further into the future. The funds are following this trend.

Even with the recent blow-ups in hedge funds during 2005 – with crude oil options trading, natural gas squeezes, and electric power financial trading failures – we are now hearing or seeing much concern about credit issues, except for some large bank credit analysts. The issue of credit risk and hedge fund performance is rising in importance, but management of hedge fund credit risk is an issue no one wants to talk about in public, including the ratings agencies. Today, Moody's KMV, Fitch and Morningstar are just venturing into rating hedge funds with their announcements to provide these services. Moody's KMV has been working on their own scoring model for hedge funds, as they think the business might suffer from the inability to get position information from hedge funds. They have only rated one energy hedge fund as far as we know. This issue would require both monitoring and a more proactive approach. Once again, the ratings agencies have been slow to react.

As more banks and funds enter energy trading, and try to push the envelope, it is unsurprising that many long-term players view the newcomers with suspicion, arguing that their presence is causing increased volatility. Because funds and banks have made highly leveraged bets that prices will stay at high levels, the argument is that something of an energy bubble has been created. So far, their strategy has appeared to pay off in the present bull market. However, we have seen this all before.

Of course, there are other immature energy commodity markets where there can still be sustained upward price movements, such as for example the downstream side of the business, where chemicals and plastic feed stock markets are more immature and as energy prices in general feed through. But the largest opportunities are likely to be in the emerging emissions and renewable energy markets, as previously discussed. Water is the next logical market extension for hedge fund trading in both equities and as a commodity.

Energy Equities

The October 2005 retreat in energy equities was much larger than the fundamentals warranted, and was as much about market sentiment as anything else. With sustained higher energy prices, the producers of that energy will continue to benefit in terms of revenues and profits. On the other hand, costs in general are rising and will begin to erode margins in the future.

In general, we see good prospects for energy and utility equities. In part, this is related to the ongoing high and volatile energy commodity prices feeding through as profit and increased activity levels spill into other sectors of the industry, such as the oilfield services segment. At the energy industry segment level, there are also some encouraging trends too. For example, we expect and already begin to see a new round of M&A activity as oil majors seek to add reserves by the acquisition of smaller independents. Additionally, we expect to see more IPO activity on the part of smaller E&P firms. On the utilities side, the repeal of PUHCA ought to accelerate M&A activity in that segment too, although there are still issues to sort through.

Greater potential is in the growing sector of energy efficiency technology companies that will see increased maturation in the search for alternative sources of energy and increased energy efficiencies. These companies include wind turbine, solar power, fuel cell, engine technologies, biomass, and biofuels. They are already tracked by a small number of hedge funds and mutual funds today. This activity also extends to traditional energy companies who are also investing more heavily in alternative energy and energy efficiency, such as BP and companies like Suncor who are involved in Canadian tar sand development.

In the midstream segment of the industry there are still the growing numbers of MLPs and Canadian income trusts that should continue to throw off reasonable earnings, as well as display some price appreciation. However, an issue to watch in this segment remains overpaying for assets and reduced profitability as a result. Watch out for the emergence of other forms of MLP, such as green "MLPs" around biomass, for example, as this segment evolves.

As with commodities, we expect to see energy equities display more volatility in the future, since it is increasingly difficult to divorce equity valuations from the underlying energy commodity price movements. Again, hedge funds in this space will need to be able to demonstrate returns in both up and down markets in the future, and we expect to see an increasing emphasis on true long/short strategies and less on long only and long bias. In other words, hedge fund strategies will become more complex and we expect to see more diversified strategies as a result, where the equity funds expose some of their assets beyond just equities into commodities, oil and gas reserves, and other diversification plays.

Recently, we have also observed more interest in innovative strategies and instruments that allow various types of energy companies to use hedge-fund-like structures to raise capital and return profits. For example, in the E&P area there is increasing interest in things like taking working interest ownership in properties and structuring the working interest ownership in a way that accelerates revenues. We also observe an increased interest in investment on the part of hedge funds that looks very like equity or venture capital. In these instances, the lock-up period for investors in the fund is necessarily longer than usual. Now and in the future, there are many energy projects seeking investors at levels too low for the usual providers of capital to be interested and these hybrid hedge/private equity funds fit the bill.

Finally, there are many energy companies and utilities in particular that can be restructured, and we are seeing the beginnings of a trend for hedge funds that specialize in restructuring to view energy and utility companies as an opportunity. By taking a significant equity or debt position in the company, the hedge fund can influence and even demand that restructuring takes place – and in the process make money.

Energy Assets and Debt

The future for investing in energy assets and debt still looks bright, despite the fact that the asking price for assets is increasing in line with the level of interest in them and energy prices. Many of the ex-merchants are still looking to sell off assets as they restructure back to core businesses, and they continue to manage huge debt accumulations.

We have seen an increase in hedge fund activities in the utility restructuring sector and expect that to continue. More importantly, there is an ongoing and urgent need to invest in the industry infrastructure at all levels, including new generation, transmission, and renewable energy projects. Increasingly, hybrid hedge/venture capital/equity funds are playing a role in this investment. We know of at least three funds that are actively seeking energy-specific projects, or looking to take on existing projects, moving forward, one of which is led by an ex-Goldman Sachs partner who has produced 75% returns in the past from this type of project. An interesting aspect of this strategy is that commodity prices can also play a role. For example, any generation project that incorporates long-term natural gas supply contracts can be profitable, based on the value of those contracts alone.

Interestingly, we also see continued potential in the E&P and midstream segments of the industry, where increasingly funds and investors are buying oil and gas reserves, or the assets associated with distributing production such as gas plants and gathering systems. There are so many smaller E&P projects being floated at the moment looking for funding that many are having difficulty finding the funds. This will continue for the next several years.

Environmental Opportunities

The next play for investors will be greener investments in the energy space, as the environmental financial market matures over the next several years. Once again, investment opportunities will be alternative energy equities, environmental companies, green hedge funds, and green MLPs. Emissions trading and renewable energy trading are truly emerging markets, but they are also starting to mature. There is also a need for more investible indexes that are both passive and active as a means for investors to play the green card. We think that the clean technology play should not be underestimated as venues for further investment in alternative energy equities, renewable energy projects, credit and emissions trading, and water.

Other Opportunities

Given today's energy issues, there are innumerable opportunities for investors in energy and energy-related areas. Hedge fund interest in uranium, coal, steel, sugar, and emissions demonstrate this, and it is not just interest in playing the commodity but in investing in the assets and equities of the companies involved.

At the same time, there is a lot of interest in the creation of new commodity indices, new ETFs, and structured products that will allow investors and hedge funds, in particular, to both find new places to put money to work, as well as offer hedging and diversification plays. We know of multiple initiatives in this area that will bear fruit in the coming months and years.

THE FUTURE FOR ENERGY AND ENVIRONMENTAL HEDGE FUNDS

The future for energy and environmental hedge funds looks bright. The fundamentals in energy have not changed. While it may take a little more work to make money, and those returns might not be the spectacular 100% plus that some of the earlier entrants obtained, they will be higher than the average hedge fund.

We are now completing year 2 of the energy hedge fund ramp-up period, and all we see are more energy and environmental hedge funds forming or extending their platform into energy. As we enter year 3, what should an investor look out for? Well, the mantra as always is superior risk-adjusted returns in new investment areas. This book has identified many of these areas. In fact, we can argue that as a diversified investor, your portfolio will under-perform if you do not have energy exposure. In fact, we suggest that it is good to look around the corner for good investment ideas, and that leads us to the emerging environmental financial markets in alternative energy and emissions trading. If you are trend followers, you will miss these opportunities. If you are waiting for traditional hedge fund metrics, you will also miss these opportunities. It may take a "leap of faith," but the extra returns are in market opportunities, not in picking over the bones of overly mature markets as capital crowds out these opportunities. The new funds in energy and environment offer better investment opportunities, and frankly, a new asset class for investors and new approaches for investing. It has less competition, since there are so many entry points in which to participate. In fact, it may make sense to focus on companies not followed by Wall Street. We think that research-oriented hedge funds win in this new environment, and in this instance, investing in the physical energy commodities may be a good bet.

SUMMARY

As we have stated several times in this book, energy is a risky business. It has become even riskier with the advent of more hedge fund trading. As the markets change in many ways, both physical and financial, it requires new strategies to manage risk. Trying to trade these markets with old play-books doesn't work. We now see markets where heating oil trades over gasoline in June, and gas spikes in August, September, and October before the shoulder period (a time of less demand).

There is a rising realization that our energy problems will not be fixed by the recently passed US energy bill, and that energy supply and distribution problems will be with us for a long time. It has taken Wall Street about a year to finally accept that we no longer have mean reversion in oil prices. Or as a trader in London quipped to us during the summer of 2005, "The lows get higher." The reality is very different from the illusion. When the paradigm breaks, not shifts, people run scared. They deny what is obviously in front of them and pretend it's not there.

Our thinking is quite simple. Energy markets don't lie. The run-ups in crude, gasoline, heating oil and natural gas, and other commodities, are harbingers of the future. The energy industry, shell shocked from price crashes in 1986 and 1998, hasn't believed it either. So, it gives back the profits to investors in dividend boosts and stock buy-backs.

Another poor business strategy is to go into US financial electricity markets without physical assets. If Goldman and Bear Stearns both own generation assets, then they must know something. That something is price discovery in illiquid markets and the ability to backstop power trades with physical assets. Several hedge funds ran into this with poorly thought-out strategies and are now down and one is out. The only safe game in town for electricity trading for hedge funds is on the well-established Nord Pool and UK power markets.

This time it's different, and human nature does not accept change. Today's energy markets do not follow traditional seasonality. They are following too many factors to quantify in multi-factor models. Black box trend-following trading ignores "common sense." This is a lacking characteristic of many mechanistic hedge fund managers used to trading the more mature and well-established foreign exchange markets. While the terms in the energy complex such as futures, options, and swaps are the same, the reality is that the energy financial markets are also very physical and complex. They react to underlying supply–demand fundamentals and are complemented by weather risk, as well as other risk factors. But how long will this bull market play last is anyone's guess, since we have never been here before. The "end of oil" cries are plain wrong. We are in not in the twilight of oil, since the cost base has risen and money will further drive production from more high-priced sources globally. But higher prices will also bring at some juncture a "desired" conservation effect. That has not happened to any great degree yet, except anecdotally in the press. But in two years we will have more than ample supply. We are not running out of anything. The price is just higher. Consumers need to accept it and manage their risk better.

Environment is an even more immature financial market that is just now getting traction globally. Green hedge funds are few but many are considering entry into this new field of opportunity in alternative energy, renewable energy trading, and emissions trading. As this takes hold globally, these emerging financial markets will have even more risk to manage as lock-up periods increase and streams of environmental credits are monetized. The monetization of credits through such green finance schemes will jump-start more market liquidity as hedge funds become the new providers of both equity and liquidity in this next emerging market.

We are also beginning to see the emergence of water hedge funds on both the equity side of the equation and the trading side of the house, through the purchase of longer date water rights. Water is another capacity-constrained commodity that hedge funds are delving into, looking for both arbitrage and opportunity. It's a space worth watching as rising environmental concerns push the envelope here. Three billion people in the world do not have access to potable water. That's opportunity.

It has taken more than three years since the collapse of the industry's merchant segment for energy commodities trading markets to recover. Now, with liquidity and market-making provided by a surprising source, energy hedge funds, energy trading is back. It's almost as if energy is the only game in town promising higher returns than world equity markets, due to its continuous price volatility across the energy-trading complex. Oil, gas, power, and coal exhibit tremendous daily and annualized price volatility. This seems to be increasing. The liquidity provided by the hedge funds is evidenced on the front end of the markets, through both NYMEX and IPE oil and gas futures trading, but is much more established in the OTC energy markets. Like the hedge funds themselves, these markets are not regulated, and have a degree of price opaqueness.

However, the current market has new entrants that are not well known. It is not highly levered. It has less investment from high net worth individuals and family office, and will gain more liquidity as the shift to institutional investment gains traction as well. The need will shift to focus on new and emerging managers to gain desired returns. There will need to be increased allocations to hedge funds in the emerging energy and environmental financial markets. Energy and environmental hedge funds are that place, as smaller funds can take advantage of arbitrage opportunities in so-called niche strategies, while larger funds can provide equity for projects, physical assets, debt, and distressed assets, as well as trading. We are already seeing the convergence of hedge funds and private investing in the clean technology segment for example. Diversification into the energy and environmental sector will prove to be a shrewd strategy for hedge fund investors. Traditional asset classes are unlikely to generate enough alpha to meet return expectations. The recurring returns will get their alpha from less-efficient markets such as energy and environment.

It is still early in this round of hedge fund activity in energy as we see the following trading plays:

- energy long/short equities and debt
- equity/commodity
- crude oil futures on exchanges and OTC markets in the United States and Europe
- natural gas futures and OTC markets in the United States
- heating oil (gasoil) futures trading
- gasoline futures trading
- electricity trading
- coal trading
- distressed generation asset plays
- midstream oil and gas acquisitions
- carbon and emissions trading
- alternative energy equities
- renewable energy trading
- ethanol trading.

Of all of these, crude oil dominates trading, as it is the most liquid market. The funds have increased intra-day trading and price volatility accordingly. They have no physical positions to cover so they are pure speculators. This has upset some oil traders and refiners.

Moreover, there are many small hedge funds that are being seeded by later funds. Man Financial and Platinum Partners are the major small fund seeders. We will see how they survive. Energy trading is a business with tremendous risks and reward, but one thing has always been certain: size matters.

The distressed asset play will require much more capital than simply trading energy as it buys iron in the ground. For example, the consortium that formed the $3.65 billion GC Power from Houston-based Centerpoint included The Blackstone Group, Hellman & Friedman, Texas Pacific group, and Kohlberg Kravis Roberts & Co. Texas Genco owned and operated 60 generating units in 11 electric power facilities. They recently flipped that package to NRG for a handsome profit estimated at 500%, with ownership of less than 15 months. With the repeal of the Public Utilities Holding Act (PUHCA) in the new US energy bill, we will see more distressed asset plays and more industry consolidation as barriers to ownership disappear. This change will include foreign hedge fund ownership in US generation assets, as demand will continue to rise in some areas of the 900,000 MW US electric power market, making for an attractive investment opportunity.

The mainstream news reports that the funds "are in" and then that the funds "are out" misjudge and understate the real importance of the entrance of hedge funds into energy trading. While it can be argued by some old-time traders and brokers that we have had commodity pools of managed futures for more than three decades, this misses the point in view of the current scale of the funds' activity. Energy is the flavor of the year. It's in the news everyday and is now seen as a business where money can be put to work. Indeed, the scale of the market shows that it has a steep market maturation process ahead of it. Twenty-six years after the first financial futures contract for energy was launched on the NYMEX, we are still only trading about half of the physical value of the $4 trillion physical energy complex. There is a tremendous opportunity for this market to grow, absorb risk capital, and actually become more volatile.

There are essentially two main types of funds entering energy trading: the macro funds with assets under management, often in excess of $2 billion that now have a proportion of their funds in energy, and the energy-specific funds created to trade energy by ex-merchant energy traders. It is the former, the macro fund traders with black boxes and macro models, that are essentially clueless about the underlying complexity of energy. They follow market trends using black box algorithms, and while so far many have done well in crude oil futures markets, at least one took a bath by shorting the market.

In fact, our research has disturbingly revealed that there may be a good deal of ignorance, and perhaps even some arrogance, on the part of these well-capitalized funds neophytes who are new to energy trading. Such trading and risk management is the most complex, volatile market in the world. Its prices are influenced by weather, geopolitical factors, supply–demand fundamentals, news, and many other factors that cannot be quantified into simple black box algorithms. Many of these funds are quite small and should have modest effects on energy-trading markets.

Meanwhile, the energy-specific funds, often a good deal smaller in terms of assets under management, are frequently founded and led by ex-energy traders. Our research has identified numerous such funds, mostly set up in the recent past. With new energy-specific funds being announced with increasing frequency, this represents an identifiable trend. In general, these funds are not limiting themselves to energy commodities markets, but are using their energy industry knowledge to participate in physical markets and other energy commodities, including electric power and natural gas. In fact, one such fund apparently made its investors around 20% in its first month of operation. This is not the norm.

Plainly, the entrance of hedge funds is re-igniting the energy-trading phenomenon. By increasing liquidity through the introduction of additional risk capital, and by improving the counterparty credit situation with strong balance sheets, the funds are providing the market some positives. However, the lack of detailed physical energy knowledge and reliance on black box models by some in the hedge fund community, combined with the lack of visibility into their activities, also ought to cause some unease and concern. The last thing the energy markets need is yet another speculative trading-led implosion.

Those that get it right most of the time are the multinational oil companies and the big two investment banks, Morgan Stanley and Goldman Sachs. These entities have maintained a consistent presence in energy-trading markets for decades and have the knowledge base to put many of the hedge funds to shame. The energy-trading winners will be those two banks and some savvy energy-trading companies that know both the energy markets *and* risk. Funds that rely simply on value at risk models, better known in some quarters as "voodoo at risk," just won't make the cut. They will fail. Granted, there will be lucky months and quarters with great returns. But we have seen this all before in the oil squeeze of North Sea Brent by Transworld Oil and its $500 million loss, the stacking and rolling strategy of MG and its $1.5 billion loss, and the quarterly gains and give-backs by many other commodity houses and oil companies. And we saw it in August, September, and October 2005 with $100 million trading losses for several funds in natural gas trading.

This is a true Darwinian game. This is survival of the energy fittest. Except for a handful of funds, they just can't stack up against the great oil trading companies like Vitol or BP and the investment banks, and since energy trading is a zero-sum game, the wealth transference could be massive. Count on more great quarters for Morgan Stanley's and Goldman Sachs' commodity shops. The other investment banks – such as Merrill Lynch, Barclays, Bank of America, and Deutsche Bank – are now playing catch up. Consistency and people make profits, not poorly executed trading strategies and opportunistic occurrences.

The positive value of the hedge funds is that they are bringing back liquidity and a risk-taking culture to the energy complex. Traditional energy companies such as the utilities are either exiting or being marginalized in this emerging, more sophisticated financial trading environment. The funds will also hire all those unemployed energy traders and they will re-center New York and London as the twin capitals of the energy-trading world.

On the downside, at least in the interim, many of the funds do not understand energy. While they have sophisticated models and approaches to risk management, there is a dangerous hint of financial arrogance in the air. They learned this during August, September, and October 2005, which showed them that energy markets are brutal and many gave back substantial gains over the entire year. Some funds have now reexamined their strategies and are now more cognizant of the risks in the energy complex. The environmental markets are even harder to understand. Quick profits will evaporate into losses quite quickly.

We see tremendous hedge fund opportunities in the energy and environmental arena, as these are immature financial markets that are starting to undergo a rapid maturation process through the participation of both hedge funds and investment banks. With these opportunities come risks. While buyer beware is still an important warning for those investors seeking better than average returns, we still think that this is the place for savvy investors to be for the next five years.

NOTES

1 BP 2005, "Putting Energy in the Spotlight," *BP Statistical Review of World Energy*, June 2005, British Petroleum.
2 See (1) above, BP 2005, p. 2.
3 IEA 2005, *Oil Market Report*, April, p. 4.
4 See (1) and (2) above.

5 See (1) above, BP 2005, p. 10.
6 Intelligence Press 2005, "BP's Browne Sees Energy Prices Stabilizing and Even Falling Long Term," news story, Tuesday, November 29, www.intelligencepress.com.
7 See (1) above, BP 2005, p. 8.
8 EIA 2005, *International Energy Outlook 2005*, p. 37, www.eia.doe.gov.
9 Reuters 2003, "Oil, Gas Output Costs Jump in U.S. Southwest – study," 11.4.2003, news story, www.reuters.com.
10 EIA 2005, *Annual Report on U.S. Oil and Gas Reserves*, www.eia.doe.gov.
11 See (1) above, BP 2005, p. 24.
12 See (1) above, BP 2005, p. 3.
13 Clayton, D. "Demand for Electric Power in China Still Outstrips Supply," ARC Advisory Group website, www.arcweb.com.
14 Renewable Energy Policy Network 2005, Renewables 2005, Annual Status Report.
15 See (1) above, BP 2005, p. 12.
16 Finch, J. 2005, "The Uranium Bull Market Keeps Getting More Bullish," November, StockInterview.com.

Glossary

Alpha – Measures the value that an investment manager produces by comparing the manager's performance to that of a risk-free investment (usually a Treasury bill).

American option – An option, which the holder may exercise any time up to and including the option's expiration date.

Annual rate of return – The compounded gain or loss in a fund's net asset value during a calendar year.

Arbitrage – A financial transaction that makes an immediate profit without involving any risk. Arbitrage opportunities arise because of minor pricing discrepancies between markets or related financial instruments.

Asian options – An option also called average price options that is a cash-settled derivative instrument whose payoff is linked to the average of the underlying commodity set at specific dates during the life of the option.

Asset-backed security – A financial instrument that is collaterized by bundled assets such as oil or gas reserves, or generation capacity.

Back end systems – Server-side software that run in conjunction with the web server, to implement whatever functionality a website is providing.

Backwardation – A market condition where the spot prices exceed the forward prices. In the energy markets it usually reflects a condition of supply and demand where there is a shortage of supply.

Basis risk – A market risk relating to differences in the market performance of two similar positions, such as one in the futures market and one in the physical market that do not move in line with the underlying exposure.

Beta – Gauges the risk of a fund by measuring the volatility of its past returns in relation to the returns of a benchmark, such as the S&P 500 index.

Black–Scholes Theory – The first successful model for pricing financial options developed by Fischer Black and Myron Scholes. The underlying assumptions of the original Black–Scholes model assumed that price was lognormally distributed with a constant mean and volatility, and that markets trade continuously with no sudden jumps in prices. The Black–Scholes model may produce misleading results in illiquid markets such as electricity.

Book – The total of all physical, futures, and derivatives positions held by a trader or company (includes documentation).

Call – An option that gives the buyers the right (but not the obligation) to enter into a long futures position at a predetermined strike price, and obligates the seller to enter into a short futures position at that price, should the option be exercised.

Cap – An options contract protecting an upside price movement against a certain fixed price.

Closed fund – A hedge fund or open-end mutual fund that has at least temporarily stopped accepting capital from investors, usually due to rapid asset growth.

Collar – Collars are a combination of caps and floor. A zero-cost collar has a zero premium.

Contango – A market condition where forward prices exceed the spot prices. In the energy markets this reflects a glut of supply.

Contract for differences – A bilateral contract where the payments are varied according to the difference of the strike price and a market spot price.

Convertible arbitrage investment strategy – A conservative, market-neutral approach that aims to profit from pricing differences or inefficiencies between the values of convertible bonds and common stock issued by the same company. Managers of such funds generally purchase undervalued convertible bonds, and short-sell the same issuer's stock.

Correlation – A measure of the degree to which changes in two variables are related, normally expressed as a coefficient between plus one and minus one. It is central to the pricing of options.

Counterparty – A counterparty is a party or organization with whom one transacts business. It is an important risk in the energy markets because of the lesser creditworthiness of many counterparties.

Credit derivative – An OTC derivative designed to transfer credit risk from one party to another by synthetically creating or eliminating credit exposures.

Credit exposure – In the event of a default this is the replacement cost of the counterparty's outstanding obligations. Because of electricity spikes and defaults in 1998 and 1999, it continues to be an important risk in energy markets.

Credit risk – The risk resulting from the uncertainty in a counterparty's ability or willingness to meet its contractual obligations.

Delta – A set of factor sensitivities used primarily to describe the risk exposures of derivative portfolios. The delta of an option describes its premium's sensitivity to changes in the underlying commodity.

Delta hedge – A delta hedge is a position when added to a portfolio that causes the portfolio to be delta neutral.

Derivative – A derivative instrument is a financial instrument that derives its value from the value of some other financial instrument or variable.

Distressed securities investment strategy – Purchasing deeply discounted securities that were issued by troubled or bankrupt companies, or short-selling the stocks of those corporations. The approach generally involves a medium- to long-term holding period.

Drawdown – The percentage loss that a fund incurs from its peak net asset value to its lowest value. The maximum drawdown over a significant period is sometimes employed as a means of measuring the risk of a vehicle.

Emerging-markets investment strategy – Investing in stocks or bonds issued by companies and government entities in developing countries. Such funds typically employ a short- to medium-term holding period and experience high volatility.

Energy hedge fund – A hedge fund that specializes in investing in some aspect of the energy industry, either as its entire focus or by using a significant proportion of its assets under management.

Energy hedge fund center – A website and free community created by the authors for the purposes of providing information on and tracking hedge fund and other alternative investments in the energy complex. See www.energyhedgefunds.com.

Enterprise risk management – The process whereby an organization optimizes the manner in which it takes risks.

European option – An option that can only be exercised on its expiration date.

Event-driven investment strategy – A strategy that seeks to anticipate certain events, such as mergers or corporate restructurings. Such funds, which include risk-arbitrage vehicles and entities that buy distressed securities, typically employ medium-term holding periods and experience moderate volatility.

Exchange-traded – A financial instrument is exchange-traded if it is traded on a formal exchange.

Exotics – Any option with a more complicated pay-out structure than a plain vanilla put or call option.

Expiry date – The date after which an option is void.

Exploration and production (E&P) segment – That part of the energy industry and the companies and business processes involved in exploring for, developing, and producing hydrocarbons.

Exposure – Every risk is comprised of two components: uncertainty and exposure to that uncertainty. Exposure is the potential replacement cost of positions with financial counterparties.

Extendible swap – A swap in which the fixed rate payer has the option to extend the payment period.

Financial engineering – A process whereby a portfolio is designed and maintained in such a manner as to achieve specified goals.

Fixed-income arbitrage investment strategy – A strategy that seeks to profit from pricing differentials or inefficiencies by purchasing a bond, annuity, or preferred stock, and simultaneously selling short a related security. Such funds are often highly leveraged.

Fixed-income investment strategy – A strategy in which the manager invests primarily in bonds, annuities, or preferred stock. The investments can be long positions, short sales, or both. Such funds are often highly leveraged.

Floor – An options contract that protects against downside price movement below a certain strike level.

Forward – A derivative agreement to purchase an underlying commodity at an agreed upon price.

Fund of hedge funds – An investment vehicle whose holdings consist of shares in hedge funds and private-equity funds. Some of these multi-manager vehicles limit their holdings to specific managers or investment strategies, while others are more diversified. Investors in funds of funds are willing to pay two sets of fees, one to the fund-of-funds manager and another set of (usually higher) fees to the managers of the underlying funds.

Futures – A standardized contract that is an exchange-traded instrument and is an agreement to purchase an underlying asset at an agreed upon price on a specified future date. The contract defines quantity, price, and time of delivery.

General partner – The individual or firm that organizes and manages a limited partnership, such as a hedge fund. The general partner assumes unlimited legal responsibility for the liabilities of a partnership.

Global-macro investment strategy – An approach in which a fund manager seeks to anticipate broad trends in the worldwide economy. Based on those forecasts, the manager chooses investments from a wide variety of markets; that is, stocks, bonds, currencies, and commodities. The approach typically involves a medium-term holding period and produces high volatility. They are sometimes called "macro" or "global directional-investment" funds.

Greeks – A set of sensitivity factors used by options traders to quantify the sensitivities of a portfolio. These include delta, gamma, vega, rho, and theta.

Hedge – A hedge is a risk which is taken; that is, offset by another risk. In other words, risk is reduced by making transactions that reduce exposure to market fluctuations.

Hedge accounting – The practice of deferring accounting recognition of gains and losses of financial market hedges until the corresponding gain or loss of the underlying exposure is recognized. Hedge accounting enables companies to incorporate the costs of hedges into the cost basis of the exposure.

Hedge fund – A private investment vehicle whose manager receives a significant portion of its compensation from incentive fees tied to the fund's performance – typically 20% of annual gains over a certain hurdle rate, along with a management fee equal to 1 to 2% of assets. The funds, often organized as limited partnerships, typically invest on behalf of high-net-worth individuals and institutions. Their primary objective is often to preserve investors' capital by taking positions whose returns are not closely correlated to those of the broader financial markets. Such vehicles may employ leverage, short sales, a variety of derivatives, and other hedging techniques to reduce risk and increase returns.

High-water mark – A provision serving to ensure that a fund manager only collects incentive fees on the highest net asset value previously attained at the end of any prior fiscal year – or gains representing actual profits for each investor.

Hurdle rate – The minimum return necessary for a fund manager to start collecting incentive fees. The hurdle is usually tied to a benchmark rate such as Libor or the one-year Treasury bill rate plus a spread.

Implied volatility – The value of volatility embedded in an option price.

Incentive fee (performance fee) – The charge – typically 20% – that a fund manager assesses on gains earned during a given 12-month period.

Inception date – The day on which a fund starts trading.

In-the-money – An option whose strike price is advantageous, compared with the current market price of an underlying commodity.

Legacy – Existing systems that must used be integrated into/inter-operate with a new distributed Web-based system.

Leverage – Any process that compounds a risk and more specifically increases exposure to a source of risk.

Liquidity – The ability to convert an asset into cash equal to its current market value.

Liquidity risk – Financial risk from a possible loss of liquidity.

Limited partnership – Many hedge funds are structured as limited partnerships, which are business organizations managed by one or more general partners who are liable for the fund's debts and obligations. The investors in such a structure are limited partners who do not participate in day-to-day operations and are liable only to the extent of their investments.

Lock-up – The period of time – often one year or more – during which hedge-fund investors are initially prohibited from redeeming their shares.

Long-biased – An approach taken by fund managers who tend to hold considerably more long positions than short positions.

Long-dated – A contract over 12 months in duration.

Long position – This is a bullish position with the expectation that by purchasing contracts the prices will increase.

Long/short investment strategy – An approach in which fund managers buy stocks whose prices they expect will increase and takes short positions in securities (usually in the same sector) whose prices they believes will decline.

Managed futures – A vehicle in which an investor gives a commodity trading advisor – usually a manager or broker – discretion or authority to buy and sell futures contracts, either unconditionally or with restrictions.

Management fee – The charge that a fund manager assesses to cover operating expenses. Investors are typically charged separately for costs incurred for outsourced services. The fee generally ranges from an annual 0.5% to 2% of an investor's entire holdings in the fund, and it is usually collected on a quarterly basis.

Mark-to-market (MTM) – A calculation of the value of financial instruments based on the current market rates or prices of the underlying.

Market-neutral investment strategy – A strategy that aims to preserve capital through any of several methods, and under any market conditions. The most common followers of the market-neutral strategy are funds pursuing a long/short investment strategy. These seek to exploit market discrepancies by purchasing undervalued securities and taking an equal, short position in a different and overvalued security. Market-neutral funds typically employ long-term holding periods and experience moderate volatility.

Market risk – The financial risk or uncertainty in the future market value of a portfolio of assets or liabilities.

Master-feeder fund – A common hedge fund structure through which a manager sets up two separate vehicles – one based in the United States and an offshore fund that is domiciled outside the United States – which serve as the only investors for a third non-US fund. The two smaller entities are known as feeder funds, while the large offshore vehicle acts as the master fund. The purpose of such an arrangement is to create a single investment vehicle for both US and non-US investors.

Mean reversion – A tendency for certain random variables to remain at or return over time to a long-run average level.

Merger arbitrage investment strategy – Trading the stocks of companies that have announced acquisitions or are the targets of acquisitions. Seeks to exploit deviations of market prices from proposed exchange formulas.

208

Midstream segment – The sector of the energy industry and the business processes and companies engaged in processing and moving hydrocarbons from the point of production.

Monte Carlo Simulation – A mathematical technique for numerically solving differential equations that is used extensively in finance for such tasks as pricing derivatives or estimating the value at risk of a portfolio.

Multi strategy – An investment style that combines several different approaches. The term often applies to funds of funds.

Netting – Netting of cash flows or obligations is a means of reducing credit exposure to counterparties.

Notional amount – The amount for a futures or other derivative instrument that is settled with physical delivery.

Offshore fund – An investment vehicle that is domiciled outside the United States and has no limit on the number of non-US investors it can take on. Although the fund's securities transactions occur on US exchanges and are executed by a US manager, or general partner, its administration and audits are conducted offshore – usually in a tax haven like the Cayman Islands. Because it is administered outside the United States, non-US investors and such US investors as pension funds and other tax-exempt entities aren't subject to US taxes.

Operations risk – The financial risk from human error, inadequate controls, or systems failure within an organization's operations function.

Option – An option is an agreement between two parties whereby one party (the option holder) has the right, but not the obligation, to buy or sell an underlying at a certain price (the exercise or strike price) from the other party (the option seller).

Out-of-the-money – An option whose underlying is below the strike price in the case of a call or above in the case of a put.

Over-the-counter (OTC) – An instrument is traded OTC if it is not traded on a formal exchange. Examples are forward contracts, swaps agreements, and customized options.

Portal – A website that provides a single "gateway" into the Internet, or into a particular area of interest on the Internet. A portal that provides a single comprehensive view to key information with links to more details, some of which may be websites external to the portal.

Premium – The cost of an option or the price paid by the buyer to the option writer for the right granted by the option.

Prime broker – A large bank or securities firm that provides various administrative, back-office, and financing services to hedge funds and other professional investors. Prime brokers can provide a wide variety of services, including trade reconciliation (clearing and settlement), custody services, risk management, margin financing, securities lending for the purpose of carrying out short sales, record keeping, and investor reporting. A prime brokerage relationship doesn't preclude hedge funds from carrying out trades with other brokers, or even employing others as prime brokers. To compete for business, some prime brokers act as incubators for funds, providing office space and services to help new fund managers get off the ground.

Private-equity fund – Entities that buy illiquid stakes in privately held companies, sometimes by participating in leveraged buyouts. Like hedge funds, the vehicles are structured as private investment partnerships in which only qualified investors may participate. Such funds typically charge a management fee of 1.5 to 2.5%, as well as an incentive fee of 25 to 30%. Most private-equity funds employ lock-up periods of five to ten years, longer than those of hedge funds.

Private placement – Issues that are exempt from public registration provisions in Section 4-2 of the Securities Act of 1933. Hedge fund shares are generally offered as private placements, which are typically offered to only a few investors, rather than the general public. They must meet the following criteria:

- The issuer must believe that the buyer is capable of evaluating the risks of the transaction.
- Buyers have access to the same information that would appear in the prospectus of a publicly offered issue.
- The issuer does not sell the securities to more than 35 parties in any 12-month period.
- The buyer does not intend to sell the securities immediately for a trading profit.

Put – The right to sell an option with the expectation that the price will go down.

Redemption fee – A charge, intended to discourage withdrawals, which a hedge fund manager levies against investors when they cash in their shares in the fund before a specified date.

Regulation D – A provision in the Securities Act of 1933 that allows privately placed transactions to take place without SEC registration and prohibits hedge funds from advertising themselves to the general public. It also outlines which parties qualify as company insiders.

Relative-value strategy – A market-neutral investment strategy that seeks to identify investments whose values are attractive, compared to similar securities, when risk, liquidity, and returns are taken into account.

Risk – This has two components: uncertainty and exposure to that uncertainty.

RiskMetrics – A trademark service of JP Morgan to support institutional value at risk analyses, including historical volatilities and correlations for a variety of risk factors.

Risk limits – A specified level of risk that an organization is willing to take that can be quantified for market and credit risk.

Securitization – A process whereby assets are pooled and security interests in the pool are sold, usually to institutional investors.

Settlement risk – The financial risk that the counterparty will fail to perform on a contract at settlement.

Sharpe ratio – A measure of how well a fund is rewarded for the risk it incurs. The higher the ratio, the better the return per unit of risk taken. It is calculated by subtracting the risk-free rate from the fund's annualized average return, and dividing the result by the fund's annualized standard deviation. A Sharpe ratio of 1:1 indicates that the rate of return is proportional to the risk assumed in seeking that reward.

Short-biased strategy – An approach that relies on short sales. Such funds tend to hold larger short positions than long positions.

Special situations investment strategy – An event-driven investment strategy in which the manager seeks to take advantage of unique corporate situations that provide the potential for investment gains.

Speculation – The opposite of hedging, in which the speculator holds no offsetting cash market position and deliberately incurs price risk in order to reap potential rewards.

Spot – A spot transaction is one in which an asset is purchased for immediate delivery. The price that is paid in a post transaction is called the spot price.

Spot month – The futures contract held closest to maturity.

Spread – The simultaneous purchase of one futures or forward contract and the sale of a different futures or forward contract. Also, refers to futures/forward contract purchase in one market and a simultaneous sale of the same commodity in some other market.

Statistical arbitrage investment strategy – A market-neutral investment strategy that seeks profit and to limit risk by exploiting pricing inefficiencies identified by mathematical models. The strategy often involves short-term bets that prices will trend toward their historical norms.

Straddle – The sale or purchase of a put or call option, with the same strike price, on the same underlying commodity, and with the same expiry.

Strangle – The sale or purchase of a put option and a call option on the same instrument, but at strike prices that are out-of-the-money.

Stress-testing – A single scenario risk measure used for analyzing the market risk of a portfolio.

Swap – An OTC derivative instrument with which two parties periodically exchange payments based upon the value of one or more market indexes. Most commonly, a swap gives a party the ability to convert a floating rate asset or liability to a fixed rate.

Swaption – An option with an embedded swap that gives the writer the option of either increasing the swap volume or increasing the period of the swap.

Systemic risk – The risk that a localized problem in the financial markets could cause a chain of events that ultimately cripple the market.

Technical analysis – The examination of patterns or futures price changes, rates of change, and changes in trading volume and open interest, often by charting, in order to predict and profit from such transactions.

Trading – The activity of trading, exchanging, and guaranteeing contracts in return for a spread or profit between the bought position and sold-out price position.

Value at risk (VaR) – A statistical risk measure that is used extensively for measuring the market risk of a portfolio or assets and/or liabilities. Value at risk is sometimes referred to as capital at risk, earnings at risk, or dollars at risk.

Value investment strategy – An approach that involves purchases of stocks that the manager deems to be priced below their intrinsic values, or are out of favor with the market, but are still fundamentally solid. Such funds typically employ long-term holding periods and experience low volatility.

Variation margin – Margin paid or collected in order to maintain a minimum margin level based on the daily fluctuations in contract value.

Venture capital – Money given to corporate start-ups and other new high-risk enterprises by investors who seek above-average returns and are willing to take illiquid positions.

Volatility – A measure of the variability of the price of the underlying commodity.

Volume – The number of transactions occurring on an exchange during a specified period of time.

Working interest – The interest of a party that holds the right to oil, gas, or minerals on a property, and that bears production costs.

Index